Race, Law, and Culture

Race, Law, and Culture

Reflections on
Brown v. Board of Education

Edited by
Austin Sarat

New York   Oxford
OXFORD UNIVERSITY PRESS
1997

Oxford University Press

Oxford   New York
Athens   Auckland   Bangkok   Bogota   Bombay   Buenos Aires
Calcutta   Cape Town   Dar es Salaam   Delhi   Florence   Hong Kong
Istanbul   Karachi   Kuala Lumpur   Madras   Madrid   Melbourne
Mexico City   Nairobi   Paris   Singapore   Taipei   Tokyo   Toronto

and associated companies in
Berlin   Ibadan

Copyright © 1997 by Oxford University Press, Inc.

Published by Oxford University Press, Inc.
198 Madison Avenue, New York, New York 10016

Oxford is a registered trademark of Oxford University Press

Library of Congress Cataloging-in-Publication Data
Race, law, and culture : reflections on Brown v. Board of Education /
edited by Austin Sarat.
p.   cm.
Essays originally presented at a conference on Brown at Forty,
held at Amherst College, December 1994.
Includes index.
ISBN 0–19–510621–0; ISBN 0–19–510622–9 (pbk.)
1. Brown, Oliver, 1918– —Trials, litigation, etc.   2. Topeka
(Kan.).   Board of Education—Trials, litigation, etc.
3. Segregation in education—Law and legislation—United States.
4. Race discrimination—Law and legislation—United States.
5. United States—Race relations.   I. Sarat, Austin.
KF4155.A2R33   1997
344.73'0798—dc20
[347.304798]   96–33875

9 8 7 6 5 4 3 2 1
Printed in the United States of America
on acid-free paper

Acknowledgments

The essays in this volume were originally presented at the conference "*Brown at Forty*," held at Amherst College in December 1994. That event was sponsored by the college's Charles Hamilton Houston Forum on Law and Social Change. The forum honors one of Amherst's most distinguished graduates, a man who played a crucial role in the struggle that eventuated in *Brown*. I am grateful for the support provided by the Houston Forum and by Amherst's former president, Peter R. Pouncey. Three colleagues at Amherst, Thomas Dumm, Martha Umphrey, and Robert Gooding-Williams, provided insightful commentaries on the papers presented at the conference. To them and other colleagues and students who made that such a stimulating event I express my appreciation.

Contents

Contributors

HAZEL CARBY is Professor of African and African American Studies at Yale University.

PEGGY COOPER DAVIS is Professor of Law at New York University.

LAWRENCE M. FRIEDMAN is Marion Rice Kirkwood Professor of Law at Stanford University.

DAVID J. GARROW is a freelance journalist, Pulitzer Prize–winning author, and lecturer. He is currently Presidential Visiting Distinguished Professor at Emory University.

PAUL GEWIRTZ is Potter Stewart Professor of Constitutional Law at Yale University.

CAROL J. GREENHOUSE is Professor of Anthropology at Indiana University.

GEORGE KATEB is Professor of Politics and Director of the Center for Human Values at Princeton University.

GARY PELLER is Professor of Law at Georgetown University.

AUSTIN SARAT is William Nelson Cromwell Professor of Jurisprudence and Political Science at Amherst College.

DAVID B. WILKINS is Kirkland and Ellis Professor of Law and Director of the Program on the Legal Profession at Harvard Law School.

Race, Law, and Culture

The Continuing Contest about Race in American Law and Culture

On Reading the Meaning of Brown

To pursue the concept of racial entitlement—even for the most admirable and benign of purposes—is to reinforce and preserve for future mischief the way of thinking that produced race slavery, race privilege and race hatred. In the eyes of government, we are just one race here. It is American.

Justice Antonin Scalia

It never ceases to amaze me that the courts are so willing to assume that anything that is predominantly black must be inferior. . . . Because of their "distinctive histories and traditions," black schools can function as the center and symbol of black communities, and provide examples of independent black leadership, success, and achievement.

Justice Clarence Thomas

When it comes to race and racial issues these are strange times, confused and confusing times, for all Americans. This is especially true when the issue of race involves relations between African Americans and Caucasians. It is especially true at a time when we celebrate the triumph of the black middle class while demonizing young black males in our inner cities.[1] More than forty years after *Brown v. Board of Education* put an end to segregation of the races by law, the question of whether Americans can live with racial differences and how we can do so, is still a pressing one.[2] Current debates about affirmative action,[3] multiculturalism,[4] and racial hate speech[5] reveal persistent uncertainty and ambivalence about the place and meaning of race in American culture and the role of law in guaranteeing racial equality. Moreover, all sides in those debates claim to be the true heirs to *Brown*, even as they disagree vehemently about its meaning.[6]

What can we learn about race, law, and culture in contemporary America, one legitimately might ask, when two Justices of the Supreme Court, who in many other respects share similar social views, take radically divergent positions about what our country should aspire to in recognizing race and racial difference? What can we learn about the legacy of *Brown* from the fact that both claim it as their own? One, Justice Scalia, advocates a kind of uniracialist ideal, while the other, Justice Thomas, the only African American on the Court, speaks in the language of black pride, if not black nationalism. And these differences certainly could be multiplied if we examined a broader array of political views.

American uncertainties and ambivalence about race go at least as far back as Tocqueville's pained observations about the three races in America and their sad inability to live together as equals.[7] In the intervening two centuries the uncertainties have not been resolved by civil war, legal prescription, mass protest, or inspiring leadership. Today conflict between blacks and whites, and conflict about black-white relations, is as vexing as it has ever been. Race, as Gunnar Myrdal reminded us, is the "American Dilemma."[8]

Uncertainty is particularly acute in the legal domain, where, over the last four decades, courts and judges have struggled to come to terms with the meaning of the Constitution's guarantee of equal protection of the law.[9] In that period the record of judicial interpretation and understanding of racial equality has taken the form of a back-and-forth movement in which first desegregation, then integration, with its accompanying need for busing and affirmative action, and now color blindness have been the prevailing ideologies.[10] At each turn courts have tried to come to terms with the following issues: Can or should the law see, or see through, the racial mosaic that is America? Is taking race into account to remedy the effects of past racial discrimination a form of racism or a step toward a more racially tolerant society? Can law lead us away from discrimination and racism? Or is it hostage to prevailing sentiments and opinions?

Race, Law, and Culture: Reflections on Brown v. Board of Education speaks to these questions. It does so by looking back on *Brown* and drawing out its implications for a wide range of today's racial issues. According to the authors whose work is assembled in this book, *Brown*'s significance involves more than even its remarkable willingness to say no to one of the great shames of American history. *Brown* was, in our century, an occasion for the rebirth of America,[11] an occasion that told a story of struggle and liberation, and pointed the way for a new engagement with the problem of difference,[12] of how men and women of different backgrounds and races might live together as equals. But *Brown* is more than this. It marked a radical departure in the style and substance of our law. And it has had a profound impact on the way Americans think about law's role in promoting social justice. The drama of *Brown*, of an appeal to law to make good on its promises, has in the last four decades been repeatedly reenacted in courtrooms across the United States.[13] And *Brown*, even today, provides a powerful template and touchstone through which contemporary racial issues can be seen.

As is now widely recognized, until 1954 the project of establishing the American Constitution was radically incomplete.[14] It was incomplete because, in both chattel slavery and then Jim Crow, the law systematically excluded people from participating fully, freely, and with dignity in America's major social and political institutions on the basis of their race. But *Brown* changed everything.[15] "*Brown*," J. Harvie Wilkinson contends, "may be the most important political, social, and legal event in America's twentieth-century history. Its greatness lay in the enormity of the injustice it condemned, in the entrenched sentiment it challenged, in the immensity of law it both created and overthrew."[16] It stood for the proposition that "race is an impermissible basis for governmental decisions."[17] Yet it did not end the indignities that the law itself had heaped on African Americans. *Brown* was at once a turning point and a source of resistance, a point of pride and an object of vilification. Its legacy, like the legacy of all great historical events, is, even today, contested and uncertain.

In *Brown*, the Supreme Court dealt with four separate cases, each of which challenged the practice of legal segregation in the schools of one state— South Carolina, Virginia, Delaware, and Kansas. In each case, African American plaintiffs sought to invalidate laws that required or permitted the segregation of black and white schoolchildren. They challenged the prevailing constitutional orthodoxy, namely that separate but equal facilities did not violate the Fourteenth Amendment guarantee of equal protection. As the Supreme Court wrote in *Plessy v. Ferguson*,[18]

> When the government has secured to each of its citizens equal rights before the law and equal opportunities for improvement and progress, it has accomplished the end for which it was organized. . . . If the civil and political rights of both races be equal, one cannot be inferior to the other civilly or politically. If one race be inferior to the other socially, the Constitution of the United States cannot put them upon the same plane.

As Earl Warren understood the question before the Court in *Brown*, it was whether the "segregation of children in public schools solely on the basis of race, even though the physical facilities and other 'tangible' factors may be equal, deprive the children of the minority group of equal educational opportunities?"[19] By posing the question this way, Warren raised the issue of whether the harms of segregation might go beyond the denial of equal tangible facilities and embrace "intangible" injuries inflicted by the legal separation of the races.[20] He answered his own question by asserting with disarming directness, "We believe that it does."[21] In the judgment of the Court,

> Segregation of white and colored children in public schools has a detrimental effect upon colored children. The impact is greater when it has the sanction of law; for the policy of segregating the races is usually interpreted as denoting the inferiority of the negro group. A sense of inferiority affects the motivation of the child to learn . . . and has a tendency to [retard] the educational and mental development of negro children and to deprive them of some of the benefits they would receive in a racial[ly]

integrated school system. . . . [T]he plaintiffs and others similarly situated . . . are by reason of the segregation complained of deprived of the equal protection of the laws guaranteed by the Fourteenth Amendment.[22]

"We conclude," Warren wrote in the single most memorable passage from *Brown*, "that in the field of public education the doctrine of 'separate but equal' has no place. Separate educational facilities are inherently unequal."[23]

These few quotations give the flavor of the remarkable restraint with which Warren's opinion is written. For all of its legal and cultural significance, and for all of the controversy that it has stirred up, it is but thirteen pages long and contains an unlawyer-like number of only fourteen footnotes.[24] Its prose is sturdy and direct, as if Warren feared saying too much, or saying it in a way that would distract attention from *what* was being said.[25] Like Lincoln's Gettysburg address, the text of *Brown* is marked by surprising brevity but also startling vision.[26] It was, in Richard Kluger's words, "the turning point in America's willingness to face the consequences of centuries of racial discrimination."[27] It altered the course of constitutional history by sweeping away the legal and philosophical underpinnings of segregation,[28] and, in so doing, took a giant step toward the realization of the vision of respect for persons that, from the beginning, has animated our constitutional vision.[29] Like Lincoln's Gettysburg address, *Brown* reminds us, again in Kluger's words, that "[of] the ideals that animated the American nation at its beginning none was more radiant or honored than the inherent equality of mankind. There was dignity in all human flesh, Americans proclaimed, and all must have a chance to strive and excel."[30]

As the editors of the *Yale Law Journal* put it in their celebration of the thirteenth anniversary of *Brown*, "No modern case has had a greater impact either on our day-to-day lives or on the structure of our government."[31] And what was true more than a decade ago is no less true today. Yet ours is a time of revision and mixed views about *Brown* and its legacy. While some commentators have noted that it has not resulted in the elimination of racism in American society,[32] or even of segregation in public education,[33] others suggests that *Brown* has been given too much credit for sparking racial progress.[34] "[F]rom a long-range perspective," Michael Klarman argues, "racial change in America was inevitable owing to a variety of deep-seated social, political and economic forces. These impulses for racial change . . . would have undermined Jim Crow regardless of Supreme Court intervention."[35]

For scholars like Klarman, *Brown* stands not as a monument to law's ability to bring about social change, but instead as a monument to its failure to do so. In their view, whatever racial progress America has achieved cannot be traced back to *Brown*. Gerald Rosenberg contends that

> courts had virtually no effect on ending discrimination in the key fields of education, voting, transportation, accommodation and public places, and housing. Courageous and praiseworthy decisions were rendered, and nothing changed. . . . In terms of judicial effects, then, *Brown* and its progeny stand for the proposition that courts are impotent to produce significant social reform.[36]

Still others remain unsatisfied with the doctrinal basis of the *Brown* opinion.[37] And some now say that the integrationist vision that is most closely associated with *Brown* is inadequate to deal with the continuing subordination of African Americans in contemporary American society.[38]

All told, the story of race, law, and culture in contemporary America is far from a happy one. As several of the authors in this book remind us, there is another legacy of *Brown* that is today seen in what Hazel Carby calls "political apartheid" and in Carol Greenhouse's description of the "criminalization" of racial minorities. And as the continuing controversy and confusion surrounding race all too dramatically reveals, *Brown* unsettled as much as it resolved; it opened up new avenues for contestation, new ideas about how Americans should think about race, new challenges for law.

While the essays in this book look back at *Brown* to assess its legal and cultural significance, they also examine its contemporary meaning and hold on the future. They do so in a time of turmoil in the American debate about race.[39] As Wilkinson argues, "America stands at a critical juncture with respect to its race relations—a juncture every bit as important as that which confronted the Supreme Court in 1954."[40] Where once the integrationist ideal and the equal opportunity that *Brown* heralded were the preeminent ideals of racial justice, today each is seriously contested.[41] Today criticism of affirmative action[42] as well as the development of black nationalism and multiculturalism undermine, or at least challenge, integration for hegemony in the story of racial progress.[43]

The essays in this book chart the ambiguous and contested meanings of *Brown* in law and culture and confront a variety of important questions about race in contemporary America: What was the legal and cultural vision contained in that decision? How have those visions been articulated in other legal struggles? What kind of story did *Brown* tell about imagination, possibility, and change? How has it transformed the very meaning of citizenship and identity in American culture? What have the four decades since *Brown* taught us about the capacity of law to foster change in cultural life? Why does the subject of race continue to haunt the American imagination and continue to play such a large role in political and legal debate? Do affirmative action and multiculturalism promise a way out of racial polarization, or do they sharpen and deepen it? What is the status of *Brown* today?

This book takes the continuing controversy about race in law and culture as an invitation to revisit *Brown*, and it takes *Brown* as a lens through which to view that controversy and the issues involved in it.[44] It does not try to assess the net effect of the case on the material conditions of life in post-*Brown* America; instead it takes stock of *Brown* as a moment in history and asks about its significance in the law and culture of the United States. The essays collected here describe the ambiguous and contested legacy of *Brown* in the realm of both law and culture as well as the way it is implicated in the uncertainties and ambivalences about race that afflict American society today. In so doing they put aside what I call an "instrumentalist" perspective[45] and instead focus attention on questions of meaning and interpretation.[46]

Instrumentalist accounts of *Brown* assess its value largely in terms of material changes brought about in the lives of African Americans.[47] They conceive of law as a tool for sustaining or changing particular aspects of social life, in this instance the integration of public education.[48] But law, Brown included, is more than an instrument for changing social life; it is in addition crucial in generating and reproducing structures of meaning or what Geertz calls "webs of signification."[49] In this view, law is "part of a distinctive manner of imagining the real";[50] it is "a mode of giving particular sense to particular things in particular places (things that happen, that fail to, things that might)."[51]

Meaning is the key word in the vocabulary of those who speak about law in interpretivist terms. "Our gaze focuses on meaning, on the ways . . . [people] make sense of what they do—practically, morally, expressively, . . . juridically—by setting it within larger frames of signification, and how they keep those larger frames in place or try to, by organizing what they do in terms of them."[52] Thinking about legal decisions in terms of the meanings generated and conveyed by them requires that scholars of race, law, and culture attend to networks of legal practices, on the one hand, and clusters of beliefs, on the other. It requires recognition that the meaning of Brown is to be found in the variety of locations and practices that comprise the legal world and that those locations and practices do not exist outside the webs of signification that, in turn, make them meaningful. To acknowledge that legal decisions have meaning-making power, independent from their ability or inability to change material conditions, is to suggest that social practices are unintelligible apart from the legal norms that give rise to them.[53] Students of law and culture believe that such decisions permeate social life and that their influence is not adequately grasped by treating them as a type of external, normative influence on independent, ongoing activities.[54] And this is as true in the area of race as it is in other domains of social life.

This perspective helps explain why instrumentalist assessments of Brown are naturally inclined to see it as failing, as "struggling to retain what seems like a tenuous grasp on the social order."[55] But for the authors in this volume the significance of Brown is that it made it possible to ask new things of law and to tell new stories about what it means to be African American.[56] Indeed, in one sense, it made it possible for the first time for blacks in this society to think of themselves as being American.[57] Brown opened up both new legal and cultural possibilities. Yet it also stirred passions that even today have not cooled. It opened up issues with which Justices Scalia and Thomas and all Americans continue to struggle. It pushed race to the center of the continuing dialogue about law and culture.

Part I of this book—"Brown and Its Legal Contexts"—contains three essays, each of which takes us back to 1954 to note the many ways Brown gave new meaning to law. In addition, they also look at the present to show how that meaning has been played out in other cases and contexts. The first essay, by Peggy Cooper Davis, examines the language used by the lawyers in their arguments before the Supreme Court in Brown. She argues that the plaintiffs' lawyers "simultaneously played on and subverted the image of the United States as a white polity." They did so by combining a carefully calculated linguistic strategy of deference to existing social, political, and legal authority with an effort to exemplify, in their own actions, ways in which African Americans could participate productively in the ongoing processes of national self-definition.

Davis describes how Thurgood Marshall, Robert Carter, and their colleagues framed their argument as a story of "plight not right" by focusing on the harms experienced by black children in segregated schools.[58] In so doing they appropriated a powerful story from the mainstream culture, a story of childhood innocence, of hope for the future played out as an investment in children. Yet their language, and the cause with which they openly affiliated themselves, told another story, a story of the meaning and significance of the Constitution as a force for social justice. These lawyers articulated a vision of the meaning of the Constitution as not being fixed in its history, but as found in a set of principles whose implications are negotiated and renegotiated at crucial historical junctures.[59] Thus they were able both to speak of the needs of their people and, at the same time, exemplify a vision of law that joined the plight of black children with the promises and possibilities of the Constitution itself.

It is this vision that stirred up great controversy in the legal academy at the time the Court made its decision in *Brown*. Some of the most famous legal commentators of the time—people like Learned Hand,[60] Herbert Wechsler,[61] and Louis Pollak[62]—praised the result, yet vehemently criticized Warren's jurisprudential style.[63] Lawrence Friedman's essay puts such criticism in context by claiming that *Brown* indeed marked a revolution in the way the Constitution up to that point had been interpreted.

Brown, Friedman argues, inhabits a legal and doctrinal world quite far removed from the world in which *Plessy* was decided. In that world, Friedman argues, an inflexible racial hierarchy coexisted with a legal style that he calls the "person-from-Pluto approach." According to that style, "the textual surface of the law, the actual rules and regulations, should be so phrased and framed that an alien from outer space, totally unaware of the realities of life in Louisiana, would not *know* from the texts of the laws whether 'whites' were on top, or 'blacks', or neither." The context of *Plessy* was one in which the state "structured its laws to meet this stylistic requirement." While occasionally the Court would strike down a statute upholding segregation, it steadfastly clung to the person-from-Pluto approach.

One of the great accomplishments of *Brown*, Friedman argues, was to discredit that approach. Warren's decision treated the southern system of segregation as a caste system. It was based on the proposition that judges could not, and should not, be blind to the social realities that were often masked by abstract legal formulae. But in this approach the very meaning of law was up for grabs. Judges, like Warren, refused to be constrained by "legal technicalities"; instead they embraced an expansive, commonsense style that was the "medium for emphasizing context, reality, for rejecting the dry formalism that made it (stylistically) possible to pretend that all was well in the house of the South." Whatever its ultimate impact on the social conditions of African Americans (Friedman contends that *Brown's* "impact . . . was completely benign"), *Brown* reoriented the way an entire generation of judges saw their role in interpreting the law.

Yet at the same time, Friedman notes that the integrationist vision is today actively contested in the political and cultural realm by what he calls "plural equality." Despite *Brown's* legal significance, integration in the social and cultural domain today fails to capture the imagination of significant numbers of racial minorities who seek to preserve their identity and culture rather than to see it transformed.[64] In this sense the case and its legacy are, in Friedman's view, as controversial as they have ever been.

David Garrow's essay takes up Friedman's argument about the legal meaning of *Brown* by systematically tracing its influence in two areas of constitutional law—due process and equal protection. *Brown*, in Garrow's view, repudiated historical intent as a methodology of interpreting the twin guarantees of the Fourteenth Amendment.[65] As a result, it "singlehandedly marks the advent of the 'modern' . . . Supreme Court." The genius of Warren's opinion in *Brown*, Garrow argues, was in displacing the question of history and putting in its place the question of how judicial power appropriately might be used to advance the cause of social justice. In the area of equal protection, *Brown's* approach was institutionalized in the Court's apportionment decision, *Baker v. Carr.*[66] In that case, the Court found political guarantees in the Fourteenth Amendment that it had, prior to *Brown*, been unwilling or unable to recognize.

For Garrow, however, the full meaning of *Brown* was not realized until the Court's decisions in *Griswold v. Connecticut*,[67] *Roe v. Wade*,[68] and, especially, *Planned Parenthood v. Casey*.[69] In those cases, the Court carried out the work of laying to rest the ghost of *Lochner v. New York*[70] that *Brown* had begun. *Lochner* had, for almost half a century, stood in the way of a complete development of the Fourteenth Amendment as a resource in the fight for liberty. *Casey* finally repudiated *Lochner* and openly embraced "substantive due process." *Brown* and *Casey*, Garrow writes, "are . . . bookends to the twofold rereading that the Court has accorded the Fourteenth Amendment—both, in *Brown* (and in *Baker*) with regard to the Equal Protection Clause, and, in *Casey* (as in *Griswold* and *Roe* before it) with regard to the new rebirth of the Due Process Clause. . . . As *Brown* and *Casey* both signify, the modern-day meanings of American constitutional protections should not be—and happily are not—fettered by the burdens and limitations of history."

Part II—"Racial Discrimination and Antidiscrimination Law"—contains two essays, both of which assess the adequacy of *Brown's* vision of the antidiscrimination principle. George Kateb begins this assessment by asking the disarmingly simple question—"What is the harm of legal segregation of the races?" In Kateb's view, the answer to that question is found first and foremost in the violation of basic rights, and, secondarily, in the damage done by segregation to the character of persons, especially members of the majority race. He criticizes Warren's answer, which focused solely on the psychological effects on children of the minority race.

Kateb suggests that Warren's opinion in *Brown* leaves open the issue of what would be wrong with legal segregation if humiliation were intended but not felt by blacks.[71] Segregation would, on Kateb's account, still be a gross and grievous wrong even if that were the case. It would be wrong because it "creates a general system that is meant not only to curtail the ability to exercise or take positive advantage of the rights of freedom and equality enjoyed by others, but also to entwine that curtailed ability with a continuous humiliated feeling of unworthiness to exercise those rights."[72]

The clearest juridical recognition of this harm, Kateb contends, is found in Harlan's *Plessy* dissent. There, Harlan argues that legal segregation is inconsistent with the guarantee of a republican form of government found in the Fourteenth Amendment.[73] Harlan was right, in Kateb's view, to treat segregation as a form of tyranny that rendered illegitimate, for both blacks and "conscientious" whites, a supposedly legitimate form of government. Moreover, the Guarantee Clause provides a basis for identifying the harm of legal segregation that does not depend on the feelings of injury of the minority race.

Kateb goes on to argue that legal segregation damages character without the people living under such a system quite knowing it. It does so by diminishing the "integrity of the person as a democratic individual." People living under legal segregation are encouraged or permitted to give in to attitudes of prejudice or hatred; those attitudes are a "specimen of group thinking" that ignores the merits of individuals. Legal segregation fortifies the tendency to love exclusiveness, which in turn expresses impatience with individual difference. Finally, legal segregation encourages people to "live a lie," namely to live as if the political system in which they were living were indeed legitimate when, as Kateb suggests, it could not be. Because it could not comprehend any of these effects, Warren's opinion in *Brown* does not provide an adequate explanation for the harm of legal segregation.

In addition, Paul Gewirtz sees *Brown* as leaving an ambiguous legacy in the area of antidiscrimination law.[74] The ambiguity of that legacy results from the fact that at the very moment when we are seeing the "triumph" of its antidiscrimination principle, that principle is being transformed from a focus on individual to group rights. *Brown* not only is largely responsible for the power of antidiscrimination as a cultural and legal principle, but it "has opened up a new range of problematic issues for our society."

Gewirtz suggests that the antidiscrimination principle now provides a primary vocabulary for speaking about social and political issues in the United States.[75] "[M]ore and more areas of social life," Gewirtz suggests, "are now treated as raising a problem of 'discrimination'—rather than viewed as raising some other kind of problem, or raising no problem at all." He argues that the power of that principle has been fueled by the civil rights revolution, the emergence of the identity politics, and a set of government policies designed to shift costs of remedying discrimination to the private sector.

In area after area—from gender, to age, to disability, to religion—Gewirtz shows how the antidiscrimination principle has displaced other ways of talking about social problems. Yet in each area he notes that the antidiscrimination principle has been transformed even as it has triumphed. "Originally non-discrimination meant an obligation to treat people the same. But today, non-discrimination is coming to mean accommodating differences." The transformation of antidiscrimination law is most vividly seen in affirmative action. Accommodating differences, Gewirtz concedes, "is simply more likely than 'formal equality' to produce speedy and broad inclusion of previously marginalized groups in important institutions." Yet he worries that "the differences that are being accommodated are differences that impose excessive costs," and that "in some circumstances we may find ourselves valorizing differences that in fact are regrettable products of oppression, differences that we should try to change rather than valorize or 'accommodate.'"

Part III of this book—"Reading the 'Realities' of Race"—moves beyond law to culture, beyond *Brown*'s impact on the articulation of legal ideas to its meaning in the life stories of African Americans and Caucasians in the United States. Here again we confront the ambiguities and uncertainties that surround racial issues in our society and that mark the meaning of *Brown*. However, now we confront them as they are played out in individual lives and in ongoing political struggles.

David Wilkins's "Social Engineers or Corporate Tools? *Brown v. Board of Education* and the Conscience of the Black Corporate Bar" begins Part III by asking what *Brown* has meant to the current generation of African American corporate lawyers. He argues that it is both an example and a trap for lawyers who are just now able to gain entry to the most powerful and prestigious corporate firms. It is an example of lawyers' commitment to the progress of all African Americans but also, in that example, a nagging reminder of the inadequacy of a life devoted to self-aggrandizement.

Wilkins describes the importance of Charles Hamilton Houston as a founding presence in the movement for black civil rights. Houston insisted that blacks, in particular an elite corps of black lawyers, had to play the leading role in that movement. He did not believe that whites, whatever their intentions, would have the commitment and the staying power to fight for racial progress. *Brown*, Wilkins argues, represented the triumph of Houston's vision. But, he asks, is that vision still relevant some forty years later? Is it still relevant to black corporate lawyers?

The answer, Wilkins suggests, is yes. Black corporate lawyers, he argues, "have moral obligations to advance the cause of racial justice that must be balanced against other legitimate professional commitments and personal goals." And, in fact, a large proportion of black corporate lawyers devote themselves to that cause. For them, the story of *Brown*, as well as the historical contributions of black lawyers to racial justice, is still very much alive in their consciousness and lives.

Carol Greenhouse explores the ambiguous cultural meaning of *Brown* in "A Federal Life: *Brown* and the Nationalization of the Life Story." How, she asks, has that case become part of the life stories of African Americans? It has indeed provided an important narrative structure, Greenhouse writes, through which recent generations of African Americans have been able to make sense of their own lives. "*Brown*," she says, "was the definition of an iconic life story for a particular generation of African Americans." For them, *Brown* was not about "the arithmetic of citizenship"; instead, it realized the narrative of an individual's life over time, a life enabled or disabled by its wants. The life story that it realized tied the progress of blacks to the power of the federal government. "After *Brown*, . . . African American lives belonged to the semiotics of the federal power and, through federal agency, to the nation as a whole."

Greenhouse illustrates the cultural narrative of race in post-*Brown* America by examining Darryl Pinckney's novel, *High Cotton*, and the confirmation hearings of Clarence Thomas. In the former, Supreme Court decisions, in particular *Brown*, are referents for the differing lives of the novel's two central characters, the narrator and his black grandfather. *Brown* held out the promise of a special future for the narrator and his generation; the crisis of the novel is the narrator's discovery that there is "no autobiographical interval" to connect him to that future.

Similarly, in the Clarence Thomas hearings, that case played a key role. Thomas explicitly linked his progress to the triumph of the civil rights movement. He asked the Senate to judge the life that that movement had made possible for African Americans. His life, like the life of the narrator in *High Cotton*, was not his own; it stood as a symbol of the nation's life in the post-*Brown* era.

Greenhouse ends her essay by suggesting that *Brown* contained another story, a "but for" story. The case constructed a narrative of possibility but also of danger: of blacks liberated to become full and productive citizens, but also another prospect of black lives, dangerous and unproductive. Today, Greenhouse worries, that other side is emerging. The life story that *Brown* now marks is a story of race and danger. "Recent cultural politics," Greenhouse notes, "has involved currents whose force is accelerated by deepening tensions between race and class . . . ; the widespread legibility of George Bush's 'Willy Horton' ad is a convenient icon of these changes." We have moved from civil rights to the criminal trial as the occasion for identifying the place of race in our national life. Racial difference is now a signal of racial danger.[76]

In the 1990s the underside of the narrative of black life implicit in *Brown* has emerged. Threat has been substituted for progress in the life story of African Americans. "The criminal trial paradigm," Greenhouse concludes, "reveals an element of the national life that *Brown* captured profoundly, and that is the extent to which one can celebrate a life story without acknowledging the life that *makes* the story."

In the face of these changes, how, Gary Peller asks, should people outside the black community respond? In answering that question he argues that the discourse about culture reflected in *Brown* was one important moment in the shifting ways that a (primarily white) educated elite has understood the significance of racial, and cultural difference. Today, Peller notes, that elite is enthralled with the ideology of cultural pluralism, what Friedman calls "plural equality." This ideology encourages respect for the autonomy and self-determination of cultural groups and deference to their conventions and choices. Nevertheless, Peller rejects it in favor of an interventionist-oriented—what otherwise might be called cultural imperialist—practice.

He argues that *Brown* was based on a recognition of cultural deprivation that justified massive intervention in the lives of southern communities. Recently, the idea of cultural deprivation as the basis for social policy has been called racist by both black nationalists and white progressives. It has been replaced by strident advocacy of cultural defense. This position, Peller argues, is the parallel in the cultural realm of laissez-faire in the market. Both, he contends, are false. Just as it was impossible in the economic sphere for individuals to be said to have simply decided for themselves, so it is impossible in the cultural sphere to ever have that kind of simple deference to a clearly identified community decision. For Peller, neither deference nor intervention can be decided by invoking formulae like respecting other people's cultures since cultures are always permeable and shifting. For him, intervention is always an open possibility, which, in the end, must be considered in light of claims of social justice.

It is to the claims of social justice, Hazel Carby suggests in the last essay in this volume, that the inheritors of *Brown* must be continuously attentive. While Peller addresses his argument primarily to white progressives, Carby inquires about the meaning of *Brown* for black intellectuals. In her view, it has had a significant impact in the cultural realm. Black literature and culture has been successfully "integrated." It is found in every college curriculum and in every suburban library. But, evoking Peller's discussion of deprivation, *Brown* has been noticeably less successful in dismantling American "apartheid."

Carby insists that cultural progress ought not be taken as a substitute for alleviating the continuing human misery of the black underclass. She warns that valorizing cultural diference is very risky. It has been, and will be, used by racists to defend a new politics of exclusion. In response, the inheritors of *Brown* should reclaim its meaning as an invitation to analyze "the relation between the production of cultural forms and the state of cultural formations, the material conditions that shape our collective as well as individual existence." She worries that cultural integration has been offered as a "pacifier, an antidote to the anger and outrage that we bitterly repress." Finally, she notes that the same legal system which brought us *Brown* has now turned its back on African Americans. Blacks must take up the cause of justice and equality that the courts refuse to defend. "Our present language of cultural integrationism, multiculturalism, must be replaced by an active politics of social, political, and economic transformation."

Carby's essay ends this collection by rejecting meaning in the name of materiality, by injecting an instrumentalist conclusion as a caution against an all-too-exclusive focus on the cultural and legal meaning of *Brown*. Hers and the other essays in this volume remind us not only of *Brown*'s significance in our national life, but also of the complexity and indeterminacy of its meanings in the contests and confrontations that mark today's racial politics. While it is clear that *Brown* gave new meaning to our Constitution and cultural life, its legacy has been, and can be, no more certain than the trajectory through which it will be narrated and renarrated in both law and culture. That case did not end our national conversation about race, law, and culture. *Race, Law, and Culture: Reflections on* Brown v. Board of Education uses it as a window into that conversation, as one way of thinking about issues such as affirmative action, multiculturalism, and the criminalization of black youth. It also gives us a chance to revisit a landmark case in the legal history of race and culture in the United States.

Notes

1. Compare Stephen Carter, *Reflections of an Affirmative Action Baby* (New York: Basic Books, 1991) and Thomas L. Dumm, "The New Enclosures: Racism in the Normalized Community," in *Reading Rodney King/Reading Urban Danger*, Robert Gooding-Williams ed. (New York: Routledge, 1993).

2. It is also the case that we are now coming to recognize the socially constructed character of race (see, for example, Lucius Outlaw, "Toward a Critical Theory of 'Race,'" in *Anatomy of Racism*, David Theo Goldberg ed. [Minneapolis: University of Minnesota Press, 1990]) and the fact that America is increasingly a multiracial society (Deborah Ramirez, "Multicultural Empowerment: It's Not Just Black and White Anymore," 47 *Stanford Law Review* [1995], 957).

3. See Michael Rosenfeld, *Affirmative Action and Justice: A Philosophical and Constitutional Inquiry* (New Haven: Yale University Press, 1991). Also Kathanne Greene, *Affirmative Action and Principles of Justice* (New York: Greenwood Press, 1989).

4. Charles Taylor et al., *Multiculturalism: Examining the Politics of Recognition* (Princeton: Princeton University Press, 1994). See also David Theo Goldberg, *Multiculturalism: A Critical Reader* (Boston: Blackwell, 1994) and Jurgen Habermas, "Address: Multiculturalism and the Liberal State," 47 *Stanford Law Review* (1995), 849.

5. Mari Matsuda et al., *Words That Wound: Critical Race Theory, Assaultive Speech and the First Amendment* (Boulder, Colo.: Westview, 1993). Also Kent Greenawalt, *Fighting Words: Individuals, Communities, and Liberties of Speech* (Princeton: Princeton University Press, 1995).

6. See Andrew Kull, *The Colorblind Constitution* (Cambridge, Mass.: Harvard University Press, 1992). Also William Van Alstyne, "Rites of Passage: Race, the Supreme Court and the Constitution," 46 *University of Chicago Law Review* (1979), 775, and Wendy Brown-Scott, "Justice Thurgood Marshall and the Integrative Ideal," 26 *Arizona State Law Journal* (1994), 535.

7. Alexis de Tocqueville, *Democracy in America*, Henry Reeve trans. (Boston: John Allyn, 1876), ch. 18.

8. Gunnar Myrdal, *An American Dilemma: The Negro Problem and Modern Democracy* (New York: Harper, 1944).

9. See Kimberle Williams Crenshaw, "Race, Reform, and Retrenchment: Transformation and Legitimation in Antidiscrimination Law," 101 *Harvard Law Review* (1988), 1331.

10. David Strauss, "The Myth of Colorblindness," 1986 *Supreme Court Review* (1986), 99.

11. J. Harvie Wilkinson, *From Brown to Bakke: The Supreme Court and School Integration: 1954–1978* (New York: Oxford University Press, 1979), 6.

12. For a discussion of the way difference is conceptualized in law see Martha Minow, *Making All the Difference: Inclusion, Exclusion, and American Law* (Ithaca, N.Y.: Cornell University Press, 1990). Also Austin Sarat & Roger Berkowitz, "Disorderly Differences: Recognition, Accommodation and American Law," 6 *Yale Journal of Law & the Humanities* (1994), 285.

13. This point is made by Lawrence Friedman, *Total Justice* (New York: Russell Sage Foundation, 1985).

14. See Charles Black, "The Lawfulness of the Segregation Decision," 89 *Yale Law Journal* (1960), 421. Also Charles Black, *The People and the Court: Judicial Review in a Democracy* (Englewood Cliffs, N.J.: Prentice-Hall, 1960).

15. Kenneth Karst, *Belonging to America: Equal Citizenship and the Constitution* (New Haven: Yale University Press, 1989), 15.

16. Wilkinson, supra note 11, at 6.

17. See Mark Tushnet, "The Significance of *Brown v. Board*," 80 *Virginia Law Review* (1994), 176. See also William Bradford Reynolds, "Individualism vs. Group Rights: The Legacy of *Brown*," 93 *Yale Law Journal* (1984), 998.

18. See 163 U.S. 537 (1896).

19. See 347 U.S. 483, 493 (1954).

20. See John Casais, "Ignoring the Harm: The Supreme Court, Stigmatic Injury, and the End of School Desegregation," 14 *Boston College Third World Law Journal* (1994), 259.

21. 347 U.S. 483, 493.

22. *Id.* at 494. The extent to which the meaning of *Brown* is separable from the arguments about the psychological effects of segregation is even today a subject of dispute. As Justice Thomas recently argued, *"Brown I* itself did not need to rely upon any psychological or social-science research in order to announce the simple yet fundamental truth that the Government cannot discriminate among its citizens on the basis of race. . . . Psychological injury or benefit is irrelevant to the question whether state actors have engaged in intentional discrimination." See Missouri v. Jenkins, 63 U.S.L.W. 4486, 4500 (1995).

23. *Id.* at 495.

24. As J. Harvie Wilkinson argues, "[T]he Court refused to lift the nation to the magnificence of the principle it had that day redeemed. It even refused to borrow eloquence. . . . In short, the opinion failed to rouse or inspire; it simply existed." Wilkinson, supra note 11, at 29.

25. This style was praised at the time of *Brown* by Albert Sacks, "The Supreme Court, 1953 Term," 68 *Harvard Law Review* (1954), 96, 98–99.

26. See Garry Wills, *Lincoln at Gettysburg: The Words That Remade America* (New York: Simon & Schuster, 1992).

27. See Richard Kluger, *Simple Justice* (New York: Knopf, 1975), x.

28. See David Garrow, "Hopelessly Hollow History: Revisionist Devaluing of *Brown v. Board of Education*," 80 *Virginia Law Review* (1994), 151.

29. *Brown* was "a crossroads, not just for an outcast race, but for an outcast region, a true testing ground for liberal values and theory, a challenge for the rule of law and the authority of the Court." See Wilkinson, supra note 11, at 6.

30. Kluger, supra note 27, at ix.

31. See 93 *Yale Law Journal* (1984), 981.

32. See Charles Lawrence, "'One More River to Cross'—Recognizing the

Real Injury in *Brown:* A Prerequisite to Shaping New Remedies," in *Shades of Brown: New Perspectives on School Desegregation*, Derrick Bell ed. (Jackson: University of Mississippi Press, 1980).

33. See Gary Orfield, *The Reconstruction of Southern Education* (New York: Wiley, 1969). John Casais notes that "[a]s the 1990s began, some eight hundred school systems in the United States were under court supervision because school authorities had operated them in a racially discriminatory manner." See Casais, supra note 20, at 259. Also Tushnet, supra note 17, at 175. "If *Brown*," Tushnet suggests, "aimed at achieving some significant distribution of children of both races in the same schools, it was indeed a failure." MaryAnn Dadisman, "Still Segregated: The Legacy of *Brown*," 21 *Human Rights* (1994), 12.

34. See Gerald Rosenberg, *The Hollow Hope: Can Courts Bring About Social Change?* (Chicago: University of Chicago Press, 1991), ch. 2.

35. See Michael Klarman, "*Brown*, Racial Change and the Civil Rights Movement," 80 *Virginia Law Review* (1994), 10.

36. Rosenberg, supra note 34, at 70–71.

37. See James Washburn, "Beyond *Brown*: Evaluating Equality in Higher Education," 43 *Duke Law Journal* (1994), 1115; Daniel Gordon, "Happy Anniversary *Brown v. Board of Education*: In Need of a Remake After Forty Years," 25 *Columbia Human Rights Law Review* (1993), 107; and Joseph Goldstein, *The Intelligible Constitution* (New York: Oxford University Press, 1992). For a useful discussion of the doctrinal controversy surrounding *Brown*, see Morton Horwitz, "The Jurisprudence of *Brown* and the Dilemmas of Liberalism," 14 *Harvard Civil Liberties—Civil Rights Law Review* (1979), 599.

38. That vision is described by Brown-Scott, supra note 6. For critiques of that vision see Barbara Flagg, "Enduring Principle: On Race, Process, and Constitutional Law," 82 *California Law Review* (1994), 935. See also Washburn, supra note 37; Frederick Hord, "African-Americans: Cultural Pluralism and the Politics of Culture," 91 *West Virginia Law Review* (1989), 1047; T. Alexander Aleinekoff, "A Case for Race Consciousness," 91 *Columbia Law Review* (1991), 1060.

39. See Drew Days, "*Brown* Blues: Rethinking the Integrative Ideal," 34 *William and Mary Law Review* (1992), 53. Also J. Harvie Wilkinson, "The Law of Civil Rights and the Dangers of Separatism in Multicultural America," 47 *Stanford Law Review* (1995), 993.

40. Wilkinson, supra note 39, at 994.

41. See Mark Tushnet, "Public Law Litigation and the Ambiguities of *Brown*," 61 *Fordham Law Review* (1992), 23.

42. For useful examples see Nathan Glazer, *Affirmative Discrimination: Ethnic Inequality and Public Policy* (New York: Basic Books, 1975); Carter, supra note 1; William Bradford Reynolds, supra note 17.

43. See Wendy Brown-Scott, "The Communitarian State: Lawlessness or Law Reform," 107 *Harvard Law Review* (1994), 1209.

44. The essays collected in this volume were first presented under the aegis of the Charles Hamilton Houston Forum on Law and Social Change, an annual event honoring Charles Hamilton Houston, of Amherst's class of 1915. Houston had an outstanding career at Amherst, and carried what he learned there into the world to struggle for social justice. His life as a lawyer and as a legal educator exemplifies a belief that our law is more than a device for maintaining social order; it is and can be a tool for changing the society that it serves. Houston played a key role in devising

the legal strategy that ultimately led to the decision in *Brown*. As Kluger put it, in the struggle for racial justice through law, Charles Houston became the critical figure that linked "the passion of Frederick Douglass demanding black freedom and of William Du Bois demanding black equality to the undelivered promises of the Constitution of the United States." Kluger, supra note 27, at 106.

45. For a good example of the instrumentalist perspective, see Harrell Rodgers & Charles Bullock, *Law and Social Change: Civil Rights Laws and Their Conse-quences* (New York: McGraw Hill, 1992).

46. For a discussion of the difference in these perspectives see Austin Sarat & Thomas R. Kearns, "Beyond the Great Divide: Forms of Legal Scholarship and Everyday Life," in *Law and Everyday Life*, Austin Sarat & Thomas R. Kearns eds. (Ann Arbor: University of Michigan Press, 1993).

47. See Wilkinson, supra note 11, at chs. 4–9.

48. As Robert Gordon has observed, "[W]riters in this tradition divide the world into two spheres, one social and one legal. Society is the primary realm of social experience. It is 'real life': What's immediately and truly important to peo-ple . . . goes on there. . . . 'Law' or 'the legal system', on the other hand, is a distinctly secondary body of phenomena. It is a specialized realm of state and professional activity that is called into being by the primary social world in order to serve that world's needs. Law is auxiliary—an excrescence on social life, even if sometimes a useful excrescence." See "Critical Legal Histories," 34 *Stanford Law Review* (1984), 60.

49. Clifford Geertz, *Local Knowledge: Further Essays in Interpretive Anthro-pology* (New York: Basic Books, 1983).

50. *Id.* at 184.

51. *Id.* at 232. As David Trubek argues, "[I]nterpretivists: understand the world in terms of . . . structures of meaning. . . . [A]n interpretivist does not split action into a soft and arbitrary core of individual volition and a hard shell of external constraint. Rather, he sees action as the result of socially constructed systems of meaning which constitute the individual, providing the grounds for behavior and defining the channels of conduct." See Trubek, "Where the Action Is: Critical Legal Studies and Empiricism," 34 *Stanford Law Review* (1984), 604.

52. See Geertz, supra note 49, at 232.

53. "The values, knowledge, and evaluative criteria embodied in the subjec-tivity of actors are not individually held units of meaning but rather are the threads or traces of a collectively held fabric of social relations." See David Trubek & John Esser, "'Critical Empiricism' in American Legal Studies: Paradox, Program, or Pandora's Box?" 14 *Law & Social Inquiry* (1989), 17.

54. In *Local Knowledge*, Clifford Geertz suggested that "law, rather than a mere technical add-on to a morally (or immorally) finished society, is, along of course with a whole range of other cultural realities, . . . an active part of it. . . . Law . . . is, in a word, constructive; in another constitutive; in a third, formational. . . . Law, with its power to place particular things that hap-pen . . . in a general frame in such a way that rules for the principled manage-ment of them seem to arise naturally from the essentials of their character, is rather more than a reflection of received wisdom or a technology of dispute-settlement." Supra note 49, at 218 and 230.

55. Susan Silbey, "Law and the Order of Our Life Together: A Sociological Interpretation of the Relationship Between Law and Society," in *Law and the Order*

of Our Life Together, Richard Neuhaus ed. (Grand Rapids, Mich.: William Eerd-mans Publishing, 1990), 20.

56. For an important recent example of this way of talking about *Brown* see Garrow, supra note 28, at 151.

57. See Karst, supra note 15. This thesis is itself not without its critics; see Michael Klarman, "*Brown v. Board of Education*: Facts and Political Correctness," 80 *Virginia Law Review* (1994), 185.

58. See also Loren Miller, *The Petitioners: The Story of the Supreme Court of the United States and the Negro* (New York: Pantheon Books, 1966).

59. This vision of the meaning of the constitution was attacked by Herbert Wechsler, "Toward Neutral Principles of Constitutional Law," 73 *Harvard Law Review* (1959), 1. For an important response see Paul Brest, "Foreword: In Defense of the Anti-Discrimination Principle," 90 *Harvard Law Review* (1976), 1.

60. See Learned Hand, *The Bill of Rights* (Cambridge, Mass.: Harvard University Press, 1958).

61. Wechsler, supra note 59.

62. See Louis Pollak, "Racial Discrimination and Judicial Integrity: A Reply to Professor Wechsler," 108 *University of Pennsylvania Law Review* (1959), 1.

63. For different responses see Brest, supra note 59; also William Taylor, "*Brown*, Equal Protection, and the Isolation of the Poor," 95 *Yale Law Journal* (1986), 1700.

64. See Henry Louis Gates, "Beyond the Culture Wars: Identities in Dialogue," *Profession* (1993), 93.

65. For criticism of the *Brown* approach see Raoul Berger, *The Fourteenth Amendment and the Bill of Rights* (Norman: University of Oklahoma Press, 1989).

66. See 369 U.S. 186 (1962).

67. 381 U.S. 479 (1965).

68. 410 U.S. 113 (1972).

69. See 112 S. Ct. 2791 (1992).

70. 198 U.S. 45 (1905).

71. For a contrasting perspective see Casais, supra note 20.

72. As Washburn argues, "The inferiority described in *Brown* should be attributed to the notions of white superiority ingrained in social structure that once demanded mandatory segregation." Supra note 37, at 119.

73. For a similar view see Lawrence Tribe, "In What Vision of the Constitution Must the Law Be Color-Blind?" 20 *John Marshall Law Review* (1986), 201.

74. Burke Marshall contends that the antidiscrimination principle is itself ambiguous as an expression of the meaning of equal protection of the law. See "A Comment on the Nondiscrimination Principle in a 'Nation of Minorities,'" 93 *Yale Law Journal* (1984), 1007.

75. See Lawrence Friedman, *Republic of Choice: Law, Authority and Culture* (Cambridge, Mass.; Harvard University Press, 1990). For a contrasting perspective see Kristin Bumiller, *The Civil Rights Society: The Social Construction of Victims* (Baltimore, Md.: Johns Hopkins University Press, 1988).

76. Judith Butler, "Endangered/Endangering: Schematic Racism and White Paranoia," in Robert Gooding-Williams ed., supra note 1.

BROWN AND ITS LEGAL CONTEXTS

PEGGY COOPER DAVIS

Performing Interpretation

A *Legacy of Civil Rights Lawyering in* Brown v. Board of Education

What A Single Sentence shows—
An Introductory Illustration

On August 22, 1861, James McCune Smith, an African American abolitionist, wrote a letter to Gerrit Smith, a European American abolitionist.
Gerrit Smith had published an arguably conciliatory appeal to the New York
State Democratic Committee, urging that it express solidarity with President
Lincoln against the Confederacy. James McCune Smith chided his colleague
in antislavery struggle for giving attention to a "dead Democratic Committee"
and neglecting to insist upon immediate emancipation as the only moral
means of restoring the Union. For James McCune Smith, the moral and
political error of Gerrit Smith's course was apparent from the terms of his
argument to the Democratic Committee. In what may be the earliest recorded
example of a critical race theory analysis of American political discourse, the
African American Smith wrote: "A single sentence . . . shows that you
fail to see 'the Situation.' You say 'for whilst the other President (Davis) is
cheered and strengthened by the entire devotion . . . to his cause of all
around him.' &c. &c. Is this true? Is it not virtually ignoring one half of those
around Jeff Davis (I mean the Slaves)?"[1] Gerrit Smith was able to imagine
Jefferson Davis cheered and strengthened by the entire devotion of all around
him, I think, because when he imagined the Confederate community—when
he imagined the political and social entity that the South had become—he
instinctively imagined a white community. When James McCune Smith
imagined the Confederate community, he envisioned black and white, slave
and free—the cheering and devoted people who chose to follow Davis and

the watchful and disaffiliated people who, even as they planned the desertion of plantation enterprise and "defections" to the Union army that would give the Union its eventual margin of victory,[2] were presumed to have no choice.

The instinct to imagine the political community of these United States as a white community continued, in the psyches of black people as well as in the psyches of white people, to exist and to affect the course of national self-definition for at least the nearly one hundred years from 1861 to 1954. It was expressed in presuppositions of the kind exposed by James McCune Smith. It was expressed as African Americans wavered between stances of affiliation and of alienation *vis à vis* the old and the reconstructed Union.[3] It was reinforced as a segregated America settled into both crude and subtle rituals of dominance and subordination.[4]

My analysis of *Brown* builds on the insight of James McCune Smith, the unwitting critical race theorist, that we Americans have had difficulty imagining a multicultural political community. This is my hypothesis: The lawyers for the African American plaintiffs who brought *Brown* to the Supreme Court simultaneously played upon and subverted the image of the United States as a white polity. In some respects, they manifested a strategic, albeit culturally ingrained, deference to social, judicial, and doctrinal authority. At the same time, however, they commanded unprecedented authority in the interpretation of constitutional doctrine. In the end, their efforts transformed our Constitution, establishing it as an open text—a text to be (real)ized in interpretive deliberation informed by previously neglected perspectives. Moreover, as they brought neglected American perspectives to constitutional deliberation, the *Brown* lawyers loosened the national imagination from its inability to conceptualize African American participation in the processes of political self-definition.

I hope to elaborate this hypothesis by taking you through an analysis of the language and structure of oral arguments offered by two of the lawyers who faced the Court in 1952: Robert Carter and Thurgood Marshall, arguing for the plaintiffs in Kansas and South Carolina. The argument of John Davis, arguing for the State of South Carolina, will also be considered, for it serves both to illustrate a defensive stance and to provide a sense of the interactive context within which Marshall conducted his argument.[5]

Before turning to the arguments, I must say a few words about how and why the structure and language of appellate argument might reveal things that are not obvious about the stances and the conscious and unconscious strategies of the participating lawyers.

Markers of Strategy and Stance

I begin by positing two stances that plaintiffs' lawyers in a case such as *Brown* might assume. Either of these stances might be assumed as a matter of conscious strategy, as a matter of culturally ingrained habit, or as a result of both factors. On the one hand, lawyers might speak (and present their clients) as full members of the political community, entitled to a voice in the articulation and interpretation of its laws. On the other hand, they might speak (and present their clients) as supplicants in need of the help and protection of the Court and the law. I will refer to these two possible stances as the stance of political self-definition and the stance of political appeal. From a stance of political self-definition, we would expect people to argue that "we" as a society are or should be committed to a certain course. From a stance of political appeal, we would expect people to present a plight and urge that the law, or some other external entity, respond to it. A politically self-defining litigant would urge an interpretation of law or a vision of social duty. A supplicating litigant would appeal for a remedy.

You will notice that the two stances are different, but they are not opposites. We might say that the opposite of an appeal is a demand, and that the opposite of self-definition is deference to text, precedent, or original intent.[6] Moreover, the stances are not mutually exclusive. One could make an appeal or a demand in terms that are politically self-defining or in terms that are text-bound, precedent-bound, or originalist.[7] Indeed, a lawyer asserting a constitutional claim is likely to alternate between the stances of self-definition and appeal, utilizing each in a wide variety of ways. These two stances are analyzed, not because they are contrasting as a matter of logic, but because they represent distinct and politically significant approaches to the assertion of a constitutional claim. When used in different degrees and patterns, the stances will create different impressions and generate different reactions—both within the context of the litigation and within broader political and social contexts.

Despite the fact that the stances of political appeal and political self-definition are neither opposite nor mutually exclusive, the two stances are distinguishable. There are patterns of speech that warrant characterization as political appeal and *different* patterns of speech that warrant characterization as politically self-defining. I will examine four of the markers by which lawyers take on the stances of political appeal and political self-definition. The first has to do with the conceptualization of the legal claim; the remaining three have to do with its articulation. Let me describe them in turn.

Conceiving and Casting the Claim

Any story can be told with a variety of casting choices. *Hamlet* can be told with or without Rosencrantz and Guildenstern, and *Rosencrantz and Guildenstern* can be told virtually without Hamlet. A closing argument in a homicide case may star the defendant and the victim—revisiting the details of the act of killing, or it may star the jurors as guardians of liberty and due process—making vivid the duty to resist the temptation to convict on less than conclusive evidence in a doubtful case.[8] These choices are often strategic. A good defense lawyer consciously or unconsciously knows the value of starring the jurors as s/he closes a difficult case; a good prosecutor consciously or unconsciously knows the value of starring the victim and defendant in a strong case.

There will often be casting alternatives even with respect to the identity and characterization of the claimants. The story of segregated public schooling that was told in *Brown* could be a story of children stigmatized and hurt by separation, a story of parents denied the appropriate benefits of citizenship, or a story of a community subordinated by caste legislation. The choice will often have implications for the stances of the litigants and lawyers.

Voicing the Claim

Displaying Authority Uses of deferential terms and of tentative forms of assertion have been associated with social powerlessness.[9] They have also been associated with subordinate status in professional interactions.[10] Although these markers are ambiguous, their cautious analysis can be illuminating. We might predict that, on the whole, a supplicant will be more deferential, whereas a political participant will be more assertive. However, we will be sensitive to the possibility that polite and tentative forms will have strategic values that are more complex than the notions of powerlessness and subordination might suggest.

Displaying Interpretive Function Students of discourse have distinguished exposition styles that call attention to the person and role of the speaker and those that mask or background the speaker. The difference is marked by an absence or presence of "frames" that comment upon the conversational situation. Some of these frames are obvious, like the introductory, self-depreciating joke to encourage audience-speaker bonding. Some are subtle, like the use of mental verbs, such as "I think that . . . ," or verbs of assertion, such as "I contend that. . . ." I will refer to mental verbs and verbs of assertion collectively as "mental state verbs."

Some analysts have noted the tentativeness conveyed by the use of mental state verbs and associated their use with deferential, powerless speech.[11] If these analysts are correct, then we would count a heavy use of mental verbs as a marker of political appeal. On the other hand, the interpretation of mental state verbs as deferential would not lead us to associate them with acts of political self-definition.

A recent and suggestive analysis of the speech of divinity students concluded that self-referencing framing devices, such as mental state verbs, are used more extensively by speakers who comfortably claim interpretive authority.[12] If this conclusion is correct, then a stance of political self-definition might be associated with the more extensive use of mental state verbs. We will need to sort out the apparent inconsistency between earlier interpretations of mental state verbs as deferential (and therefore suggestive of political appeal) and this more recent interpretation of mental state verbs as markers of a sense of interpretive authority (and therefore suggestive of political self-definition).

Analysts of legal and political texts have noted that speakers often choose to employ direct, as opposed to indirect, framing devices when they want to draw attention to the hierarchical eminence of a text. For example, a statute might be set off in quotes, maintaining its original form and deictic anchoring ("The statute provides: 'Under rendition of a verdict of guilty, the court shall enter an order requiring that a sentencing investigation be conducted by the Department of Probation.'"), or it might be paraphrased, allowing the speaker to alter its original form and perspective ("Your Honor is required, under the statute, to order a presentence investigation.")[13] The first form reinforces the status of the text, while the second calls attention to the existence of an interpreter. We might expect lawyers working from a stance of political self-definition to use indirect framing devices, thereby seizing interpretive authority. On the other hand, the framing strategies of lawyers working from a stance of political appeal will not be predictable in this respect, for one might appeal to the authority of law or to the discretion of the court.

Displaying Affiliation   The use of personal pronouns allows a lawyer to display or mask affiliation with the client, with the bench, with professional colleagues or with the political community. The lawyer who says, "I ask this on behalf on my client," takes a different stance from the lawyer who says, "We are injured by the defendants' acts." The first highlights an independent professional role; the second expresses solidarity with the claimant. The lawyer who highlights a professional role beyond service as the voice of the client seems positioned for political self-definition. The lawyer who voices directly the plight of his client seems positioned for political appeal.

The lawyer who says in oral argument, "We must look to the meaning of equality in a society committed to democracy and universal education," takes a different stance from the lawyer who says, "The Constitution does (or does not) prohibit segregation." The first takes a stance of political self-definition by expressing affiliation with the political community and implicitly inviting the justices to share in an interpretive inquiry, while the second masks affiliation and implicitly denies interpretation. The first invites partnership with the bench in an interpretive effort; the second suggests that the meaning of the constitutional text is closed.

Let us turn to the *Brown* arguments and analyze, first, the choices made in casting the claim and then, the displays of authority, interpretive function, and affiliation that occurred as the claim was voiced.

Whose Claim? Casting the Litigation Narrative

The Plaintiffs' Star Negro Children

The plaintiffs' decisions in conceiving and casting their claim can only be understood against the backdrop of precedent. We begin, therefore, with a review of casting decisions in prior, similar claims brought to the Supreme Court—specifically, of decisions about who would be cast as the aggrieved

party. This is a review of rhetorical choices, not a review of the law of standing. Principles of standing do not constrain the choices discussed. Indeed, in
several of the cases (and in the *Brown* cases) claimants in two or more categories were named in the pleadings, but claimants in only one category were
featured in the rhetoric of the Court or of counsel.

In 1899, people of color, describing themselves as parents of school-age
children, citizens and residents, property owners, and taxpayers, sued to challenge a decision to close the only public high school in Richmond County,
Georgia, open to children who were not white. When relief was denied in the
courts of Georgia, they took their claim to the Supreme Court, arguing that
they, their children, and the African American community were denied equal
protection of the laws. At each stage of the litigation, they emphasized their
status as citizens, property owners, and taxpayers, and claimed an entitlement
to equal schooling for their community. The Supreme Court of the United
States, echoing the Supreme Court of Georgia, found that Richmond County
school authorities had acted appropriately with respect to the interests of black
children:

> The *colored school children* of the county would not be advanced in the
> matter of their education by a decree compelling the defendant board to
> cease giving support to a high school for white children. The board had
> before it the question whether it should maintain, under its control,
> a high school for about 60 colored children or withhold the benefits
> of education in primary schools from 300 children of the same race. It
> was impossible, the board believed, to give educational facilities to
> the 300 colored children who were unprovided for, if it maintained a
> separate school for the 60 children who wished to have a high-school
> education. *Its decision was in the interest of the greater number of colored
> children.*[14]

The court did not address the board's responsibility vis-à-vis the petitioning
parents. This rhetorical choice is unusual. In subsequent cases, both litigants
and justices cast education claims as the claims of adults.

In 1923, a Nebraska teacher challenged laws that prohibited conducting
elementary school classes in languages other than English. The Supreme
Court ruled in his favor, reversing the Supreme Court of Nebraska on the
grounds of the right of the teacher to pursue his calling without undue state
interference and the right of parents to direct the education of their children
without undue state interference.[15] The rights and interests of children were
not mentioned.

In 1925, certain private schools challenged an Oregon law requiring that
all elementary school children attend public schools. The Supreme Court
upheld the challenge, relying upon the right of the plaintiff to pursue its
business interests and the right of parents to direct the education of their
children.[16] The rights of children were not mentioned.

In 1927, an association of Japanese language schools operating in Hawaii
challenged a law that would have placed the curricula of those schools under
government control and vastly restricted opportunities to teach languages

other than English. Affirming the holding of lower federal courts, the Supreme Court found the law unconstitutional in that it interfered with a Japanese parent's "right to direct the education of his own child without unreasonable restrictions."[17] The rights of children were not mentioned.

Also in 1927, a Chinese father and child claimed the child's right to attend a white public school in Bolivar County, Mississippi. The Supreme Court agreed that both father and child had rights with respect to the availability of public schooling for the child, but also agreed with the Supreme Court of Mississippi that the federal Constitution afforded no right for a Chinese student to attend a white school.[18]

In 1940, a father and his minor children brought suit to challenge a Pennsylvania law requiring that public school children pledge allegiance to the flag of the United States as part of their school-day routine. Although the matter had been argued in terms of the rights and interests of both parents and children, the Supreme Court considered the matter in terms of parental rights. It upheld the right of the state to interfere in this way with the right of parents to direct the upbringing of their children.[19]

In 1943, West Virginia parents raised the same claim that had been rejected three years earlier when it was raised by Pennsylvania parents and their children. On this occasion, the Supreme Court reversed itself, holding that the requirement of a pledge of allegiance interfered too greatly with the right of parents to direct the upbringing of their children.[20] Although the opinion addressed at length the rights of *individuals* to protection against state coercion, the rights of children, as such, were not addressed.

In 1948, the Supreme Court considered the case of Vashti McCollum, a citizen, taxpayer, and parent who objected to the use of public school classrooms, during school hours, for religious instruction. Resting on the interests of parents as taxpayers in seeing that their taxes do not contribute to activities in their children's schools that those parents deem inappropriate, the Court upheld McCollum's claim.[21]

These are all of the cases I have found in which the Court considered, before 1952, the manner in which public education was provided. In each case, a parental right was claimed. In several, the rights of children went unmentioned. In all but one, the rhetoric of the Court carried, at least in part, the theme of parental rights. Interestingly, in the single case in which the Court's narrative highlighted children rather than parents, the petitioning families were African American.

In 1996, many of us feel concern that the rights of children would still remain unexpressed, or only vicariously expressed, in cases touching their interests in important ways. But let us set aside that concern for a time and consider the strategic choices of the *Brown* lawyers as they worked in the fourth and fifth decades of this century to end school segregation. Past rhetoric of the Court and the practice of litigants arguing before the Court with respect to the education of children would have suggested that the claim be framed as a right of African American parents, citizens, and taxpayers to full benefit of systems established for the education of children within their communities.

This framing would have resonated well with the history of the Fourteenth Amendment and with the history of the people who sought relief. Like so many great ideals of the United States' political system, the ideal of family liberty was refined and deepened by the struggle against the enslavement and caste oppression of African Americans.[22] Slavery required that men, women and children be bound more surely by ties of ownership than by ties of kinship. Slavery supported itself by annulment of marital, parental, and paternal rights. Drafters and advocates of the Fourteenth Amendment had vivid impressions of what it meant to be denied rights of family, for the denial of those rights was a hallmark of slavery in the United States. These men and women regarded the denial of family liberty as a vice of slavery that inverted concepts of human dignity, citizenship, and natural law. They regarded the Fourteenth Amendment as the instrument that would reenshrine family liberty as an inalienable aspect of national citizenship, and they regarded rights of parental authority and autonomy as central to the concept of family liberty. Eric Foner describes this expectation as he reports former slaves' reactions to the socializing authority of the slaveholder class. Foner reports that after Emancipation Georgia freedman James Jeter was beaten "for claiming the right of whipping his own child instead of allowing his employer and former master to do so."[23] He also quotes the following complaint, made to the governor by a black North Carolinian in 1869:

> I was in my field at my own work and [Dr. A. H.] Jones came by me and drove up to a man's gate that live close by . . . and ordered my child to come there and open that gate for him . . . while there was children in the yard at the same time not more than twenty yards from him and jest because they were white and mine black he wood not call them to open the gate. . . . I spoke gently to him that [the white children] would open the gate. . . . He got out of his buggy . . . and walked nearly hundred yards rite into my field where I was at my own work and double his fist and strick me in the face three times and . . . cursed me [as] a dum old Radical. . . . Now governor I wants you to please rite to me how to bring this man to jestus.[24]

Foner recognizes "political meaning" in this encounter, a meaning that is influenced both by Lewis's refusal "to let a stranger's authority be imposed on his family" and by his assumption that government would provide a remedy for the assault on his person and his dignity.[25]

Despite the intertwined history of the Fourteenth Amendment and the African American parent class—and despite the body of precedent conceptualizing rights with respect to public schooling as rights inhering in parents, there was good reason to conceptualize the *Brown* claim as a claim of children harmed. The image of children harmed was credible and compelling, while the image of African American citizens claiming entitlement resisted cultural expectations.

We do not know whether these factors were consciously considered. We do know that parental voices were not scripted into the arguments. The story was not of a denial of the rights of citizen-taxpayers; it was a story of children being harmed. It was a story of plight, rather than one of right. Speaking first among counsel for the plaintiffs, Robert Carter argued:

> [T]he statute requires appellants to attend public elementary schools on a segregated basis . . . [and] the act of . . . segregation in and of itself denies them equal educational opportunities.

> Negro children are denied equal protection of the laws, and they cannot secure equality in educational opportunity.

> [W]here public school attendance is determined on the basis of race and color, . . . it is impossible for Negro children to secure equal educational opportunities.

> Negro children are . . . put in one category for public school purposes, solely on the basis of race and color.

> [T]his type of segregation makes it impossible for Negro children and appellants in this case to receive equal educational opportunities.

> [T]he restrictions which the appellants complained of place them and other Negro children . . . at a disadvantage with respect to the quality of education which they would receive, and . . . as a result . . . the development of their minds and the learning process is impaired and damaged.

> [T]hese restrictions imposed disabilities on Negro children and prevented them from having [equal] educational opportunities.[26]

Thurgood Marshall argued:

> [T]he humiliation that these children have been going through is the type of injury to the minds that will be permanent as long as they are in segregated schools, not theoretical injury, but actual injury.

> I have yet to hear anyone say that they denied that these children are harmed by reason of this segregation. Nobody denies that, at least up to now. So there is a grant, I should assume, that segregation in and of itself harms these children.

> [State imposed segregation] affects the individual children.

> I know of no scientist that has made any study, whether he be anthropologist or sociologist, who does not admit that segregation harms the child.[27]

With one brief exception, neither attorney argued from the right of African American parents, who were also plaintiffs below, to protect their children against a system that subordinated and stigmatized them, to assure that their children were socialized to full citizenship, to choose integrated classrooms for their children, or to enjoy the full benefits of schools supported by their tax dollars. The exception was a reference to the most prestigious African American within the Justices' ken; Marshall said during the course of his argument: "[I]f Ralph Bunche were assigned to South Carolina, his children would have to go to a Jim Crow school. No matter how great anyone becomes, if he happens to have been born a Negro, regardless of his color, he is relegated to that school."[28]

The plaintiffs' decision to star Negro children had the decided benefit of creating a maximally sympathetic claim. It highlighted suffering children and cast the Court as the entity that could alleviate their suffering. But the choice was not cost free. The decision to highlight suffering children and to keep their parents offstage imposed constraints on the litigation. It drew the Court's focus from the fact that the harm complained of was an element of caste-based subordination that affected, not just schoolchildren, but an entire race. It masked the indignity of being forced, as an African American, to support schools that stigmatized one's race as well as one's children. It increased the chance that remedies would be determined by public officials on a majoritarian basis rather than by African American communities and their parents. And it reduced the liberating potential of the litigation campaign, depriving the lawyers of opportunities to promote, and to advance realization of, a full citizenship role for African American adults. We will see presently how compensating political gains were built into the form and content of the arguments of Carter and Marshall.

The State Casts a Villain

The plaintiffs' decision to highlight the children and to keep their parents offstage also facilitated certain responsive arguments. Davis characterized the choice to segregate as a choice made by an adult majority to protect "their" collective children from "what may be an unwelcome contact."[29] The implication was that local political majorities would better protect the interests of children than would the children's representatives in the litigation. Since the plaintiffs had not scripted parents as the children's representatives, it was easier for Davis to argue that the children's interests were adequately considered by the local majority that chose segregation. It was also easier for Davis to cast—and to make villains of—those who spoke for change in the children's behalf. In Davis's narrative, the children's representatives were activist lawyers who argued against segregation. He referred, for example, to the plan to desegregate as "Mr. Marshall['s] . . . redistricting program." At another point in the argument, Davis asserted that Marshall had "some plan . . . by which the districts will be redistricted again with resulting benefit to all concerned." Later in his argument, Davis returned to the theme of the activist agitator for "mixed schools." He described the plight of the State of South Carolina as follows:

> Now, South Carolina is unique among the states in one particular. You have often heard it said that an ounce of experience is worth a pound of theory. South Carolina does not come to this policy as a stranger. She had mixed schools for twelve years, from 1865 to 1877. She had them as a result of the Constitutional Convention of 1865, which was led by a preacher of the Negro race, against whom I know nothing, who bore the somewhat distinguished name of Cardozo, and he forced through that convention the provision for mixed schools.[30]

In fact, the provision for public schooling adopted by the South Carolina Convention of 1865, the first in the South to contemplate universal education, had broader, and interracial, support.[31] Moreover, Cardozo's position with respect to the provision was complex and consistent with sensitivity to the competing goals of ending enforced segregation and promoting parental autonomy. He had argued as follows to the Convention:

> Before I proceed to discuss the question, I want to divest it of all false issue of the imaginary consequences that some gentlemen have illogically thought will result from the adoption of this section with the word "compulsory." They affirm that it compels the attendance of both white and colored children in the same schools. There is nothing of the kind in the section. It simply says that all the children shall be educated; but how, it is left with the parents to decide. It is left to the parent to say whether the child should be sent to a public or private school. There can be separate schools for white and colored. It is left so that if any colored child wishes to go to a white school, it shall have the privilege of doing so. I have no doubt, in most localities colored people will prefer separate schools, particularly until some of the present prejudice against their race is removed.[32]

But the story of a multicultural coalition for educational reform consistent with the exercise of parental authority did not suit Davis's narrative strategy. The image of inept government by carpetbaggers and former slaves was summoned, and the possibility of parental choice was ignored. Playing upon the misinterpretations of Reconstruction history that were prevalent at the time, Davis argued that South Carolina promptly and properly recognized the adoption of mixed schooling as "the most unwise action of the period."[33]

As Anthony Amsterdam has demonstrated in his brilliant analysis of the narrative and lexical structure of the Davis and Marshall arguments, Davis spun around the character of the activist lawyer a tale of a foolish and insatiate beneficiary who asks more of the Court than reason and law require and understandably comes to grief.[34] As Amsterdam has also noted, Davis characterized the social scientists who testified that segregation caused emotional harm to children as equally foolish partners in the misguided venture to desegregate. Amsterdam captures the flavor of Davis's characterization of the law and social science partnership that presumed to challenge the states' decisions to segregate: "Marshall has enticed a bare handful of poor actors— professional types and impractical visionaries all—who, having each observed a few children playing with a few dolls, are willing to hazard vastly mentalistic conclusions . . . [in order to] inveigle the Justices of the Supreme Court of the United States to take momentous action."[35] As we shall see, Davis contrasts these poor actors who would urge a new understanding of equal protection with legions of more official, more representative, and wiser actors who have a settled and long relied-upon an understanding of equal protection. As we shall also see, the plaintiffs' lawyers are nonetheless able to subvert the image of the activist lawyer in league with misguided social scientists and turn it to a liberating purpose.

Whose Constitution? Voicing the Legal Argument

Let us return to our themes of political self-definition and political appeal and
see how the plaintiffs have positioned themselves thus far. The decision to
write the story of segregated schooling with an emphasis on the suffering of
children and without reference to parents places the plaintiffs in a stance of
political appeal. The suffering of children cries out for remedy, but the voices
of children do not carry well the message of political self-definition. Moreover, Davis has undermined the possibility that the plaintiffs will be credible
in a stance of political self-definition by portraying the children's legal representatives as foolish and insatiate, and by passing unusually harsh judgment
on the quality of their legal and social science claims.

We look now to aspects of the voicing and articulation of the constitutional arguments to see whether these initial positionings hold. We will find
the self-positioning of the plaintiffs and their lawyers as political supplicants
deepened by superficial markers of deference, but transformed by more subtle
linguistic patterns.

Displays of Authority and Deference

Speakers display authority or deference by the use (or avoidance) of a variety of
linguistic markers, including talkativeness, interruptions, topic control, and
uncertainty signs (hedging frames, hesitation forms, question intonation, in-
tensifiers, and polite forms).[36] In the context of formal legal argument, the
most frequent and revealing deference markers are polite forms, the avoidance
of interruptions, and two kinds of hedging frames: mental state verbs and
authority frames. We first explore these markers of deference for their suggestion of supplication or political appeal. In some instances, however, we will
find suggestions of appeal laced with suggestions of interpretive power.

Polite Forms   Polite forms of speech have been associated with relative powerlessness in legal discourse.[37] Polite forms are not, however, an invariable
sign of deference. Moreover, the simple frequency of politeness markers is an
inadequate measure of either politeness itself or of deference.[38] Nonetheless,
politeness markers in the context of a ritualized process like appellate legal
argument, taken in combination with other markers and interpreted in light of
the text as a whole, can provide a rough indication of attorney stance. In this
study, I have chosen markers that seemed to have consistent, and at least
superficially deferential, meaning at each use and seemed, as a result, consistent with a stance of appeal. They consist of requests for permission to speak
and uses of honorific or formalized titles. These markers appeared 24 times, or
52.5 times per 10,000 words, in Carter's speech and twice, or 1.1 times per
10,000 words in the speech of Justices addressing Carter. They appeared 60
times, or 99.7 times per 10,000 words, in Marshall's speech and twice, or 1.2
times per 10,000 words, in the speech of Justices addressing Marshall. If we

combine the politeness markers in the speech of Carter and Marshall, we find that they appear at a rate of 79.4 per 10,000 words. They appeared 11 times, or 30.26 times per 10,000 words in Davis's speech. They did not appear in the speech of Justices addressing Davis.

It is not, of course, surprising that politeness markers were significantly more frequent in the speech of litigants than in the speech of judges. As I have reported in other contexts,[39] deference markers are more frequently used by persons participating in the legal process in a role that is considered subordinate. Nor is it surprising that the justices were more likely to use polite terms when speaking with litigants who used polite terms heavily. It is common for speakers to adjust their styles in response to the styles of conversational partners.[40] It is interesting that Carter and Marshall used polite terms significantly more than did Davis. This difference standing alone is entirely inconclusive. It is, however, consistent with the hypothesis that the plaintiffs' lawyers felt less of a sense of ownership and entitlement with respect to the process of asserting a constitutional interpretation or claim. Moreover, it is consistent with an attitude of supplication.

Interruptions   Because there is no audio or video recording of the *Brown* arguments, it is impossible to determine the frequency of interruptions as precisely as one would like. There are, however, sixteen reasonably unambiguous interruptions in the text of the arguments we are considering. The Justices interrupted Carter five times, or 10.9 times per 10,000 words. They interrupted Marshall ten times, or 16.6 times per 10,000 words. Marshall once interrupted a Justice; no other litigator did so. There were no interruptions of the Davis argument. For purposes of this analysis, it is appropriate to exclude interruptions that are nonsubstantive—that constitute, for example, an effort at conversational repair, an expression of support, or a timing error rather than an attempt to seize the floor or change the topic.[41] We therefore exclude an interruption of Carter to announce a luncheon recess, two supportive interruptions of Marshall, and Marshall's supportive interruption of a Justice. We find, then, that Carter was interrupted four times, or .87 times per 1,000 words; Marshall was interrupted eight times, or 1.33 times per 1,000 words; and Davis and the Justices were not interrupted.

The failure of the litigants to interrupt the Justices seems to reflect deference in the same way that their use of polite terms reflects deference. It is an indication of the litigants' subordinate role. It is a reflection of the custom that appellate argument be structured to accommodate the questions of Justices rather than the presentation preferences of the parties.[42] The Justices' behavior of interrupting plaintiffs' counsel but not interrupting Davis may be seen as an indication that the Justices regarded Davis with a greater measure of respect and saw him as a more legitimate participant in the interpretive process. On the other hand, it is wise to be mindful of the litigator's maxim that a silent bench is an unresponsive one. It may be that the interruptions of Carter and Marshall were signs of mutual engagement in an interpretive drama.

Mental Verbs and Verbs of Saying   As indicated above, these mental state verbs allow a speaker to stop short of direct assertion, framing a statement as product of the mind of the speaker rather than presenting it as unfiltered fact in the world. Compare the direct statement, "The sky is blue," and the framed statements, "The sky seems blue," or "I think the sky is blue," or "I swear, that sky is blue." The framed statements are said to mark uncertainty because they signal that the assertion reflects a fallible thought process. Although mental state verbs have been classified by some scholars as signs of deference or powerlessness, they are ambiguous and versatile expressions. In my own research, I have found that they can represent not only uncertainty, but also an openness to negotiation in the domains in which they are used and an openness to the thoughts and opinions of a listener.[43] Since they highlight the speaker's interpretive process, they will be of interest in our inquiry concerning the ownership of interpretive authority.

The analysis of mental state verbs is confined to those portions of the speech of the litigants addressed to legal argument (as opposed to reports of the proceedings below or characterizations of the evidence). In these passages, Carter and Marshall use mental state verbs or their equivalents[44] more then three times as frequently as does Davis. Carter uses them 91 times, or 19.9 times per 1,000 words. Marshall uses these framing devices 110 times or 18.3 times per 1,000 words. Davis uses them 20 times, or 5.5 times per 1,000 words.

By contrast, Davis makes six interpretive assertions with respect to the Fourteenth Amendment that are direct, rather than filtered through mental state verbs:

> The right of a state to classify the pupils in its public schools on the basis of sex or age or mental capacity, or race, is not impaired or affected by that Amendment.

> [The question of school segregation] is an administrative or a political question, and not a judicial one.

> Changed conditions may bring things within the scope of the Constitution.

> When . . . [matters] come within the field of interstate commerce then they become subject to congressional power.

> [Congressional power] is defined in terms of the Constitution itself.

> Circumstances . . . do not alter, expand or change the language that the framers of the Constitution have employed.[45]

Carter makes two such statements:

> The Constitution does not, in terms of protecting, giving equal protection of the laws with regard to equal educational opportunities, does not stop with the fact that you have equal facilities, but it covers the whole educational process.

> The Amendment was intended to protect Negroes in civil and political equality with whites.[46]

Marshall makes four direct, interpretive statements about the Constitution, but each of them asserts the same proposition—that the Court is the exclusive arbiter of the meaning of the Constitutional text:

> [Leaving a question of personal and present constitutional right to the legislature] is directly contrary to every opinion of this Court.

> [W]hen a statute is tested, it is not tested as to what is reasonable insofar as South Carolina is concerned, it must be tested as to what is reasonable as to this Court.

> [T]he ultimate authority for determining . . . [the rights of minorities] is this Court.

> [W]hether or not I, as an individual, am being deprived of my right is not legislative, but judicial.[47]

Davis's legal arguments are spoken in certain, direct terms. The legal arguments of Carter and Marshall are in the negotiable, and arguably deferential, terms of thinking and saying. Davis seizes authority to announce the meaning of the constitutional text. The plaintiffs' lawyers are more circumspect, making direct interpretive assertions that are modest in their implications or explicitly assign interpretive authority exclusively to the Court.

Authority Frames   I use the term "authority frame" to describe framing devices that place interpretive authority outside the mind of the speaker, attributing it to a source that bears what Bakhtin referred to as "hierarchical eminence."[48] Carter and Marshall, arguing for the *Brown* plaintiffs, and Davis, arguing the position of the states, make roughly equal, but very different, use of authority frames.

Precedent is more clearly on Davis's side, and he takes pains to emphasize that fact. A single example serves to illustrate:

> It would be an interesting, though perhaps entirely useless, undertaking to enumerate the numbers of men charged with Official duty in the legislative and the judicial branches of the Government who have declared that segregation is not per se unlawful. The members of Congress, year after year, and session after session, the members of state constitutional conventions, the members of state legislatures, year after year and session after session, the members of the higher courts of the states, the members of the inferior federal judiciary, and the members of this tribunal—what their number may be, I do not know, but I think it reasonably certain that it must mount well into the thousands, and to this I stress for your honors that every one of that vast group was bound by oath to support the Constitution of the United States and any of its Amendments. Is it conceivable that all that body of concurrent opinion was recreant to its duty or misunderstood the constitutional mandate, or was ignorant of the history which gave to the mandate its scope and meaning? I submit not.[49]

It is against this legion that Davis pits his adversaries—the mutually misguided lawyers and social scientists bent on social reform:

> Now, what are we told here that has made all that body of activity and learning of no consequence? Says counsel for the plaintiffs . . . , we have the uncontradicted testimony of expert witnesses that segregation is hurtful. . . . These witnesses severally described themselves as professors, associate professors, assistant professors, and one describes herself as a lecturer and adviser on curricula. I am not sure exactly what that means.[50]

Davis's combination of direct assertions and authority frames has the effect of painting the constitutional question as settled. By contrast, Carter and Marshall craft their uses of authority frames both to give hierarchical eminence to principles upon which they wish to rely, and to express interpretive possibilities. A typical example is presented when Carter bolsters with judicial authority a claim having to do with classification. The language of the passage nicely combines Carter's and Marshall's more frequent use of mental frames and a reliance on the authority of precedent;

> It is our position that any legislative or governmental classification must fall with an even hand on all persons similarly situated. This Court has long held that this is the law.[51]

A more striking example is provided as Marshall simultaneously personalizes the resort to precedent and humanizes the precedent itself. Observe the many devices by which Marshall suggests in this passage that the lawyer's act of citation and the judges creation of precedent are both products of interpretive work:

> I know lawyers at times have *a hard time finding a case in point*. But in the reply brief, *I think* that we have a case in point that is *persuasive* to this Court. It is the case of Elkison v. Deliesseline, a decision *by Mr. Justice William Johnson*, apppointed to this Court, if I remember, from South Carolina. The decision was rendered in 1823. And in 1823, Mr. Justice Johnson, in a case involving the State of South Carolina, which provided that where free Negroes came in on a ship into Charleston, they had to put them in jail as long as the ship was there and then put them back on the ship—and *it was argued* by people arguing for the statute that this was necessary, it was necessary to protect the people of South Carolina, and the majority must have wanted it and it was adopted. *Mr. Justice Johnson made an answer* to that argument in 1823, which *I think* is pretty good law as of today. *Mr. Justice Johnson said:*
>
> > But to all this the plea of necessity is urged; and of the existence of that necessity we are told the state alone is to judge. Where is this to land us? Is it not asserting the right in each state to throw off the Federal Constitution at its will and pleasure? If it can be done as to any particular article it may be done as to all; and, like the old confederation, the Union becomes a mere rope of sand.[52]

Displaying Interpretive Function

The work that framing devices do in expressing interpretive possibility can be more fully explored if we revisit mental verbs, considering them in this instance not as signs of simple uncertainty, but as displays of interpretive function, and examining them as a category of *self-referencing* frames.

In a sociolinguistic study of the work of divinity students, Frances Smith suggests that when students feel entitled to assert interpretive authority as they explicate the Bible, they will make their voices visible by the use of framing devices.[53] Smith compared the sermons of male and female students and found that the women, who revealed in questionnaire responses an ambivalence about the appropriateness of assuming the role of clergy, concealed their interpretive authority by avoiding self-references and mental state verb frames. Men, who revealed in questionnaire responses no ambivalence about the appropriateness of their assuming the role of clergy, highlighted their interpretive role with the use of mental state verb frames and other self-referencing devices.

For purposes of my analysis of the *Brown* arguments, I distinguish two types of self-referencing frames: metaframes that expose the speaker as organizer of the conversational flow, and expository frames that use mental state verbs or their equivalents to expose the speaker as source of the assertions contained in the body of the argument. We have seen that the plaintiffs' attorneys were far more likely to use expository frames than was Davis. The situation is reversed with respect to metaframes.

Davis devotes 425 words to metaframing, making in explicit, self-referencing terms a detailed outline of his argument. These examples come from his opening:

> I want to address myself during the course of this argument to three propositions, and I will utilize the remaining minutes of the afternoon to state them.

> The first thing which I want to contend for before the Court is . . .

> The second question to which I wish to address myself is . . .

> Third, I want to say something about the evidence offered by the plaintiffs upon which counsel so confidently relied.[54]

Carter devotes 158 words to metaframes, and they are incidental rather than organizing. Examples include:

> as I indicated . . .

> I am reading from the quote of the statute from page three . . .

> as I indicated before . . .

> Just before the recess, I was attempting to show . . .[55]

Marshall devotes only 50 words to metaframes, and they, too, are incidental rather than organizational. Davis, then, seizes control of the course and structure of his argument and makes conspicuous his role in doing so. Carter and Marshall, on the other hand, do not fix the course of their arguments with metaframes.

We find, then, a stark difference in patterns of metaframing and patterns of mental state verbs. Davis, whose language has seemed more expressive of comfortable authority, uses metaframing heavily, thus marking his control of the flow of discourse, but he declines to use mental state verbs. Carter and Marshall, on the other hand, make little use of metaframing; they are relatively inactive or inconspicuous in the control of the flow of discourse. Yet, their speech is full of mental verbs.

This result suggests that the self-referencing language patterns that have been highlighted in the Smith research can take distinct forms, each carrying different implications for the stance of the speaker. Metaframing seems to express authority and comfort as an organizer of a discursive event, but it seems unrelated to interpretive function. On the other hand, mental state verbs seem directly related to interpretive function, but ambiguously related to the speaker's authority and comfort, either as an organizer of the conversational flow or as an interpreter of authoritative texts. Indeed, contrary to the Smith results, mental state verbs may suggest *uncertainty* with respect to both the authority of the speaker and the content of the speaker's message.[56]

In the *Brown* arguments, it appears that mental state verbs served the function of displaying—and their absence served the function of masking—interpretive possibility. It was in Davis's strategic interest to represent the legal arguments as fixed and the interpretive question as closed. Precedent was on his side. Whether he operated by instinct or by design, it made sense for him to urge that the work of interpreting the Equal Protection Clause as it related to segregation was finished. Thus, although Davis displayed comfortable *discursive* authority by extensive use of metaframes, he masked *interpretive* authority—speaking in certain terms that were consistent both with interpretive confidence and with a strategic need to inhibit the Justices' interpretive instincts. In the terms of Davis's argument, we see that the question at bar is one that prior cases have resolved. As Davis himself put it: "[I]f, as lawyers or judges, we have ascertained the scope and bearing of the equal protection clause of the Fourteenth Amendment, our duty is done. The rest must be left to those who dictate public policy, and not to the courts."[57]

On the other hand, it was in Carter's and Marshall's strategic interest *to make of the arguments a performance of interpretive process in which lawyers and Justices shared, in the present tense, the work of worrying over the proper reading of an open text.* It would be a process in which the Justices had final authority, but it would be a process in which legal reality was thought about, rather than fixed. It would be a process that evoked deliberative politics,[58] rather than an image of a Herculean judge.[59] It would be a process like that described by Jerome Bruner in a reflection upon pedagogy and stance. "Stance marking in the speech of others gives us a clue about how to use our minds," Bruner said. He proceeded to describe a great teacher of his youth:

I recall a teacher, her name was Miss Orcutt, who made the statement in class, "It is a very puzzling thing not that water turns to ice at 32 degrees Fahrenheit, but that it should change from a liquid into a solid." . . . She was not just *informing* me. She was, rather, negotiating the world of . . . possibility. . . . Miss Orcutt . . . was a human event, not a transmission device. It was not that my other teachers did not mark their stances. It was rather that their stances were so off-puttingly and barrenly informative.[60]

It is possible that the women in the Smith study had more profound reason than Smith realized for failing to assert themselves as interpreters of the biblical tradition: It is possible that they were not only unable to assert, but also unable to recognize interpretive power—that they saw themselves as reporters of revealed truth rather than as participants in an interpretive process. The *Brown* lawyers, by contrast, were capable of seeing (or required, in light of their adversarial task to assert) the openness of the constitutional text and of demonstrating that openness by speaking of the text in language that implied a world of possibility. Thus, in their avoidance of metaframes, they backgrounded themselves as presenters, but, in their overwhelmingly disproportionate use of expository mental state verbs, they demonstrated the openness of the interpretive process.

Displaying Affiliation

By their strategic use of markers of affiliation, Davis and the plaintiffs' attorneys give texture to their respective roles as information transmitter and participants in a human and political event.

Davis made cautious and limited use of the first person plural. The "we" who in Davis's argument had ascertained the scope and bearing of the Equal Protection Clause were the broad professional community of lawyers and judges. But this was a backward-looking reference, offering no vision of continuing communal effort. Davis made two other references to himself as part of the larger legal community—one a reference to "our duty" in the same sentence, and the other a reminder of the Court's prior statements that "it is the duty of the interpreters [of the Constitution] to place ourselves as nearly as possible in the condition of the men who framed the instrument."[61] Davis six times linked himself and the Justices, but these uses of the pronoun "we" were narrowly collaborative, never relating to a shared act of interpretation: "we have . . . uncontradicted testimony," "we heard yesterday." He never linked himself with his client. He once spoke of himself as part of the larger political community ("Is it not a fact that the very strength and fiber of our federal system is local self-government?")[62]

The plaintiffs' lawyers used the first person plural more expansively, to suggest a political and legal community in which they, and their clients, shared. Carter and Marshall linked themselves with the justices 28 times (5 in Carter's case and 23 in Marshall's case). The plaintiffs' lawyers used the pronoun not only in the more limited fashion of Davis, but also to describe joint interpretive activity: "[They say] we are bound by *Plessy*," Carter argued. Marshall said, in terms that warmly invited collaboration, "[W]e do not have to get to *Plessy* . . . we do not have to get to any other case, if we lean right on these two cases."[63]

In a contrast that is perhaps more significant, Carter and Marshall three times identified themselves with their clients, whereas Davis never did so. Carter began his argument:

> It is the gravamen of our complaint . . . that the appellees have de-prived—that we have been deprived of the equal protection of the laws.[64]

Later, he referred to the decision the Court would render as one that "can be handed down in our favor" on a particular basis.[65] Marshall said, early in his argument,

> Our position is not that we are denied equality in these cases. . . . We are saying that there is a denial of equal protection of the laws.[66]

He closed his argument by making the claim entirely personal—a question of "whether or not I, as an individual, am being deprived of my right." This closing statement also incorporated two of Marshall's six uses of the first person plural to refer to the larger political community. The full closing was:

> [T]he rights of minorities, as has been our whole form of government, have been protected by our Constitution, and the ultimate authority for determining that is this Court. I think that is the real difference. . . . [W]hether or not I, as an individual, am being deprived of my right is not legislative, but judicial.[67]

The remaining self-incorporating references to the larger political community were:

> [W]e cannot have the individual rights subjected to this consideration of what the groups might do.

> [U]nder our form of government, these individual rights of minority peo-ple are not to be left to even the most mature judgment of the majority of the people.

> [T]he ultimate authority for the asserted right by an individual in a mi-nority group is in a body set aside to interpret our Constitution, which is our Court.[68]

These references circle back to—and mitigate—the choice to frame the claim as a claim of children to be relieved of suffering. As they used affiliative pro-nouns to link themselves and their clients, Carter and Marshall stood with the children as representatives of a people. As they used affiliative pronouns to po-sition themselves as part of the political community, they gave African Ameri-can people a voice in the process of political self-definition and constitutional construction. As their words bespoke the openness of the constitutional text, they made political self-definition and constitutional construction possible.

Conclusion

Neither the drafters of the Fourteenth Amendment, the Congress members who voted for it, nor the state bodies that ratified it can be said to have acted with a confident expectation that the amendment would outlaw segregation. *Brown* stands, therefore, as proof that our Constitution means more than its framers imagined. It stands as proof that our constitutional principles are ideals, the just implications of which are to be negotiated through political and legal processes in which both majority and minority voices can be heard and empowered. And *Brown* stands solidly. As Ronald Dworkin has written,

> [T]he [*Brown*] decision has by now become so firmly accepted, and so widely hailed as a paradigm of constitutional statesmanship, that it acts as an informal test of constitutional theories. No theory seems acceptable that condemns that decision as a mistake. (I doubt that any Supreme Court nominee would be confirmed if [s/]he now said that [s/]he thought it wrongly decided.)[69]

The interpretive performances of Carter, Marshall and their colleagues worked subtly but surely to produce *Brown*'s guarantee of a living constitution, unfrozen and responsive to evolving standards of civic decency.

The plaintiffs' victory in *Brown v. Board of Education* was a landmark in the movement that began with resistance to slavery and continued after emancipation as resistance to surviving ideologies of color and caste. Robert Carter recently described the interplay between lay people who were the heart of the movement and the lawyers who took center stage in trials of civil rights cases across the South. He recalled the social impact when African American lawyers took authority as officers of the court:

> I remember one instance when in Mississippi we had the superintendent of schools on the witness stand. I was questioning him and he asked me a question, and I said, "Oh, no. You don't ask me questions; I ask you questions, and you respond." And the judge said, "That's right," and the audience, the blacks, they fell out.[70]

> The first time I tried a case in Mississippi there was the same kind of thing, with Connie Motley. . . . [B]lacks had never seen a black woman lawyer in the court before, never seen a black lawyer in the court before. And here we were, you know. And Connie and I weren't tolerating any nonsense from anybody inside the courtroom.

> So the court trials were being enacted in barbershops around afterwards and so forth. . . . [I]t was . . . *inspiration. [It was]* . . . *theater.*[71]

The *Brown* victory was not only a moment in a political and social movement, but also the culmination of a litigation strategy carefully designed to upset the doctrine of separate but equal and to open the meaning of the Equal Protection Clause to new interpretive possibilities. When we focus on the litigation strategy, rather than on the movement, we see that civil rights lawyering had the object and effect of modeling a new professional stance.

Within the movement, the lawyers who brought the *Brown* cases dramatized and inspired civil and political assertiveness. Within the profession, they dramatized and inspired work in open dialogue to interpret constitutional aspirations in light of broadened perspectives and evolving circumstances.

The legal profession was in the 1950s (and remains to a considerable extent today) captured by professional habits born of narrowly positivist assumptions about the nature of law. Lawyers were (and are) inclined to argue law as if right answers were locked away in a vault (or a cave). Conversations in the law—in appellate argument, in bargaining, or in counseling, to take three important examples—sounded (and sound) more like debates over the last term of a syllogism than debates over the meaning of a text. The nature of the task facing lawyers working within the civil rights movement, and the traditions and ideologies that informed the movement, posed a challenge to narrowly positivist presuppositions. Civil rights lawyers saw the Fourteenth Amendment as a polyvalent text—a text born of neglected history, expressive of indistinct aspirations, and in need of interpretation in an open political process. On the surface, the lawyers for the *Brown* plaintiffs manifested a strategic, albeit culturally ingrained, deference to social, judicial and doctrinal authority. On close reading, however, we see the ways in which they seized authority to participate in the shaping of doctrine. Their words modeled interpretive deliberation informed by previously neglected perspectives and aspirations. And the Justices followed their model.

Notes

1. C. Peter Ripley ed., 5 *The Black Abolitionist Papers*, 113–14 (Chapel Hill: University of North Carolina Press, 1985).

2. See W. E. B. Du Bois, *Black Reconstruction: An Essay Toward a History of the Part Which Black Folk Played in the Attempt to Reconstruct Democracy in America, 1860–1880* (Philadelphia: A Saifer, 1935), 55–121. Among other indicia of the impact of African American actions upon the outcome of the hostilities, Du Bois offered the testimony of a Virginian before the Committee on Reconstruction: "I had a conversation with one of the leading men in . . . [a southern] city, and he said to me that the enlistment of Negro troops by the United States was the turning-point of the rebellion; that it was the heaviest blow they ever received. He remarked that when the Negroes deserted their masters, and showed a general disposition to do so and join the forces of the United States, intelligent men everywhere saw that the matter was ended." Id. at 120. Du Bois also offered the testimony of a Union general: "Freedom for the slave was the logical result of a crazy attempt to wage war in the midst of four million black slaves, and trying the while sublimely to ignore the interests of those slaves in the outcome of the fighting. Yet, these slaves had enormous power in their hands. Simply by stopping work, they could threaten the Confederacy with starvation. By walking into the Federal camps, they showed to doubting Northerners the easy possibility of using them as workers and as servants, as farmers, and as spies, and finally, as fighting soldiers. And not only using them thus, but by the same gesture, depriving their enemies of their use in just these fields. It was the fugitive slave who made the slave-

holders face the alternative of surrendering to the North, or to the Negroes." *Id.* at 121.

3. This pattern is most prominently illustrated by the change in Frederick Douglass's position from rejection of the Constitution as a racist document to affiliation with its human rights priority and struggle to loosen its inconsistent embrace of slavery.

4. These rituals were tellingly described in anthropological studies of the South in the early 1940s: "According to . . . [prevailing] dogma, and to a large extent actually, the behavior of both Negroes and white people must be such as to indicate that the two are socially distinct and that the Negro is subordinate. Thus . . . [i]n places of business the Negro should stand back and wait until the white has been served . . . , and in entering or leaving he should not precede a white but should stand back and hold the door for him. On the streets and sidewalks the Negro should 'give way' to the white person." Allison Davis, Burleigh Gardner, & Mary Gardner, *Deep South: A Social and Anthropological Study of Caste and Class* (Chicago: University of Chicago Press, 1941), 22–23.

5. The Carter argument was the lead argument for the opponents of segregation and was coordinated closely with the Marshall argument. Interviews with Robert Carter, notes on file with the author. The argument of the counsel directly opposing Carter was unrepresentative because of the state's ambivalent position concerning the litigation and has therefore not been included in this preliminary analysis.

6. One can also imagine that the decision to adopt an originalist, text-bound, or precedent-bound position is itself an act of political self-definition. A litigator's rhetoric will sometimes reflect this possibility.

7. Uses of deictic markers—more specifically, of pronouns of affiliation— increase the possibilities of making coherent arguments in a variety of modes: A lawyer who is identified with the client might not plausibly argue that *the Court* must read the Constitution to "grant *us* relief." However, a lawyer who is identified with the profession or the political community might plausibly argue that "*we*" must read the Constitution to grant *the client* relief.

8. See, Anthony Amsterdam & Randy Hertz, "An Analysis of Closing Arguments to a Jury," 37 *New York Law School Law Review* (1992), 55.

9. Peggy Cooper Davis, "Conceptual Legal Criticism," 66 *New York University Law Review* (1991), 1635, 1647–54.

10. See id. at 1664–67 (concerning the differentiation of lawyers' and clients' speech); Candice West, "When the Doctor Is a Lady: Power, Status and Gender in Physician-Patient Encounters," 7 *Symbolic Interaction* (1984), 87 (concerning the differentiation of doctors' and patients' speech).

11. See Davis, supra note 9, at 1652–54.

12. Frances Lee Smith, "The Pulpit and Woman's Place: Gender and the Framing of the 'Exegetical Self' in Sermon Performances," in *Framing in Discourse*, Deborah Tannen ed. (New York: Oxford University Press, 1993).

13. See, Elizabeth Mertz, "Consensus and Dissent in U.S. Legal Opinions: Narrative Structure and Social Voices," 30 *Anthropological Linguistics* (1994), 369, 378 and authorities cited.

14. Cumming v. Richmond County Board of Education, 175 U.S. 528, 544 (1899) (emphasis added).

15. Meyer v. Nebraska, 262 U.S. 390 (1923).

16. Pierce v. Society of Sisters, 268 U.S. 510 (1925).

17. Farrington v. Tokushige, 273 U.S. 284 (1927).

18. Gong Lum v. Rice, 275 U.S. 78 (1927).

19. Minersville v. Gobitis, 319 U.S. 586 (1940).

20. West Virginia v. Barnette, 319 U.S. 624 (1943).

21. McCollum v. Board of Education of Champaign County, 333 U.S. 203 (1948). See also Doremus v. Board of Education of Borough of Hawthorne, 342 U.S. 29 (1952), in which the Court denied certiorari in a case raising the question whether a parent had standing to challenge school practices that arguably did not compromise her beliefs or those of her child. At the time of the denial of certiorari, the plaintiff no longer had a school-age child.

22. People of color in the academy have long argued—often to uncomprehending audiences—that the ideals of United States constitutional democracy have been born and nurtured in struggle, first against slavery, and then against caste oppression. For a review of the arguments, see, Derrick Bell, Address at the Schomburg Center for Research in Black Culture, New York (Dec. 7, 1991). For a recent, and well-received, version of the arguments, see Orlando Patterson, *Freedom* (New York: Basic Books, 1991).

23. Eric Foner, *Reconstruction: America's Unfinished Revolution 1863–1877* (New York: Harper and Row, 1988), 120.

24. Id. at 122 quoting, A. D. Lewis to William W. Holden, June 5, 1869, North Carolina Governor's Papers.

25. Id. at 122–23.

26. Philip B. Kurland & Gerhard Casper, eds., 49 *Landmark Briefs and Arguments of the Supreme Court* 279–83 (1975).

27. Id. at 315, 320, 323, 342.

28. Id. at 339.

29. Id. at 339. Subsequent quotes in this paragraph are in id. at 330 and 327.

30. Id. at 337. Davis apparently refers to Francis L. Cardozo, the son of a prominent Jewish businessman and economist and a free black mother. Cardozo, an educator, minister, and carpenter, studied at the University of Glasgow and at Presbyterian seminaries in Great Britain. Eric Foner, *Freedom's Lawmakers* (New York: Oxford University Press, 1993), 41. Cardozo, along with 75 other African Americans, was a representative to the 124-member South Carolina Constitutional Convention of 1865. W. E. B. Du Bois, *Black Reconstruction*, 389 (1962 edition).

31. Du Bois, supra note 30, at 397.

32. Id. at 398.

33. Kurland & Casper, supra note 26, at 337. See Peggy Cooper Davis, "Contested Images of Family Values: The Role of the State," 107 *Harvard Law Review* (1994), 1348, 1358–60.

34. Anthony G. Amsterdam, "Telling Stories and Stories About Them," 1 *Clinical Law Review* (1994) 9, 21–23.

35. Id. at 23. Amsterdam does not exaggerate Davis's tone of contempt and condescension toward social scientists. Consider Davis's own words: "I may have been unfortunate, or I may have been careless, but it seems to me that much of that which is handed around under the name of social science is an effort on the part of the scientist to rationalize his own preconceptions. They find usually, in my limited observation, what they go out to find." Kurland & Casper, supra note 26, at 336–37.

36. See Davis, supra note 9, at 1647–54.

37. See John M. Conley et al., "The Power of Language: Presentational Style in the Courtroom," 1978 *Duke Law Journal* (1979) 1375, 1379–80.

38. See Bent Preisler, *Linguistic Sex Roles in Conversation: Social Variation in the Expression of Tentativeness in English* (New York: Mouton de Gruyter, 1986), 9.

39. See Davis, supra note 9, at 1664.

40. See H. Giles, "Social Psychology and Applied Linguistics: Towards an Integrative Approach," 35 *ITL: A Review of Applied Linguistics* (1977) 27.

41. See Davis, supra note 9, at 1649.

42. Compare the customs with respect to closing arguments to a jury.

43. Peggy C. Davis, "Law and Lawyering: Legal Studies with an Interactive Focus, 37 *New York Law School Law Review* (1992) 185, 199–202; Davis, supra note 9, at 1667.

44. "Report frames," which report in terms of the speaker's mental state are counted as mental verbs. Examples include "My view is that . . ." and "According to my contention. . . ."

45. Kurland & Casper, supra note 26, at 324, 332. Davis makes an additional direct, interpretive statement about the Constitution ("It is true that the Fourteenth Amendment was addressed primarily to the states."), but it is uncontroversial and is therefore not counted as argument.

46. Id. at 285, 294. Carter also makes four statements concerning the Court's prior interpretations of the Constitution.

47. Id. at 311, 340, 346.

48. V. N. Volosinov, *Marxism and the Philosophy of Language* (New York: Seminar Press, 1973), 123.

49. Kurland & Casper, supra note 26, at 335.

50. Id. at 335.

51. Id. at 281.

52. Id. at 313. (Emphasis added.) The juxtaposition of Marshall's and Davis's speeches makes clear that the lawyers differed not only in strategy and professional stance, but also in the styles of their personalities and subcultures. Resonances between style and litigation stance no doubt deepened the effect upon the Justices of the lawyers' performances.

53. Frances Lee Smith, "The Pulpit and Woman's Place: Gender and the Framing of the 'Exegetical Self' in Sermon Performances, in Deborah Tannen ed., supra note 12, at 146.

54. Kurland & Casper, supra note 26, at 325.

55. Id. at 282, 283, 284.

56. This analysis suggests that the Smith results with respect to mental state verbs may reflect the male and female students' different senses of interpretive possibility (or of the authority of the text) rather than their sense of security or insecurity as interpreters.

57. Kurland & Casper, supra note 26, at 331.

58. See Jurgen Habermas, *Between Facts and Norms: Contributions to a Discourse Theory of Law and Democracy* (Cambridge, Mass.; M.I.T. Press 1995); Frank I. Michelman, "The Supreme Court, 1985 Term—Foreword: Traces of Self-Government," 100 *Harvard Law Review* 4 (1986); Frank I. Michelman, "Law's Republic," 97 *Yale Law Review* 1493 (1988).

59. See Ronald Dworkin, *Law's Empire* (Cambridge, Mass.; Belknap Press, 1986).

60. Jerome Bruner, *Actual Minds, Possible Worlds* (Cambridge, Mass.; Harvard University Press, 1986), 126.

61. Kurland & Casper, supra note 26, at 331. This reference is, of course, ambiguous because of its placement in a quote of the Court's language.

62. Id. at 339. Davis, who referred to himself forty-nine times in the first person singular, used first person plural references only twenty-five times.

63. Id. at 284, 315.

64. Id. at 279.

65. Id. at 289.

66. Id. at 309.

67. Id. at 346.

68. Id. at 319, 339, 346.

69. Ronald Dworkin, "The Bork Nomination," *New York Review of Books,* August 13, 1987.

70. Robert L. Carter Oral History Project, Interview #1, vol. 1 (February 1, 1992), 15.

71. Id. at 12–13. See also Donald Nieman, "From Slaves to Citizens: African-Americans, Rights Consciousness, and Reconstruction," forthcoming *Cardozo L. Rev.* (describing spectators at the district court argument of the South Carolina case). Nieman quotes a spectator who had driven two hours to watch the argument in a packed courthouse: "I never did get to sit down in the courtroom, but I never did get tired that day."

2

LAWRENCE M. FRIEDMAN

Brown in Context

For those of us above a certain age, it is startling to realize that *Brown v. Board of Education*[1] has celebrated its fortieth anniversary. The subject of this great case, as everybody knows, was race segregation in the schools; and, as everybody knows, the Court declared this practice unconstitutional.[2] *Brown* was only the first in a long line of important civil rights cases, which ended up outlawing every aspect of the southern system of apartheid—and attacking much of the more subtle northern system as well. It says something, perhaps, about this momentous decision that it is hard for most people to imagine what the world was like before *Brown*. Is there any Supreme Court case, in this century, that has sunk down deeper roots? I can't imagine anybody trying to overrule *Marbury v. Madison*,[3] and the school segregation case is not very far behind.

Of course, the case did not always sit so securely on its pedestal. It was, in fact, extremely controversial from the word go. There were those, black and white, who immediately hailed it as a great step forward, when the Court handed it down in 1954.[4] Quite predictably, white supremacists vilified it; one irate man from Mississippi, steamed up over this decision, referred darkly to the "malignant powers of Communism, atheism and mongrelization," which were presumably responsible for Warren's dreadful act.[5]

There was also a certain amount of timid hand-wringing among the apostles of judicial restraint. Some of these handwringers were found in the upper ranks of American legal education. Also among the critics was no less a figure than Judge Learned Hand, who, in a notable lecture series, voiced some rather vague doubts about the decision—hinting that it went too far, and that it encroached on what was properly the job of the legislative branch.[6]

Probably the most famous hand-wringing exercise was Herbert Wechsler's, in his much-cited article about "neutral principles" of constitutional law (whatever those might be).[7] The "problem" of the *Brown* case, according to Wechsler, "inheres strictly in the reasoning of the opinion." After gnawing away at this or that aspect of the case, Wechsler asks, plaintively, whether there was "a basis in neutral principles for the holding" of the case. "I should like to think there is," he says, "but I confess that I have not yet written the opinion. To write it is for me the challenge of the school-segregation cases." Imagine! The challenge was not segregation, not racism, not social justice, not American democracy, not human suffering or human dignity; nor race relations or social justice—but whether the opinion could possibly meet the high technical criteria of Professor Herbert Wechsler.[8]

The learned gentlemen who found fault with *Brown* never went so far as to defend segregation (at least not the learned gentlemen who lived above the Mason-Dixon line); but they certainly criticized the Supreme Court for over-reaching, or for violating sacred canons of style and craftsmanship. Even some scholars who were friendly toward *Brown* were unhappy about what they considered the poor quality of the text. Louis H. Pollak, to take one notable instance, agreed that the opinion left a lot to be desired; Earl Warren had fallen down on the job. But Pollak felt that one *could* write a satisfactory opinion, and in fact he tried his hand at that enterprise.[9] It has never quite replaced the actual opinion, however.[10]

By now, as we said, *Brown* is firmly ensconced in the pantheon of sainted cases. William L. Taylor called it a "resounding success"; a case that "validated the role of the judiciary as a catalyst in helping to renew and revitalize our political processes."[11] Drew Days probably expressed the prevailing view about its impact and importance. The decision, he said, along with "the integrative ideal that it embraced have opened opportunities for black advancement that were previously unthinkable"; the case "transformed our entire society in other ways too numerous to recite."[12]

Exactly how much transforming has gone on in this society is, of course, a difficult empirical question. The immediate impact included resistance, violence, and an upsurge of Klan nastiness (the federal response, at least initially, was extremely vacillating and feeble).[13] There is certainly room for debate on the question of how much influence *Brown* actually had on the course of events; among the notable skeptics is Gerald Rosenberg, who has argued that the actual impact of the case has been vastly overrated.[14] Richard Delgado and Jean Stefancic agree: the *Brown* decision, according to them, was swallowed up by a massive social context it was unable to control or affect.[15] Black scholars, too, can be forgiven for wondering how much the *Brown* decision really accomplished, in the light of some of the events of the last forty years. After all, *Brown* did not put an end to racism in American society; moreover, millions of blacks are still engulfed in poverty, live out their lives in black ghettos, and are in all respects at the bottom of the social ladder.[16]

Curiously enough, some of the criticism about the style and language of the decision (as opposed to its impact) seems to come these days from the left, not the right. Because so many blacks lead dismal lives, and because racism shows no signs of disappearing, it is no wonder some people have jumped to the conclusion that *Brown* itself must have been fatally flawed—or even that *Brown* might be one reason why the country is in such a bad fix today.[17] *Brown*, according to one recent writer, was not a progessive decision at all; rather, it "served to deaden political debate and to legitimate the status quo."[18]

I myself have little patience with this line of argument, and similar ones,[19] at least as far as they concern the actual decision in *Brown*, rather than what America has made of it. After all, an attack of this sort has to be based rather narrowly on the text of the case, on the words, on the logic, on the construction and the style, the reasoning, the doctrine, the shape of the opinion. (Nobody on the left is going to argue that the *result*, that is, outlawing segregation in the schools, was a bad thing, as far as it went.) In my view, arguments based on text wildly exaggerate the impact of text. They assume that the language and the reasoning made a critical difference, as opposed to what the decision *did*, that is, its result, outcome, or decree, as the lay public understands and understood it. But anybody who feels that a more tightly crafted and better reasoned opinion in *Brown* would have had a bigger (or even different) impact on life in rural Mississippi (or Washington, D.C., for that matter) than what Warren actually wrote, can't be living on this planet.

In fact, most of the people for and against racial equality or desegregation or whatever—99 plus percent of them—have never read Warren's opinion, know nothing about its reasoning or style, and never laid eyes on it in fact. This is nothing unusual. Reading *Roe v. Wade*[20] is not a prerequisite for picketing an abortion clinic—or, by the same token, for picketing the pickets. I dare say very few people on either side of the abortion debate have the foggiest notion about the *legal* issues at stake. This is true, of course, of *all* famous Supreme Court decisions. The general public does not read advance sheets.

There is of course a more sophisticated version of the text theory, a kind of trickle-down version. Considerations of craft, logic, and choice of argument sail over the heads of the general public; that much is obvious. But issues of doctrine and form matter greatly to legal elites; and these elites talk to other kinds of elites, and sooner or later a climate of opinion is formed, a kind of party line of the intelligentsia. This then finds its way into *Time Magazine* and other middle-brow periodicals, and ultimately influences just about everybody, at least everybody in the middle-class.

This version is (on the surface) more plausible; but there is no evidence that the first few steps actually occur. The "craftsmanship" objections to the *Brown* opinion basically began and ended in the world of the legal mandarins, as far as I can tell. This is a fairly closed little world.[21] Similarly, with regard to *Roe v. Wade*, my other example. Scholars in high places have lambasted the decision on craft and technical grounds;[22] but I remain unconvinced that any of this attack has made the slightest difference in the actual *debate* (sometimes violent) over abortion. People do not shoot doctors because of the Tenth Amendment to the Constitution or because they think there is no textual basis for a right of privacy.

Another version of this argument is the claim that somehow the kind of argument made in a leading case "traps" people *in* that argument; it sticks to them like glue, and when (for whatever reason), that line of argument leads down the wrong path, they are stuck with it. Epstein and Kobylka, in their study of the abortion and death penalty cases, come to a conclusion of this sort: the "framing of the legal arguments tendered before the Court" was important to the resolution of these issues; but "initial 'liberal' victories were forged and then lost, in significant part, because their defenders doggedly clung to their understanding of the Court's logic."[23] I am extremely skeptical about this explanation, as applied to the political history of abortion or the death penalty, simply because I doubt whether the later political history of these issues owes anything to the Court's logic, or what defenders understood of it, or to the particular line of argument (which is in any event soon forgotten). I also doubt very much the relevance of this point for race relations; I cannot imagine that so volcanic and fundamental a matter as how blacks and white relate to each other gets "stuck" in a line of "liberal" argument obscurely secreted in a judicial decision.

People on both sides of the issue often refer to the "symbolic" meaning of the segregation decision; but even here there are disguised empirical problems. Everybody talks about "symbolic" meanings, decisions, impacts, and so on;[24] but I often find myself wondering exactly what "symbolic" means. In general, symbolism is in the eye of the beholder. One person's symbol is another person's blunt instrument. Sometimes the word means nothing more than "not economic." Is prayer in the schools a symbolic issue? It is not an economic (dollars and cents) issue, but in other regards, I would hardly call it symbolic. Many people want children to say prayers in school because they think prayer is good for children and their moral development. There is nothing "symbolic" about this point. These parents want concrete behaviors and concrete results.

I would never deny that some issues *are* symbolic; flag burning, I suppose, is one example. That is, the meaning it carries has little or nothing to do with any *instrumental* impact; it is not as if anybody wants to stamp out burning flags because it is economically wasteful, or causes fires, or because flags are an endangered species. But segregation in the schools is very different. *Brown*, like other significant cases, did send out a definite *message*; it had a social meaning for its audience. This message, in essence, was unmistakable. It was clear, for example, that *Brown* was not just an isolated case; in any event it soon became clear. The meaning of the case went far beyond schools.[25] I think "signal" may be a better word to apply to *Brown* than "symbol."

In any event, the value of a symbol, ultimately, whatever meaning you assign to the word "symbol," rests on the behavior it stimulates or legitimates; if the symbolic stone does not cause the water to ripple, it wears out even as a symbol. And "symbolic" is a word often applied to a case (or other action) that was *intended* to have an instrumental impact, but which in fact did not, for one reason or another. In this sense, of course, it can be argued that *Brown* has become purely symbolic.[26]

It might seem odd, then, after eagerly debunking the passions of law professors, and their obsession with legal texts, that I propose to go on and devote a large part of this essay to the text of *Brown* (and, as we shall see, the texts of other cases). The craft, the line of argument, the legal mumbo jumbo may be unimportant, as far as *impact* is concerned, or the way the case is received by the wider public; it does not follow that these aspects of a case might not be interesting in some other regard.

I will be using these opinions, then, not to show that they influenced anybody outside the legal academy, but as social and legal indicators; and, in a way, to debunk the high priests of legal craftsmanship. In fact, *Brown* inhabits a different world, as to style and substance, than *Plessy* inhabited, along with certain of the pre-*Brown* cases on race. This essay is meant to explore these worlds. In the debates over *Brown*, over the last forty years, style and substance have been hopelessly conflated.

Sociology and Other Crimes

Style and substance, for example, are both implicated in the charge that the *Brown* decision was "sociological," which is apparently one of the worst insults one can level at an opinion. The idea that *Brown* was "sociological" did not come exclusively from white southerners. James Reston, writing in the *New York Times* the day after the decision was handed down, intoned solemnly that the decision relied "more on the social scientists than on legal precedents." (How he knew this is not disclosed.) The heading of his article was "A Sociological Decision: Court Founded Its Segregation Ruling on Hearts and Minds Rather Than Laws."[27] The decision, according to Reston, "read more like an expert paper on sociology" than a judicial opinion.

I will pass over the question of whether "sociology" and "hearts and minds" are the same thing. Reston's point about "social scientists" must refer, of course, to the famous footnote 11. This is the footnote which cites a gaggle of social scientific studies. Of course, social scientists themselves, being only human, were eager to claim a lot of credit for the results of *Brown*. The other side—the states'-righters and white supremacists—was eager to heap scorn on this aspect of the case.[28] The "nine sociologists" had clearly stepped out of the proper role of judges and become dastardly usurpers.

What is true is that the *style* of the opinion offended some people (though nothing compared to the way the result offended them); and one of the tasks of this essay is to examine that style. Whether the famous footnote 11 is an aspect of that style or is part of the substance of the case is not worth quibbling about. It is hard to imagine the judges of the late nineteenth century citing social science. Of course, there was not very much of it to cite. But their worldview precluded such adventures.

As I said, the style of *Brown* is worth examining, in a bit more detail. But I prefer to sidle up to the subject rather than confront it directly. I will begin, therefore, with a dose of history.

The Strange Case of Jim Crow

One logical starting point, of course, is the case of *Plessy v. Ferguson*[29]—the case that established the "separate but equal" doctrine, and thus legalized segregation.[30] *Brown* did not in fact overrule this case, at least not in so many words; but it totally superseded it. The facts of the *Plessy* case are well known. It concerned Jim Crow rules in railroad cars.[31] A light-skinned black protested when he was pushed to the back of the bus, so to speak. The Supreme Court upheld the Louisiana Jim Crow law, in a sweeping and notorious decision.[32]

The majority opinion, written by Justice Henry Brown, declared (among other things) that legislation was "powerless to eradicate racial instincts or to abolish distinctions based upon physical differences." It was incorrect (said Brown) to say that "the enforced separation of the two races stamps the colored race with a badge of inferiority." If blacks so interpreted it, that was unfortunate, but entirely their own doing.

Did Brown really believe this line? Could he have been so intolerably naive? I rather doubt it. The opinion in *Plessy* reflects what I like to call the person-from-Pluto approach. It is, in the first place, frankly racist. It considers blacks (and black-white relations) a "problem"; and imagines that the solution is segregation and a caste system. But it also recognizes that the rule of law, not to mention American constitutional doctrine, demanded some attention to formalities and niceties. The textual surface of the law, the actual rules and regulations, should be so phrased and framed that an alien from outer space, totally unaware of the realities of life in Louisiana, would not *know* from the texts of the laws whether "whites" were on top, or "blacks," or neither. So long as a state structured its laws to meet this stylistic requirement, the Supreme Court was not inclined to interfere.

This rather formalistic approach characterizes much of the work of the Supreme Court in race cases in the years after the Civil War. Blacks rarely won these cases. One rather significant exception was *Strauder v. West Virginia*.[33] West Virginia, by law, restricted jury service to white males over the age of twenty-one. The defendant, who was black, was convicted of murder and sentenced to death; the jury, of course, was all white. The Supreme Court struck down the law, as a violation of the equal protection clause. Overt discrimination was apparent on the face of the statute. Yet, in *Virginia v. Rives*, decided at about the same time, the Court refused to interfere in a case from a state where no black had ever served on the jury—in this case, however, the local statute was neutral on its face.[34] It was the person-from-Pluto approach.

What could possibly justify such an attitude? It is easy to call it hypocrisy, or to pin the label of "formalism" on it, and assume that the judges of the time were simply formalists; but I think it better to try to explain it in social terms. "Formalism" after all can either be a frame of mind (this is, I think, very rarely the case), or it can be a posture, a strategy. The legal system in the nineteenth century was replete with what we might call double systems, in which a yeasty and grimy reality lay under the surface of a smooth formality. As one example of many, consider police brutality. Suspects in the nineteenth century were routinely beaten or otherwise mishandled; the "third degree" was positively epidemic.[35] But a goodly number of the respectable citizenry thought of it (if they thought at all) as a necessary evil. If you made brutality and torture legal and legitimate, you would in the first place run afoul of the Constitution and positive law. You also might get far too much of a good thing. But if you demanded a kind of surface posture of humility before legal rules, meanwhile winking at a bit of subterranean violence, you were able to achieve what some might think the optimal mix of legality and toughness.

Most of the white South—and the white North for that matter—truly believed that the status of blacks in the late nineteenth century constituted a "problem," especially for the South. The solution was a kind of caste system; not to mention a docile supply of black farm labor. Perhaps, then, the situation called for a mixture of suppression and surface legality—somewhat like the status of police brutality. The Court's bland words were a cloak for ideas of this type, consciously or not. It is certainly clear from the language he used that Justice Brown, and his colleagues no doubt, did not believe in the equality of the races, separate or not. This inclined them to think the white southern solution was, in this imperfect world, about as good as one might do. These justices were certainly not inclined to interfere.

The only dissenter in the *Plessy* case was John Marshall Harlan; his famous dissent, passionate and eloquent, has, however, in a kind of historic irony, gotten most of its mileage out of one single phrase. "Our Constitution," he said, "is color-blind." The irony is that this phrase has become a slogan for those who reject the whole idea of affirmative action. It has come to mean a rigid refusal to take race into account in framing employment or educational policy or whatever.[36] In the actual opinion, Harlan meant something quite different, or so it seems to me (not that "affirmative action" was an issue in 1896). To understand what this meaning was, it is important to read the whole opinion, which is sensitive at all times to *context*. Unlike his colleague Justice Brown, Harlan made it clear that he was acutely aware of southern reality. The "color-blind" phrase must therefore mean, not indifference to race, but a rejection of white supremacy and the legacy of slavery—quite a different nuance.[37]

What lay behind *Plessy v. Ferguson?* There were, perhaps, some important intellectual roots; this was the era of scientific racism. Physical anthropologists, for example, tended to believe in a kind of evolutionary scheme, in which the white race was the most advanced, the most civilized, and the blacks were left behind at the post.[38] Scientific racism, however, was not the *source* of plain ordinary racism; it was, on the contrary, more likely the *effect* in intellectual circles of the pervasive racism of the day. The average white certainly thought of the average black as lazy, intellectually backward, and in general inferior; and he or she held this opinion long before the vogue of scientific racism. American whites, in general, had never been in favor of racial equality; even those who disapproved of slavery were, on the whole, lukewarm about a truly "color-blind" society.

What *Plessy* stood for, then, was a kind of racial caste system. The case stood for white supremacy. What justified white supremacy, in the minds of men like Justice Brown, was the conviction that nature intended this to be the case. Moreover, the two races could not and should not mix. Certainly, the legal system could not and should not do anything to promote "mixing" (or anything that led to social or economic equality); on the contrary, it could and should do whatever was in its power to do, which would maintain the caste system, north and south. Justice Brown understood that the South in particular would find its own ways to accomplish this dreadful end, and that segregation was an important aspect of caste. The formalism of his opinion was a way of saying to the South: Full steam ahead; we will not disturb you in your task.

Stages along the Way: The Peonage Cases

The *Plessy* case put a stamp of approval on segregation, and the southern states eagerly took advantage of the opportunity.[39] In the years afterward, segregation statutes multiplied; segregation came to cover every aspect of southern life, and the web of statutes and ordinances in the South played a part in supporting the system.

Segregation was, however, only one leg of the southern system. Labor arrangements made up the other leg. Here law and custom joined together to keep blacks, in essence, tied to the soil. To put it bluntly, the southern labor system was a form of serfdom.[40] There were, of course, national laws against "peonage";[41] and slavery had been officially abolished by the Thirteenth Amendment to the Constitution. Getting rid of slavery was, to be sure, a great social advance; and it meant a great deal to southern blacks—that is undeniable. When slavery ended, the mass of blacks could legally marry, own property, and, to a limited degree, run their own lives. But their rights and powers continued to be severely circumscribed. For one thing, most blacks were desperately poor. They were farm workers—sharecroppers or contract laborers. Practically speaking, they were tied to the soil. An elaborate structure of laws, designed to preserve intact "the southern way of life," buttressed the labor system. The point of these laws was to keep blacks "in their place."

Everywhere in the South, when the Reconstruction period ended, white supremacy parties took control, and stripped blacks of the right to vote. Black political power, such as it was, withered and died. The black population was systematically disenfranchised, through a combination of terror and legal maneuvering. Soon blacks had no power on city councils, or in state legislatures. There were no black police in southern cities. The system of justice, civil and criminal, was exclusively in the hands of whites.[42] There was thus no escape, legally speaking, for any black who might protest against the sheer unfairness and oppression of the labor system.

In *Bailey v. Alabama*,[43] decided in 1911, the Supreme Court confronted one of these rare rebels. The precise question in *Bailey* was the validity of one of the nastier Alabama statutes. This law rather blandly stated that it was a crime to defraud an employer, by entering into a labor contract, getting an advance, and then failing to live up to the contract (or give back the money). This failure itself would be "prima facie evidence" of intent to defraud. Moreover, the courts did not allow the accused to testify "as to his uncommunicated motives, purpose or intention." The idea, plainly, was to make it (in effect) a crime for a black farm laborer to quit his job; it was the custom to make small cash advances, and the typical black laborer would be hard pressed to pay such advances back.

Was the statute constitutional? Or was it, rather, a form of peonage? If so, it was a violation of the Thirteenth Amendment, and of the antipeonage laws that Congress had passed to carry the amendment into effect.[44] That was the issue in the case, which went up to the Supreme Court. The Court's opinion in *Bailey* is a good example of the conflict between style and substance. For whatever reason, the Court felt constrained to adopt the person-from-Pluto style; or perhaps it would be accurate enough just to call the style of this opinion formalistic. Charles Evans Hughes, speaking for the Court, announced, sweepingly, that in the case "no question of a sectional character is presented, and we may view the legislation in the same manner as if it had been enacted in New York or in Idaho." He added, for good measure, "We at once dismiss from consideration the fact that the plaintiff in error is a black man. . . . The statute, on its face, makes no racial discrimination, and the record fails to show its existence in fact."[45]

Of course, all this was arrant nonsense. The Court was perfectly aware that there were no such statutes in New York, let alone Idaho; and it must have been perfectly aware that the statute was applied 100 percent to black laborers. The Court not only knew these facts; it was eager to act on them. At least that is what the result suggests. The Court denounced the statute as a form of peonage, in violation of a statute of 1867.[46] The antipeonage laws embraced "all legislation which seeks to compel the service or labor by making it a crime to refuse or fail to perform it."[47] The Alabama law, with its "presumption" of fraud, was a "convenient instrument" for the kind of coercion which the statute was trying to outlaw. The law threatened the "freedom of labor upon which alone can enduring prosperity be based."[48] It therefore had to fall.

Why did the Court pretend that *Bailey* had nothing to do with black workers in the South? The formalism, such as it was, did not prevent the Court from reaching the result it wanted; but the style was not wholly irrelevant. My guess is that the Court was a bit shy about confronting so deeply entrenched a system. Far better to deal with it case by case, than to attack it frontally; and to find some reason, other than race (an incendiary topic) for striking down the statute.[49] Or perhaps what bothered the Court was not the racism of the statute so much as its repugnance; they might have felt that it was an offense against a free labor market—as odious as slavery, in its own way.[50] In the event, *Bailey* accomplished nothing—the South ignored it or bypassed it; and the federal government had no particular zeal about any follow-up. But this can hardly be blamed on the Supreme Court, which, then as now, has no easy way to monitor or enforce its decisions.

The case-by-case approach was a tactic that the Court came to use in school segregation situations as well—in a series of cases, beginning in the 1930s, the Court struck down *particular* arrangements, on the grounds that they did not meet the separate-but-equal standard. In so doing, the Court did not need to confront head-on the question of segregation per se. The best known cases were the ones that concerned higher education.[51] In *Sweatt v. Painter* (1950),[52] the Court held, quite sensibly, that a new school for black law students in Texas was certainly not "equal" to the University of Texas, a school that had "those qualities which are incapable of objective measurement but which make for greatness in a law school," qualities such as the "reputation of the faculty, experience of the administration . . . traditions and prestige."[53] In *McLaurin v. Oklahoma*,[54] McLaurin, who was black, was admitted to the University of Oklahoma as a graduate student (through court order), but was segregated there—even in the cafeteria. But setting McLaurin apart from the other students, said Chief Justice Vinson, would "impair and inhibit his ability to study, to engage in discussion and exchange views with other students, and, in general, to learn his profession." This, then, was not equality either.

In a sense, the handwriting was on the wall. *Sweatt v. Painter* was not a person-from-Pluto case. The "qualities" that could not be measured at the University of Texas were not surface qualities; they were not mere text, mere formality. On paper, it was possible to create a law school "equal" in size, money, and facilities to the University of Texas (maybe); but it was no more equal in context and reality than a robot or a department-store dummy is equal to a living, breathing soul.

The March of Science

Meanwhile, over the years, some social and behavioral scientists had been chipping away at the intellectual side of racism. In some sense, the high point of scientific (or pseudoscientific) racism, and the eugenics idea, was attained in the 1930s, in Hitler's Germany.[55] Hitler's crackpot ideas were directed, above all, at the Jews, whom he later slaughtered by the millions. He had nothing but contempt for blacks, of course; but there were almost none around in Germany for him to murder; and he had to make do with the dark-skinned Gypsies instead.[56]

The stench arising from the Third Reich was one factor, and a significant one, in the move to put scientific racism into cold storage. In any event, in the twentieth century, even before Hitler, social scientists and anthropologists in increasing numbers began to argue that race was not a meaningful category.[57]

There were physical differences between the (conventionally defined) races to be sure; but they were utterly inconsequential. Race was, to use a common phrase, nothing more serious than "pigmentation of the skin."

These ideas were in the air in the 1940s and 1950s; and indeed they were argued to the Court, in such cases as *Shelley v. Kraemer*.[58] There were, of course, other historical factors at work, and probably far more powerful ones: most notably, perhaps, the civil rights movement itself. Blacks in the North voted and had at least a modest amount of political influence. The Supreme Court was a much more liberal body after the 1930s than it was before; Vinson's and Warren's Courts were New Deal and post–New Deal institutions. Slowly, too, there were political changes; Truman desegregated the armed forces, for example. The time, as they say, was ripe for change.

In essence, *Brown* reflected all these currents of change. The opinion also rejected scientific racism, and then went on to throw aside the person-from-Pluto style as well. Warren's opinion examined the southern system as a *system*; that is, as a context, a way of life, an arrangement of caste. It is in this regard that one has to understand the insistence on psychological harm to black students. A truly "separate but equal" system would not create any psychological harm in itself.[59] But logic was not the point; reality was. The opinion started out with what everybody knew: there was a caste system in the South. In *that* kind of system, feelings of inferiority might well arise—simply because the subordinate caste is clearly labeled and treated as subordinate. Segregation and the whole surrounding context operated to maintain and reinforce the caste system—to insist that blacks were the inferior race.

Of course, not everybody had abandoned scientific racism; and both scholarly and popular ideas of race figured in the furious attacks on *Brown* in the years following the decision, though often in a somewhat muted form. For example, a report of the "Alabama Interim Legislative Committee on Segregation in the Public Schools," dated October 18, 1954, solemnly asserted that there are "profound psychological and cultural differences, *including differences in aptitudes*, between the white and negro races in Alabama" (emphasis added).[60] These ideas are certainly alive and well today, even in some academic circles; the mainstream of science has, however, rather clearly repudiated any notions of higher and lower races. Yet the more "scientific" aspects of the race question—on both sides—strike me as no more decisive today than they were in the nineteenth century. The intellectual battle over *Brown*, and over race relations, is an afterthought, icing on the cake; the real battles are social, political, cultural; and they run very deep.

The academic reaction to *Brown* was, as I indicated at the outset, somewhat mixed. There was always a good deal of admiration, among liberal academics, and certainly among black scholars, for the decision itself. But there was also criticism, some of it a bit diffident, some of it not. This criticism, at base, was probably nothing more than social conservatism, but it took the form of criticizing style and craftsmanship. It was the bold way *Brown* rejected formalism and the person-from-Pluto approach, its emphasis on "nonlegal" factors, that constituted the sublime affront to legal tradition. Of course, there were those (like Albert Sacks) who praised the opinion for its "straightforward simplicity," and its sensitivity to "the need for preserving and enhancing one of the country's most valuable assets—the quality of its human resources."[61] But the clean, honest style was a slap in the face of the legalists.

Alexander Bickel, in a well-known passage, attacked both the Warren Court, and Warren's personal behavior as a Justice: "When a lawyer stood before him arguing . . . on the basis of some legal doctrine or other, or making a procedural point," Bickel says, Warren "would shake him off saying, 'Yes, yes, yes, but is it . . . *right?* Is it *good?*'" The Warren Court, Bickel said, "took the greatest pride in cutting through legal technicalities, in piercing through procedure to substance. But legal technicalities," according to Bickel, "are the stuff of law."[62]

But are they? If Warren was "cutting through legal technicalities," what was he cutting *to?* Bickel suggests that Warren was guided, not by "law," but by a kind of commonsense morality. Personally, I see nothing wrong with that; but in fact I doubt that this is what Warren was doing, or thought he was doing, certainly not in the segregation cases. What he was piercing, in those cases, was the veil of lies about the position of blacks in southern society. He was refusing to use the person-from-Pluto approach. The "commonsense" style of *Brown* is the medium for emphasizing context, reality, for rejecting the dry formalism that made it (stylistically) possible to pretend that all was well in the house of the South.

Another good example of the same approach is Warren's opinion in *Loving v. Virginia*,[63] which struck down antimiscegenation laws. The argument (not a bad one, technically) *for* the laws was that they were truly separate but equal. It was just as much a crime for a white to marry a black as vice versa. There was no "discrimination." But Warren brushed this argument aside. His language was blunt: miscegenation laws were "designed to maintain White Supremacy," and that, of course, was unacceptable. But of course nothing in the text of a miscegenation law *says* anything about white supremacy; and there is nothing in the wording of a miscegenation law that would allow a little green creature from Pluto to tell what the racial situation was in Virginia, and why miscegenation fell under the ban. However, for those of us who live in the United States, and who are not little green creatures from Pluto, it is obvious that Warren was exactly right. Miscegenation laws are laws against "race mixing," and these laws are about theories of black inferiority, and the prevention of fraternization between the races; and the whole point of these laws is white supremacy and how to maintain and sustain it.

In any event, to return to Bickel, one can legitimately ask: suppose we concede that Earl Warren was not really concerned with legal technicalities. Who then *was* interested in these niceties? Certainly not the general public—white or black; but that seems obvious. Certainly not the southern senators who fulminated against *Brown* on the floors of Congress. Presumably lawyers and judges. But is this so? Was it "legal technicalities" that the *Plessy* Court was really interested in? Did it uphold Jim Crow laws because it was concerned with procedures and doctrines? It hardly seems likely. Was it the *Bailey*

Court that focused on purity of doctrine? That seems equally unlikely, especially in the light of Holmes' mordant dissent. Does *any* court—any high court—behave as Bickel suggests it should?

I think we simply do not know. I do not want to go so far as to say that no court, ever, is interested in procedural technicalities, craftsmanship, rigorous adherence to stare decisis and the rest of it.[64] But in highly charged cases, in "political" cases, I would suggest that very few of them are. And certainly the United States Supreme Court is, and always has been, political (in the best and broadest sense of the word).

To be sure, when the Court abandons the style of formalism, in whole or in part, it renders itself a bit more naked—more exposed to the eagle eyes and sharp tongues of academic critics. But it would be nonsense to suppose that the Warren Court was the first court to decide cases according to its notion of what is right and good. In *Plessy v. Ferguson*, formalism served as a cover for nineteenth-century race ideas, and for white supremacy. The *Bailey* case showed that formalism could be used to cover or disguise a movement in the opposite direction. The obsession with style and form is a disease of law professors, and perhaps of judges making Law Day speeches; there is no proof that it goes much beyond that.

Of course, style is not accidental. What seemed a natural way of writing to Warren would have seemed unnatural to Hughes. It would be a fair question to ask why this shift in judicial style took place; and to explore its deeper, larger meaning. What audience was Warren addressing? Why did he craft the opinion as he did?[65] These are interesting questions; but they are indeed questions of style, not questions of substance. To ask these questions, is not to assume that the Warren Court was result-oriented to a degree *different* from the result orientation of other courts, in other times and places. It is possible—probable, I think—that many of these courts hid behind a formalist mask. Whether this was conscious, unconscious, or subconscious behavior is impossible to tell.

And what about footnote 11? What about all the "sociology" in *Brown?* (Actually it was social psychology, for the most part; but nobody bothered to draw such fine distinctions.)[66] There is, of course, abundant evidence that the Court did rely on something other than "legal" precedents, in reaching its decision; but the something was not the studies cited in footnote 11. What drove the decision was the strong sense that segregation was just plain wrong; and probably the sense that segregation was bad for the country in the long run. But these were hardly novel ideas. Certainly, many people in the country, including many whites, were horrified by segregation.[67] Moreover, the idea that segregation is wrong is hardly "sociology." What we know about the actual arguments in front of the Court suggest that the material cited in footnote 11 played no appreciable role at that level.[68]

The idea that race segregation might, under the circumstances, make people feel they were stigmatized, was itself nothing particularly new; such an idea had even found its way into judicial opinions.[69] Footnote 11 was probably inserted by Warren to rebut the nonsense in *Plessy* that a sense of inferiority arose out of segregation only because blacks so imagined it.[70] There seems to be an honest debate over whether the studies used the right meth-odology or actually proved anything.[71] But it is hard to imagine that the decision actually turned on whether these were good studies, bad studies, or irrelevant studies.

I would be very surprised, in fact, if Warren had read the works cited in footnote 11. I imagine he conceived of them as "authority"; and that they were treated as such. When a court cites a string of cases, it often distorts them, or uses them for purposes they were never designed to serve. There is certainly no guarantee that a judge who cites a long string of cases has actually read them. In any event, when a judge misrepresents or "distinguishes" prior cases, and does it cleverly, this is called "craftsmanship"; if she does it cleverly enough, she becomes a famous judge. Cardozo, for example, was an absolute master at making mincemeat out of precedents. His fame rests in part on this talent. Warren, I suspect, had no idea footnote 11 would be scrutinized so care-fully—or so literally.

Aside from little ripples in the academy, then, the footnote probably made no difference of any sort. It surely made no difference to the public; and certainly not in the white South. It is hard to imagine that leaving the footnote out would have mollified a segregationist. Of course, there were cries of rage that fastened on the footnote: the Court had abandoned law in favor of "soci-ology."[72] William Simmons, one of the panjandrums of the White Citizens' Councils, solemnly warned an audience that "when any court takes leave of the law and starts rendering edicts based on sociology, it is high time for all Americans to wake up."[73] Even some of *Brown*'s friends thought the footnote was a mistake.[74] But this, I believe, rests on a deep misunderstanding of the *way* cases work their impact.

After *Brown*

If *Brown* is in bad odor, at least in some circles, it may be because integration itself is in bad odor. Blacks and their allies in the *Brown* generation were engaged in a struggle with segregation—at the time, the South was a segre-gated, caste-ridden society; and the North was no paradise for black people either.

Race prejudice is a deep, primitive, dark emotion, and a rather pervasive one in American society. At the surface level, it tends to justify itself with stereotypes and lies about black people. These stereotypes have weakened over the years, but they still have considerable vitality with millions of American whites—even in some high circles, as Charles Murray's book, *The Bell Curve*, indicates.

At a time when blacks were battling to open some of the doors that were shut tight against them, liberals on race issues insisted that race did not matter; that racial differences were trivial, superficial. Race was "pigmentation" and nothing more. Sometimes race was even less than that; the "one-drop" rule meant that many "blacks" were men and women who were very light-skinned and got most of their genetic equipment from whites.[75] As Thurgood Marshall himself argued at one point before the Court in *Brown,* "there are Negroes as white as the drifted snow, with blue eyes, and they are just as segregated as the colored man."[76]

Race, therefore, was an irrational category; blacks and whites essentially shared a common humanity; some blacks were not even black; the system of segregation was evil, in that it held blacks down artificially, and kept their sameness and humanity from coming to light. Warren wrote, in *Brown,* that, in his day, "many Negroes have achieved outstanding success in the arts and sciences as well as in the business and professional world."[77] Blacks had, in short, made contributions to mainstream American civilization. They *belonged* there, that is, in the mainstream. This meant that, if we could only get rid of segregation, these contributions to American life would grow and grow—to the betterment of all the races.

What is missing from *Brown,* and from the first generation of cases, is any sense that blacks constituted a "nation." *Brown* was a product of the last days of the "melting pot" philosophy of citizenship.[78] Indeed, arguments for black liberation were arguments, on the whole, that whites kept blacks, forcibly, from participating in American society—that whites *prevented* assimilation. Black separatist movements, like that of Marcus Garvey, were very much the exception.

In the late 1940s, at the time when *An American Dilemma*[79] was written, the situation of black Americans was truly deplorable: millions of blacks were poor, illiterate, oppressed, ground down. As we mentioned, blacks could not vote in most of the South; they had no share in government or the system of justice. Most jobs were closed to blacks; blacks were even segregated in the army and navy, and barred from major league baseball; they could not even sing at the Metropolitan Opera. Race riots during the Second World War broke out when factories, in a time of acute labor shortage, dared to hire black workers for something other than sweeping the floor.[80] No wonder that the most powerful thrust of the civil rights movement was aimed at breaking down some of the terrible barriers that stood in the way of black progress.

What was emphasized, in other words, was not the uniqueness of black culture, or the claims of blacks as a "nation"; but demands more pressing and immediate. These were about the right of blacks to have a stake in America, the right to sit at the table and take part in the general festivities; the right to decent schooling, decent jobs; the right to go to the park or eat at Woolworth's. It was natural for Warren to stress what blacks could and should contribute, what they could bring to bear on America's general culture.

It would take us much too far afield to explore what has happened to this notion. The civil rights movement of the day rested on an assumption, or several assumptions, about what American society was all about. Today at least, there is a strong rival assumption (or set of assumptions). People who are prevented from assimilating quite rightly demand the right to assimilate—if they want to. But assimilation as a regnant idea is considerably frayed about the edges. For one thing, the sheer persistence of racism in some areas of

American life was bound to disillusion blacks (and some whites). Such episodes as the Boston fury over busing led many blacks to wonder why they wanted integration anyway: Was it worth the trouble? Did it pay off for their kids?[81] In general, the "melting pot" ideal is much, much weaker today than it ever was before. Assimilation faces a powerful rival, which I have elsewhere called *plural equality*.[82]

The "left" critique of *Brown*, then, is essentially a rejection of one sort of idea about race in America. It rejects the ideal of assimilation, as a goal for black people. It questions whether assimilation is either possible and desirable. More accurately put, it is a rejection of the idea that race is *only* something physical in America: "pigmentation of the skin." Race is culture, it is destiny, race is a component of a particular *nation*. Hence it is absurd to pretend that there can be a race-blind or color-blind America.[83] Indeed, Neil Gotanda goes so far as to say that color-blindness would amount to "abolition" of black culture, and abolition of a people's culture is "by definition, cultural genocide."[84]

The antiassimilationist idea is much more powerful today than ever before in our history. America is a "rainbow" of races and ethnic groups; or, if you will, a cacophony of voices. The ideal is not the melting-pot but power sharing. The ideal is a kind of Balkan federation of groups, only without the shooting wars. Each group will be free to develop and exploit its own distinctiveness. None will be asked to jump into the melting-pot and drown. This version of the multicultural state, perhaps, is what plural equality, in the end, is all about. But in such a climate, the "integrationist" ideal so powerfully expressed in *Brown* appears shopworn and old-fashioned. In our day, after all, black leaders (and some white ones) have seriously considered such tactics as setting up all-male black academies, as vessels for imparting self-respect and an atmosphere in which the "national" culture can flourish.[85]

Plural equality, in other words, calls integration into question. In so doing, of course, it casts a kind of dubious light backward on *Brown*, which was innocent of any real notion of plural equality, as it has come to be understood. *Brown* was about integration, assimilation, and the American mainstream. That stream is a lot muddier today. Hence it is no surprise to find a recent critic accusing *Brown* of trying "to make black people white people with black skin."[86] Of course, a proposition of this kind would have shocked and horrified Earl Warren—and probably Thurgood Marshall as well.

Conclusion

In this brief essay, I have tried to do two things. I have tried to put the *Brown* decision into social context. Of course, there are many social contexts, and I have chosen to talk about only one or two of them.

In many ways, too, most of this essay is not about *Brown* at all but about legal mandarins. I traced a stylistic line, from *Plessy* to *Brown*, and discussed some of the reasons that lay behind that style—and also the reaction to this style. At least some of the legal scholars who weighed in on this issue were probably quite sincere. I am sure Herbert Wechsler thought of himself this way: high-minded, principled, committed to the rule of law. He, and others, were genuinely bothered by what they saw as deficiencies in the Warren opinion. But they were, I believe, almost certainly misguided. All this stylistic stuff was totally irrelevant to the *impact* of the decision—and certainly irrelevant to the moral and political issues that lay behind *Brown*, which have accompanied it, and which will pursue it into the future. What changed since *Plessy* was not so much judicial technique as America itself; and therefore the law changed with it. What mattered in both cases—*Plessy* and *Brown*—was the result, not the opinion. It is a deadly sin of law professors to imagine that their little internal quarrels have a vital effect on the actual *impact* of cases. No one has shown or can show that this is so.

We can also ask, what has changed since *Brown?* Many things, of course; and among them is the decline and fall of the ideal of assimilation—not integration, but assimilation. This makes *Brown* look a little dubious—at least to some people. Of course, these modern critiques of *Brown* are a bit anachronistic, and not a little unfair; but there they are. To me, it does not seem quite just to judge *Brown* outside of its own time. For its period, it was bold, clear sighted, and infused with genuine morality.[87] The people who criticized it then were, frankly, mostly bigots; the handful of timid academics we can simply ignore. The impact of the case, as far as I can see, was completely benign. Whether it had enough of an impact, however, is a vexed question. That *Brown* did not put an end to racism is perfectly obvious; it is also perfectly obvious that millions of blacks still lead segregated lives. But this is not the same as arguing that *Brown* somehow impeded progress or did more harm than good, or did *any* harm at all. A lot of gods turn out to have clay feet; a lot of hero worship is misguided. But I still think *Brown*—and Earl Warren, not to mention the plaintiffs, and their lawyers—deserve a moment of silent appreciation, forty or so years down the road.

Notes

I want to thank Stanley Mallison, Sharon Phelan, and Peter Bouckaert for their research help.

1. 345 U.S. 483 (1954).
2. *Brown* itself announced a general principle, and set the case down for reargument on the question of how that principle would be carried out. In the second *Brown* decision, 349 U.S. 294 (1955), the Court sent the issue back to the local federal courts, who were told to "require that the defendants make a prompt and reasonable start toward full compliance"; if such a start were made, the courts could give "additional time." Schools were to be open on a nondiscriminatory basis, and this was to be done "with all deliberate speed."
3. U.S. (1 Cranch) 137 (1803).
4. The decision is "another long step toward making real that equality of

opportunity which . . . has been denied to so many of the children of our Negro citizens. It pushes along the effort to bring our democratic professions and our actual social practices into accord. . . . The decision . . . is a great thing for colored Americans. . . . It is a great thing for the south. . . . It is a great thing for all of us." *Christian Century* (Chicago Ill.), June 2, 1954, at 662, 663.

5. Letter to *Time Magazine*, June 14, 1954, at 10, from Robert B. Patterson of Indianola, Mississippi.

6. Learned Hand, *The Bill of Rights* (Cambridge, Mass.: Harvard University Press, 1958), 54. Hand suggested, in rather veiled language, that the Court had overturned a legislative judgment on the basis of "its own reappraisal of the relative values at stake," id., and the implication was that the Court, in so doing, was assuming "the role of a third legislative chanber," id., at 55. See also Gerald Gunther, *Learned Hand: The Man and the Judge* (New York: Knopf, 1994), 656–57.

7. Herbert Wechsler, "Toward Neutral Principles of Constitutional Law," 73 *Harvard Law Review* (1959), 10. Wechsler's article was much commented on; see, among others, Derrick A. Bell, Jr., "*Brown v. Board of Education* and the Interest-Convergence Dilemma," 93 *Harvard Law Review* (1990), 518.

8. During the hearings on the proposed confirmation of Robert Bork (he never made it, of course), Bork was asked about his views of Bolling v. Sharpe, 347 U.S. 497 (1954), the companion case to *Brown. Bolling* struck down segregation in the schools of the District of Columbia—which required a bit of fancy footwork, because the Fourteenth Amendment does not apply to the District (not being a "state"). Bork voiced considerable doubt about the case, which he suspected was "propelled by a feeling that if we are going to do this to all of the States, we cannot let the federal government do it." But he was troubled: "I have not thought of a rationale for it." Quoted in Paul Brest and Sanford Levinson, *Processes of Constitutional Decisionmaking* (3rd ed., Boston: Little, Brown, 1992), 601.

9. Louis H. Pollak, "Racial Discrimination and Judicial Integrity: A Reply to Professor Wechsler," 108 *University of Pennsylvania Law Review* (1959), 1. A very different—and tongue-in-cheek—exercise in rewriting *Brown* is David P. Berten, "*Brown v. Board of Education of Topeka*: An Econolegal Opinion," 1989 *Wisconsin Law Review* (1989), 589, an attempt to show how a follower of the law-and-economics movement would have handled the issue.

10. Bruce Ackerman, interestingly, finds *Brown* rather bland—a "legalistic effort to 'cool' the debate, not a populist or prophetic effort to 'heat' it up"; he suspects that this blandness has been "a secret source of disappointment to the partisans of the Court's prophetic mission." Bruce Ackerman, *We the People*, vol. 1, *Foundations* (Cambridge, Mass.: Balknap Press of Harvard University Press, 1991), 143.

11. William L. Taylor, "*Brown*, Equal Protection, and the Isolation of the Poor," 95 *Yale Law Journal* (1986), 1700, 1734.

12. Drew S. Days, III, "*Brown* Blues: Rethinking the Integrative Ideal," 34 *William & Mary Law Review* (1992), 53, 74.

13. There is a large literature, of course, on the civil rights movements, Southern (and northern) disorder, and the federal response. See, for example, Michal R. Belknap, *Federal Law and Southern Order: Racial Violence and Constitutional Conflict in the Post-*Brown *South* (Athens: University of Georgia Press, 1987).

14. Gerald N. Rosenberg, *The Hollow Hope: Can Courts Bring About Social*

Change? (Chicago: University of Chicago Press, 1991); Michael J. Klarman, "*Brown*, Racial Change, and the Civil Rights Movement," 80 *Virginia Law Review* (1994), 7, also feels that the significance of *Brown* has been seriously overestimated; the case did not, Klarman thinks, play a direct role in bringing about "transformative racial change"; indeed, its immediate impact was that it crystallized "southern white *resistance* to racial change," and propelled "southern politics dramatically to the right on racial issues." Id. at 10, 11.

15. Richard Delgado and Jean Stefancic, "The Social Construction of *Brown v. Board of Education*: Law Reform and the Reconstructive Paradox," 36 *William & Mary Law Review* (1995), 547.

16. For a measured overview of the position of blacks in American society in our times—a kind of revisiting of Myrdal—see Gerald D. Jaynes and Robin M. Williams, Jr., eds., *A Common Destiny: Blacks and American Society* (Washington D.C.: National Academy Press, 1989); see also Derrick A. Bell, *Faces at the Bottom of the Well* (New York: Basic Books, 1922).

17. *Brown*, writes Leslie Dunbar, has "failed. Law is not sufficient unto itself"; but Dunbar nonetheless admires the vision of the case, which was "meant to bring us closer." The political successes of black leaders in the South are "direct progenies" of the case; and the reasons for the failure are economic and political. Leslie W. Dunbar, "Not by Law Alone: *Brown* in Retrospect," 70 *Virginia Quarterly Review* (1994), 205.

18. Louis Michael Seidman, "*Brown* and *Miranda*," 80 *California Law Review* (1992), 673, 715. The Court, according to Seidman, offered the country a "deal"; the facilities available to blacks would no longer be separate—but this removed from the larger society the duty to make them "equal." Hence, once "white society was willing to make facilities legally nonseparate, the demand for equality had been satisfied and blacks no longer had just cause for complaint. The mere existence of *Brown* thus served . . . to legitimate current arrangements." Id. at 717.

Another (rather milder) form of this critique is the argument that *Brown* "gave birth to our current civil rights policy: formal equal opportunity," which is flawed and bound to fail because it ignores subtle, deep-seated institutional racism. I call this "milder" because it does not explicitly blame *Brown* for the mess that follows. Roy L. Brooks and Mary Jo Newborn, "Critical Race Theory and Classical-Liberal Civil Rights Scholarship: A Distinction Without a Difference?" 82 *California Law Review* (1994), 787, 798.

J. Harvie Wilkinson argues that *Brown* "dealt blacks an unwitting slight. . . . Separate . . . was *inherently* unequal. If this holding on the surface buoyed black morale, its undercurrents, in time, just as certainly depressed it. For *Brown* implied first, that black schools, whatever their physical endowments, could not equal white ones; second, that integration was a matter of a white benefactor and a black beneficiary." Wilkinson, *From* Brown *to* Bakke: *The Supreme Court and School Integration: 1954–1978* (New York: Oxford University Press, 1979), 46.

19. Gerald Rosenberg, supra note 14, argues that the courts (he is speaking of the *Brown* court as a prime example) "lure" social reformers, and trap them into a line of wasted effort. The courts "can seldom produce significant social reform." But the reformers "spend precious resources in litigation," which means that courts actually "limit change by deflecting claims from substantive political battles, where success is possible, to harmless legal ones where it is not." Furthermore, while Rosenberg "found no evidence that court decisions mobilize support-

ers of significant social reform, the data suggest that they may mobilize opponents." Id. at 341.

What, however, was the alternative? Rosenberg argues that legislation, not litigation, was what made a difference in school desegregation and the like. But appeals to legislatures, before *Brown*, were (for various reasons) total failures. One wonders how much headway civil rights could have made in, say, the Jackson, Mississippi, city council; the Arkansas legislature; or, for that matter, the United States Congress, without the leadership of the courts.

20. 410 U.S. 113 (1973).

21. It is certainly possible, even probable, that some opponent of racial equality heard about the dithering in the academy, and used it or cited such stuff in argument; but surely as nothing more than a makeweight. There is one aspect of the opinion that was seized upon by enemies of racial equality—the citation of social science evidence. But here too it is hard to imagine that this use of evidence made much difference, one way or another. See below, text at notes 66–71.

22. See, for example, John H. Ely, "The Wages of Crying Wolf: A Comment on *Roe v. Wade*," 82 *Yale Law Journal* (1973), 920.

23. Lee Epstein & Joseph F. Kobylka, *The Supreme Court and Legal Change: Abortion and the Deah Penalty* (Chapel Hill: University of North Carolina Press, 1992), 311.

24. Here I should cite the classic work by Joseph Gusfield, *Symbolic Crusade: Status Politics and the American Temperance Movement* (Urbana: University of Illinois Press, 1963).

25. Walter White, secretary of the NAACP, interviewed in *U.S. News and World Report*, was quite clear on this point: After all, as he pointed out, the *Plessy* case "dealt with interstate railroad travel but soon was applied to other phases of life. We believe that this is going to happen in the present . . . cases . . . —that [the holding] will affect relationships not only in schools but in other ways." *U.S. News and World Report*, May 28, 1954, at 55.

26. On this question, of course, the literature about the *impact* of *Brown* is directly relevant. See Rosenberg, supra note 14.

27. *New York Times*, May 18, 1954, at 14, col. 4.

28. See below, text at nn. 72–73.

29. 163 U.S. 537 (1896); see Charles A. Lofgren, *The* Plessy *Case: A Legal-Historical Interpretation* (New York: Oxford University Press, 1987).

30. The reference in the heading to this section, of course, is to C. Vann Woodward's famous book, *The Strange Career of Jim Crow* (New York: Oxford University Press, 1955). The book deals with the history of race segregation in the South.

31. See Gilbert Thomas Stephenson, "The Separation of the Races in Public Conveyances," 3 *American Political Science Review* (May 1909), 180, for an account of these laws.

32. The case was decided on May 18, 1896; there were reports in many newspapers, but they were rather matter-of-fact. Except for the black press, the decision did not seem to evoke much comment; most newspapers simply reported the holding, and the dissent, without editorializing—for example, *Atlanta Constitution*, May 19, 1896, at 3; *New York Times*, May 19, 1896, at 1.

33. 100 U.S. 303 (1979).

34. Virginia v. Rives, 100 U.S. 313 (1879). *In Ex parte Virginia*, however, 100 U.S. 339 (1879), the Court allowed the prosecution of a Virginia judge, under

a federal statute, for excluding blacks from juries; see also Neal v. Delaware, 103 U.S. 370 (1880).

35. See, for example, the classic study, Zechariah Chafee, Jr., et al., *The Third Degree* (New York: Arno Press, 1969); Ernest J. Hopkins, *Our Lawless Police: A Study of the Unlawful Enforcement of the Law* (New York: Viking Press, 1931).

36. "The curious ideological phenomenon is that color-blindness has become an abstraction that has taken on a life of its own, one that can turn around to disappoint the hopes of the very people on whose behalf it arose initially." Alan D. Freeman, "Antidiscrimination Law: A Critical Review," in David Kairys ed., *The Politics of Law: A Progressive Critique* (New York: Pantheon Books, 1982), 96, 101. See Adarand Constuctors, Inc. v. Pena, 115 S. Ct. 2097 (1995).

37. The passage before Harlan's famous phrase reads as follows: "[In] view of the Constitution, in the eye of the law, there is in this country no superior, dominant, ruling class of citizens. There is no caste here." It would be hard to squeeze an argument against affirmative action out of these words—not that this point, of course, is crucial.

38. See Herbert Hovenkamp, "Social Science and Segregation Before Brown," 1985 *Duke Law Journal* 624.

39. Segregation in schools was almost universal in the South; also in public transportation, and in such things as waiting rooms and the like, e.g., Virginia provisions, calling for separate areas for the races on steamboats "in the sitting, sleeping, and eating apartments," and "separate and noncommunicating rooms for the white and colored races" at the wharves. Code of Va., §§ 4022, 4026 (1919). Prisons, too, were segregated, e.g., Miss. Code, § 3625, at 1021 (1906) ("separate apartments for both eating and sleeping").

40. On the Southern labor system, and the peonage cases, see Pete Daniel, *The Shadow of Slavery: Peonage in the South, 1901–1969* (Urbana: University of Illinois Press, 1972); Daniel A. Novak, *The Wheel of Servitude: Black Forced Labor After Slavery* (Lexington: University Press of Kentucky, 1978); William Cohen, "Negro Involuntary Servitude in the South, 1865–1940," 42 *Journal of Southern History* (1976), 42.

41. 14 Stat. 546 (Act of Mar. 2, 1867) declared "unlawful" the "holding of any person to service or labor under the system of peonage."

42. See Edward L. Ayers, *Vengeance and Justice: Crime and Punishment in the 19th Century American South* (New York: Oxford University Press, 1984), especially chs. 5 and 6.

43. 219 U.S. 231 (1911); see Daniel, supra note 40, ch. 4; Novak, supra note 40, ch. 5.

44. See Benno C. Schmidt, Jr., "Principle and Prejudice: The Supreme Court and Race in the Progressive Era. Part 2: The Peonage Cases," 82 *Columbia Law Review* (1982), 646.

45. Id. at 231.

46. The statute had been upheld in Clyatt v. United States, 197 U.S. 207 (1905), as a valid exercise of congressional power under the Thirteenth Amendment. In the actual case, however, the Supreme Court reversed the conviction of the defendants on rather technical grounds. Clyatt and the other defendants had gone to Florida, it was alleged, to seize and return to "peonage" two blacks, Gordon and Ridley. Justice Harlan, dissenting, referred to "barbarities of the worst kind against these negroes," and argued for affirming the convictions. Id. at 223.

47. Id. at 243.

48. Id. at 245. The decision evoked a somewhat mordant and characteristic dissent by Oliver Wendell Holmes, Jr. Holmes seemed to be saying, Look, if you really think or say you think that this is not a case about southern blacks, then all of your reasoning is ridiculous. Breach of a contract is a wrong, he argued, and "if a State adds to civil liability a criminal liability . . . it simply intensifies the legal motive for doing right, it does not make the laborer a slave." Id. at 247.

In a sense then, Holmes could be defended (if one wants to; I prefer not to) as striking a blow against formalism. But it seems a bit callous to strike such a blow at the expense of poor and suffering black farmworkers. On Holmes's stance in this case, and his attitude toward the rights of blacks in general, see G. Edward White, *Justice Oliver Wendell Holmes: Law and the Inner Self* (New York: Oxford University Press, 1993), 335–43.

49. In Buchanan v. Warley, 245 U.S. 60 (1917), the Supreme Court struck down an ordinance of Louisville, Kentucky, which did not allow any "colored person" to occupy a house on a block where the majority of the residents were white, or vice versa. But the decision emphasized *property* rights; the ordinance took away a person's right to buy and sell, without "due process." The decision did not, in other words, attack *segregation* as an evil—at least not overtly. See the discussion in Benno C. Schmidt, Jr., "Principle and Prejudice: The Supreme Court and Race in the Progressive Era: Part 1: The Heyday of Jim Crow," 82 *Columbia Law Review* (1982), 444, 498–523.

50. Only three years before, in 1908, the Supreme Court confronted a Kentucky statute that made it a crime to operate a college "where pupils of the white and negro races are both received as pupils." Berea College was such a place, and it ran afoul of the statute. The Supreme Court, however, upheld the statute in Berea College v. Kentucky, 211 U.S. 45 (1908); and Harlan, the only dissenter in *Plessy v. Ferguson*, was the only dissenter here. The spirit of *Plessy*, then, was alive and vigorous in the age of *Bailey*—at least for some issues.

51. See, for example, Missouri *ex rel*. Gaines v. Canada, 305 U.S. 337 (1938). Missouri had a scheme to pay black students to go to law school out of state, rather than allow them into the state's law schools. The Supreme Court struck the scheme down.

52. 339 U.S. 629 (1950).

53. Id. at 634.

54. 339 U.S. 637 (1950).

55. On the eugenics movement in general, see Mark H. Haller, *Eugenics: Hereditarian Attitudes in American Thought* (New Brunswick, N.J.: Rutgers University Press, 1963); on its relationship with the Third Reich, see Stefan Kühl, *The Nazi Connection: Eugenics, American Racism, and German National Socialism* (New York: Oxford University Press, 1994).

56. On the slaughter of this ethnic group, see Michael Burleigh and Wolfgang Wippermann, *The Racial State: Germany, 1933–1945* (Cambridge: Cambridge University Press, 1991), ch. 5. After the First World War, the French occupied the German Rhineland area; and, inevitably, their soldiers fathered some children with German women. Among the soldiers were black colonial troops from African colonies. These children were sterilized during the Nazi period, see id. at 128–30.

57. Hovenkamp, supra note 38 at 668–71.

58. 334 U.S. 1 (1948); see Hovenkamp, supra note 38 at 671.

59. Nor would the kind of self-segregation that, for example, proposed black academies would foster, or the "historically black" colleges in the South; of

course, Warren and his Court (and the litigants) could have had no such schools in mind.

60. The report is printed in 7 *Alabama Law Review* (1954), 64, 65, as an appendix to an article by Prof. Jay Murphy, of the University of Alabama Law School, "Can Public Schools Be 'Private'?" 7 *Alabama Law Review* (1954), 48. Murphy quotes the sentence quoted above, and remarks: "If the Committee means that one race is inherently superior or inferior to another then this, of course, is not supported by scientific authority. . . . [E]veryone knows that one reason why the Negro citizen lacks the acquired educational skills, and the respectable kind of jobs, in the state is the fact that adequate educational and job opportunities have been denied him." Id. at 60.

61. Albert W. Sacks, "The Supreme Court, 1953 Term," 68 *Harvard Law Review* (1954), 96, 98–99. Sacks also liked the delicacy with which the Court dealt with (or ignored) *Plessy*. The Chief Justice did not try to show that the Court "had once blundered. His point, rather, was that these prior decisions were simply outmoded in present-day society."

62. Alexander M. Bickel, *The Morality of Consent* (New Haven: Yale University Press, 1975), 120–21.

63. 388 U.S. 1 (1967).

64. Judges themselves seem a bit confused about this point; some judges apparently think "nonlegal" factors are very important in the decision of cases, while others deny this point. See Henry R. Glick, *Supreme Courts in State Politics: An Investigation of the Judicial Role* (New York: Basic Books, 1971).

65. Clearly, whatever else he had in mind, Warren must have been aware of the need to persuade, to legitimize; after all, that is what an *opinion*, as opposed to a decision, is all about. Warren, in the view of one commentator, evoked "familiar images," in order to "change the focus of public awareness from race to education," and thus "gain some acceptance" for the decision. Kathryn A. Bellman, "Language and Rhetoric in *Brown v. Board of Education*" (unpublished Ph.D. dissertation, University of Nebraska, 1990), 125.

66. See Richard Kluger, *Simple Justice* (New York: Alfred A. Knopf 1976), chap. 14, for the background.

67. My impression—I can't call it anything more than that—is that northern whites, though racist through and through for the most part, were disgusted by *segregation*, separate water fountains, separate train waiting rooms, and that sort of thing. Similarly, many northerners in the period before the Civil War, who did not particularly like blacks, found slavery disgusting.

68. Kluger, supra note 66 at 705–6.

69. For example, Mendez v. Westminister School District of Orange County, 64 F.Supp. 544 (D.C., S.D. Cal., 1946). Orange County followed the practice of shunting Mexican-American children into separate schools. The district judge, McCormick, declared the practice unlawful: "methods of segregation . . . foster antagonisms in the children and suggest inferiority among them where none exists." The segregation, moreover, retards the learning of English, and prevents a "commingling of the entire student body" in such a way as to form a "common cultural attitude . . . which is imperative for the perpetuation of American institutions and ideals." Id. at 549. The case was affirmed on appeal. See Charles M. Wollenberg, *All Deliberate Speed: Segregation and Exclusion in California Schools, 1855–1975* (Berkeley: University of California Press, 1976), 129–30.

70. Kluger, supra note 66 at 706. It is important to note the context in which

Warren cited the studies. He quotes a "finding" in the Kansas case that segregation gives black children a "sense of inferiority," and adds, "Whatever may have been the extent of psychological knowledge at the time of *Plessy v. Ferguson*, this finding is amply supported by modern authority."

71. In a well-known article, Edmond Cahn argued that they were, in fact, bad studies: "When scientists set out to prove a fact that most of mankind already acknowledges, they may provide a rather bizarre spectacle." Cahn felt that the decision was plainly right, but that "our fundamental rights" should not "rise, fall, or change along with the latest fashions of psychological literature. Today the social psychologists . . . are liberal and egalitarian in basic approach. Suppose, a generation hence . . . they were to present us with a collection of racist notions and label them 'science.' What then would be the state of our constitutional rights?" Cahn, "Jurisprudence," 30 *New York University Law Review* (1955), 150, 159, 167. The studies, and the role of the social scientists, were defended by Dr. Kenneth C. Clark, one of the most notable of the social scientists consulted, in "The Desegregation Cases: Criticism of the Social Scientist's Role," 5 *Villanova Law Review* (1959), 224.

72. See text accompanying supra note 27.

73. Quoted in Numan V. Bartley, *The Rise of Massive Resistance: Race and Politics in the South During the 1950's* (Baton Rouge: Louisiana State University Press, 1969), 84. The Court, in Simmons's view, was telling the people of the South that they had to run "their public schools according to the theories of certain social revolutionaries." Id. The equation of "sociology" with "socialism" was and is rather common among the ill-informed or deliberately misinformed.

Southern opponents of the decision had to argue, of course, that the decision—handed down by the highest court of the land—was somehow not really law. But if it wasn't law, it had to be something else; why not call it sociology?

74. Kluger, for example, thinks so; the inclusion of the footnote was "gratuitously obnoxious." Supra note 66 at 707. On this score, he quotes Alexander Bickel as saying that it was a "mistake" to include the footnote. "No matter how it had been done, no doubt the enemies of the opinion were certain to seize upon it and proclaim the ruling unjudicial and illegal."

75. This was one of Homer Plessy's auxiliary arguments—that he was not really black at all. He was thus challenging Louisiana's definition of blackness; the Supreme Court brushed this argument aside as purely a matter of state law.

76. Quoted in Anthony G. Amsterdam, "Thurgood Marshall's Image of the Blue-Eyed Child in *Brown*," 68 *New York University Law Review* (1993), 226, 232; on the "one drop" rule, see F. James Davis, *Who Is Black? One Nation's Definition* (University Park: Pennsylvania State University Press, 1991).

77. Brown v. Board of Education, 347 U.S. 483 (1954), at 490.

78. Lawrence M. Friedman, "Law and Social Change: Culture, Nationality, and Identity," in *Collected Courses of the Academy of European Law*, vol. 4, bk. 2 (The Hague: Martinus Nijhoff, 1993), 237. Milton M. Gordon, *Assimilation in American Life: The Role of Race, Religion, and National Origin* (New York: Oxford University Press, 1964).

79. Gunnar Myrdal et al., *An American Dilemma* (New York: Harper & Brothers, 1944).

80. Doris K. Goodwin, *No Ordinary Time* (New York: Simon & Schuster, 1994).

81. See, for example, J. Harvie Wilkinson, *From* Brown *to* Bakke: *The Supreme Court and School Integration, 1954–1978* (New York: Oxford University Press, 1979), ch. 8.

82. Lawrence M. Friedman, *The Republic of Choice: Law, Authority, and Culture* (Cambridge, Mass.: Harvard University Press, 1990).

83. This point of view is only strengthened by the fact that conservatives have now eagerly embraced the idea that we should suddenly become extremely color-blind. Justice Scalia insists, for example, that any such thing as affirmative action is anathema. Racial preferences only "reinforce a manner of thinking by race that was the source of the injustice and will . . . be the source of more injustice still." And he makes the amazing statement that it was not "blacks, or Jews, or Irish" that were "discriminated against, but . . . individual men and women . . . who were discriminated against," as if race or ethnicity had nothing to do with the discrimination these individuals suffered. Scalia, J., concurring in City of Richmond v. J. A. Croson Company, 109 S. Ct. 706 (1989).

84. Neil Gotanda, "A Critique of 'Our Constitution is Color-Blind,'" 44 *Stanford Law Review* (1991) 1, 60. He goes on to say that "the color-blind assimilationist program implies the hegemony of white culture." Id.

85. See the discussion in Richard Cummings, "All-Male Black Schools: Equal Protection, the New Separatism, and *Brown v. Board of Education*," 20 *Hastings Constitutional Law Quarterly* (1993), 725; see also Sonia R. Jarvis, "*Brown* and the Afrocentric Curriculum," 101 *Yale Law Journal* (1992), 1285. Obviously, such academies raise gender questions as well as race questions—and have been attacked on this basis—but these questions are beyond the scope of this paper.

86. Jerome M. Culp, Jr., "Black People in White Face: Assimilation, Culture, and the *Brown* case," 36 *Willima & Mary Law Review* (1995), 665, 682. The Court, Culp argues, saw "the world mainly through lenses of the white majority." Id.

87. This is not an argument for excusing, say, *Plessy v. Ferguson*, on the grounds that it was simply a product of its time, though of course it was that.

Hovenkamp argues that criticism of the Supreme Court's race cases from 1896 on is "based on a myopic legal history." The Court was not "dominated by uninformed and outmoded bigotry. . . . [T]he Court closely tracked prevailing scientific opinion on race." Supra note 38 at 664. I disagree. Harlan's dissent, in *Plessy*, is also racist—*by modern standards*—but was noble and far-sighted, in its time. By the same token, Justice Brown's opinion in *Plessy* was mean-spirited and full of bigotry. That bigots could cite some supposed "scientific" support for their bigotry is irrelevant. We judge *Plessy* (and *Brown*) not by 1996 standards, but, as far as we can, by the standards of their own time. For its day, *Brown* was progressive and humane; for its day, *Plessy* (as the dissent makes clear) was not.

3

DAVID J. GARROW

From *Brown* to *Casey*

The U.S. Supreme Court and the Burdens of History

One of the most important lessons of the U.S. Supreme Court's resolution of *Brown v. Board of Education*[1] (*Brown I*)—both for the Court itself and for attentive commentators—is the clear and indeed almost explicit manner in which *Brown* signifies and symbolizes the post-1954 Court's repudiation of historical intent and meaningful evidence of historical intent[2] in its reading and application of the reach and meaning of the Fourteenth Amendment—both, in *Brown*, with regard to the Equal Protection Clause, and, in later cases, with respect to the Due Process Clause as well.[3]

Brown I was, of course, both constitutionally inevitable and *morally* correct, in much the same way that we now almost universally recognize both *Korematsu v. United States*[4] and *Bowers v. Hardwick*[5] as morally *repugnant* to any judicially unbiased reading of the Fourteenth Amendment. But the *Brown I* opinion was and is readily criticizable because of the narrowly and exclusively integrationist vision it articulated. Some African American commentators rightfully criticize this vision as being largely if not wholly blind to the possibility or certainty of independent, *separate* black success—without exposure to or integration with white people—in elementary and secondary schooling and other venues if public authorities actually were to provide *truly equal* resources and incentives.[6]

But separatist critiques of *Brown*, valid as they are, in our context are tangential to a full appreciation of how *Brown* for better or worse—and I *do* believe we can still find some reluctant rug rats, no matter how shy, who privately if not publicly believe the latter—single-handedly marks the advent of the "modern" or present-age Supreme Court. Many people have grown up believing that while *Marbury v. Madison*[7] is of course *the* formative U.S. Supreme Court decision of all time, *West Coast Hotel Co. v. Parrish*[8]— perhaps in conjunction with Chief Justice Stone's (or Louis Lusky's) famous footnote 4 in *Carolene Products*[9]—signals the beginning of the judicial modern age.

But that belief—a belief that was inculcated in at least two successive generations of American judicial scholars—is now all but indisputably out of date, for not only does *Brown* rather than the "constitutional revolution" of 1937 demarcate our modern era, but *Brown* also—just as importantly—paved the way toward the Warren Court's two other landmark antihistorical rulings—*Baker v. Carr*[10] and *Griswold v. Connecticut*[11] (and to their even better known progeny, *Reynolds v. Sims*[12] and *Roe v. Wade*[13])—which dramatically expanded the constitutional scope of the Fourteenth Amendment. Absent *Brown*, decisions with *Baker* and *Reynolds*'s muscularity are difficult to imagine; absent the most important of *Brown*'s own immediate progeny, namely *Cooper v. Aaron*,[14] the Warren Court's *Marbury*, much of the post-1954 Court's understanding of its own role—a role that at present has culminated in *Planned Parenthood of Southeastern Pennsylvania v. Casey*[15]—would have evolved in a decidedly different fashion. In short, *Brown I*, in tandem with *Cooper*, not only marks the beginning of modern America's official condemnation of racial discrimination, it also marks the beginning of a wide-ranging transformation of modern American life, brought about by a host of High Court decisions that have all relied on the Justices's dramatically expansive—and aggressively antihistorical—reading and application of the Fourteenth Amendment's Equal Protection and Due Process Clauses. From schooling to electoral districting to abortion, modern America is to a significant degree the product of muscular judicial utilization of the Fourteenth Amendment. It is also the product of constitutional analysis that has jettisoned the constraints of history, and—from *Brown* through *Baker* and *Reynolds* to *Griswold*, *Roe*, and *Casey*—I believe we can persuasively argue that it is a *better* America, precisely because of how the Court *has ignored* the Constitution's historical limitations in fashioning a Fourteenth Amendment jurisprudence that is responsive to the present day rather than to the institutional burdens of history.[16]

Careful students of *Brown* can of course easily recall how the Supreme Court initially hoped—and sought—to find clear Fourteenth Amendment historical support for resolving the fundamental question that *Brown* and its companion cases[17] presented. Following the first oral arguments in the *Brown* cases, the Court formally propounded five questions to the parties' attorneys. The first two questions asked for historical evidence regarding whether the framers of the amendment intended, or did not intend, for it either to prohibit, or to allow for the future prohibition of, racially segregated public schooling. The third question, however, voicing a presumption that the answers to the first two would "not dispose of the issue," posed the core issue bluntly: "[I]s it within the judicial power, in construing the [Fourteenth] Amendment, to abolish segregation in the public schools?"[18] Eleven months later, on May 17, 1954, the Court baldly—but compellingly—declared that indeed it was.

As we now know, the NAACP Legal Defense and Educational Fund litigators—and their many scholarly collaborators—were at first deeply (and justifiably) concerned by the Court's preliminary focus on historical queries whose answers would not hasten, and might well hinder, judicial acceptance of the NAACP's basic contention.[19] But by the time of *Brown* et al.'s rearguments in December of 1953, the Justices themselves privately no longer regarded the answers to those two historical queries as being potentially determinative. Felix Frankfurter had had one of his outgoing law clerks, Alexander M. Bickel, prepare an exhaustive historical research memo, and Frankfurter had distributed the impressive product to all his colleagues. Although counsel at the time were quite unaware of how Bickel's handiwork had firmly directed the Justices away from any potential history-based solution to their American dilemma, we nowadays—thanks in part to Mark Tushnet's careful analysis—can fully appreciate how by that December the historical questions "were no longer that important" to the Court itself.[20]

Even though there was (thanks to Robert Jackson and particularly Stanley Reed) no internal consensus on *how* to decide *Brown* when the Justices met for their decisive conference on December 12, 1953, there nonetheless *was* an unspoken consensus that the fundamental question before them was the previous June's "question three"—"[I]s it within the judicial power . . . to abolish segregation in the public schools?"[21] And, when Earl Warren delivered the Court's impressively unanimous opinion in *Brown* five months later, there again—and now for the whole country to see—was an explicit consensus that the core of this question, like others yet to come, concerned not evidence or documentation of "historical intent" but instead the nature and reach of "the judicial power."

Warren's opinion, in two early paragraphs that understandably are not among *Brown*'s best-remembered passages but that latter-day scholars should not overlook, deftly but decisively dismissed the decisional relevance of the Fourteenth Amendment's own history. Warren noted how *Brown*'s reargument "was largely devoted to the circumstances surrounding" the Fourteenth Amendment's 1868 adoption. "It covered exhaustively consideration of the Amendment in Congress, ratification by the states, then existing practices in racial segregation, and the views of proponents and opponents of the Amendment. This discussion and our own investigation convince us that, although these sources cast some light, it is not enough to resolve the problem with which we are faced. At best, they are inconclusive."[22]

"An additional reason for the inconclusive nature of the Amendment's history" vis-à-vis school segregation, Warren added, was the relatively undeveloped state of public education, especially in the South but also in the North, in 1868. "As a consequence, it is not surprising that there should be so little in the history of the Fourteenth Amendment relating to its intended effect on public education."[23]

So ended the *Brown* Court's analysis—and dismissal—of whether its con-

stitutional adjudication of governmentally imposed racial segregation in public schools was or should in any way be bound by the constraints of history.
Taken at their relatively modest face value, most readers pass over those two
paragraphs without attributing any special import to them, and such an
evaluation—within the four actual corners of the *Brown* opinion—is perfectly
appropriate. In a more long-range frame of reference, however—one that
encompasses particularly the years from 1962 (*Baker*) through 1973 (*Roe*)—
the *Brown* Court's affirmative jettisoning of the Fourteenth Amendment's
historical tie-lines marked the onset of a period of judicial freedom (and, some
correctly would say, judicial *sovereignty*) that dramatically transformed American life for the better. [24]

In 1954 itself, nothing highlighted the Court's Farragut-like approach to
mandating constitutional rights[25] more than its companion ruling in the fifth
of the *Brown* family of cases, Washington, D.C.'s *Bolling v. Sharpe*. Since the
Fourteenth Amendment applied its Equal Protection Clause only to the
states, and not to the federal government, the *Brown* Court found itself having
to identify some non–Fourteenth Amendment constitutional grounds for
avoiding the utterly incongruous paradox of striking down *state*-mandated
school segregation while not being able to void identical governmental policy
imposed by *federal* authorities. With a doctrinal dexterity that again may be
more significant in historical retrospect than it appeared to be in 1954, the
Court—lacking any federally applicable equal protection language—unani-
mously turned to the Fifth Amendment's Due Process Clause. "[T]he concepts of equal protection and due process, both stemming from our American
ideal of fairness, are not mutually exclusive," Chief Justice Warren wrote.
While "'equal protection of the laws' is a more explicit safeguard of prohibited unfairness than 'due process of law' . . . discrimination may be so un-
justifiable as to be violative of due process."[26]

Without expressly acknowledging that the Due Process Clause's key word
was of course "liberty," the *Bolling* opinion, while conceding that the Court to
date had not defined "'liberty' with any great precision," nonetheless went on
to emphasize that the concept was "not confined to mere freedom from bodily
restraint. Liberty under law extends to the full range of conduct which the
individual is free to pursue, and it cannot be restricted except for a proper
governmental objective. Segregation in public education is not reasonably
related to any proper governmental objective, and thus it imposes on Negro
children in the District of Columbia a burden that constitutes an arbitrary
deprivation of their liberty in violation of the Due Process Clause."[27] Any
commentators inclined to allege that the new era—or "Second Reconstruction"—of substantive due process first began to rear its assertedly ugly
head only in *Griswold v. Connecticut*[28] had best be reminded that as early as
May, 1954, *Bolling*'s quite uncontroversial language signaled that a highly
expansive approach to due process–based constitutional liberty could well go
forward hand in hand with *Brown*'s heralding of a new era of equal protection.[29]

Even more so than anything in *Brown* itself, the almost explicit point of

Bolling is that the traditions and niceties of doctrine *do not matter*—or, at the very most, matter relatively little—when and where the Court becomes convinced that a fundamental, moral holding needs to be made. But *Brown* and *Bolling* historically should not be weighed or evaluated apart from their most immediate and important progeny, namely the unprecedented "joint" opinion in the 1958 Little Rock school case of *Cooper v. Aaron*.[30] But, much as we today ought to remind each other that 1992's *Planned Parenthood v. Casey*[31] was not *just*—or perhaps even *principally*—about abortion, likewise we need to remember that *Cooper* was not just—or primarily—about school desegregation. Instead, *Cooper*, like *Casey*—and, I think one can argue, also like *Brown*—was fundamentally about the constitutional authority *and* the political role of the Supreme Court itself.

Cooper's most important paragraph spoke to what the Court called "some basic constitutional propositions which are settled doctrine":[32]

> Article VI of the Constitution makes the Constitution the "supreme Law of the Land." In 1803, Chief Justice Marshall, speaking for a unanimous Court, referring to the Constitution as "the fundamental and paramount law of the nation," declared in the notable case of *Marbury* v. *Madison*, 1 Cranch 137, 177, that "It is emphatically the province and duty of the judicial department to say what the law is." This decision declared the basic principle that the federal judiciary is supreme in the exposition of the law of the Constitution, and that principle has ever since been respected by this Court and the Country as a permanent and indispensable feature of our constitutional system. It follows that the interpretation of the Fourteenth Amendment enunciated by this Court in the *Brown* case is the supreme law of the land, and Art. VI of the Constitution makes it of binding effect on the States "any Thing in the Constitution or Laws of any State to the Contrary notwithstanding."[33]

Cooper is arguably the Court's most important declaration of its own authority and role since *Marbury*, but at least a small fringe of critical commentators, even some who cannot bring themselves to publicly attack *Brown* or *Bolling*, nonetheless feel able to denounce *Cooper*—and particularly that crucial passage in *Cooper*—as one of the Warren Court's "most troubling opinions" because of how it posited "a radical new notion of the status of judicial decisions."[34] *Cooper*, these critics allege, "was not the fulfillment of *Marbury* but rather its perversion,"[35] but the contrarian novelty of such a facially fallacious contention may best be understood as having more to do with *Cooper*'s own most important progeny—namely the 1992 "trio" opinion of Justices O'Connor, Kennedy, and Souter in *Casey*[36]—then perhaps with *Cooper* itself.

But the substantive expansiveness of *Brown*'s application of equal protection was merely the first installment in a new, multipart constitutional scenario. *Colegrove v. Green*[37] should perhaps not be spoken of in the same sentence as *Plessy v. Ferguson*,[38] but if any decision since 1954 can be seen as equal to *Brown* in long-term historical significance, then—as Earl Warren himself repeatedly said[39]—*Baker v. Carr*[40] is certainly the case. Justice Brennan's opinion for the *Baker* Court undeniably took far greater care in clearing away the preexisting judicial underbrush than had Warren's in *Brown*, but the full flowering of equal protection application to the principle of "one person, one vote"—and the Court's explicit citation of *Brown* as helpful precedent for that holding[41]—only came two years later in Warren's opinion for the Court in *Reynolds v. Sims*.[42] The Equal Protection Clause, Warren and five of his colleagues held in *Reynolds*, "guarantees the opportunity for equal participation by all voters in the election of state legislators. Diluting the weight of votes because of place of residence impairs basic constitutional rights under the Fourteenth Amendment just as much as invidious discriminations based upon factors such as race, *Brown* v. *Board of Education*, 347 U.S. 483. . . ."[43]

Baker, *Reynolds*, and *Reynolds*'s companion cases[44] all strive far more assiduously than *Brown* and *Bolling* to comport themselves in seeming accommodation with existing precedents. But both textually and historically, *Baker* and *Reynolds*—and perhaps *Reynolds* all the more so, in light of its unwillingness to accept or apply a "federal analogy" whereby only the lower chamber of a bicameral legislature would have to be apportioned into equally populated districts[45]—stand in even more undeniable tension with any intent-based reading of the Fourteenth Amendment's Equal Protection Clause than does *Brown*.[46]

But if critical acceptance of *Brown* is now universal, and approval of *Baker* and *Reynolds* widespread but not unanimous,[47] dissent with regard to *Bolling*'s best known (but rarely if ever acknowledged) descendant, *Griswold v. Connecticut*, is still treated with professional respect, if only because of the undeniable line of derivation that then leads from *Griswold* to *Roe v. Wade*. *Griswold*, like *Brown* and *Baker*, is accepted as *morally* correct even by those who reject its doctrinal grounding, but *Griswold*'s mottled reputation is largely the result not of William O. Douglas's widely recognized compositional shortcomings,[48] but of a far more significant jurisprudential legacy—namely the ignominious heritage of *Lochner v. New York*[49]—that until recently only *Bolling*, of all the new, noneconomic substantive due process liberty decisions of the past forty years, has escaped from unscathed.

This issue may well be the most important and indeed defining constitutional question of the present age, the question that ought to, and hopefully will, separate this present generation of commentators—namely, people who have come to academic maturity in the years since 1973—from the two generations (both children of 1937) that have preceded us.

Perhaps the rudest way in which to pose the question is also the most revealing: Why for more than a half-century has *Lochner v. New York* been almost universally viewed as a far more infamous constitutional precedent than, say, *Korematsu v. United States?*[50] *Lochner*, as most everyone well knows, is widely accepted as *the* symbolic ruling of the "old" conservative Court that prevailed from at least as early as 1895[51] through 1936[52] until it was vanquished in the early months of 1937.[53] *Lochner* and its many progeny were resoundingly routed by the constitutional revolution of 1937 (or, more correctly, by the constitutional revolution that began in 1937 and culminated in

1941–1942),[54] but the universally acknowledged *ghost* of *Lochner* survived in buoyant health well into the 1960s.[55] Only perhaps in 1973, and then far more certainly in 1992, did clear and convincing evidence finally appear that *Lochner*'s ghost was no longer badly frightening the occupants of America's most exalted judicial corridors.

In *Griswold*, of course, the Court in form if not in substance shied away from any prospect of encountering *Lochner*'s ghost in language that epitomizes how powerful and long-lasting the jurisprudential overreaction of the 1937 revolution proved to be. As Justice Douglas warned,

> Coming to the merits, we are met with a wide range of questions that implicate the Due Process Clause of the Fourteenth Amendment. Overtones of some arguments suggest that *Lochner* v. *New York* . . . should be our guide. But we decline that invitation as we did in *West Coast Hotel Co.* . . . We do not sit as a super-legislature to determine the wisdom, need, and propriety of laws that touch economic problems, business affairs, or social conditions.[56]

In *Griswold*, however, Connecticut's anticontraception statute "operate[d] directly on an intimate relation of husband and wife and their physician's role in one aspect of that relation,"[57] and hence Douglas, along with six of his eight colleagues, fled from *Lochner*'s ghost only in form rather than in substance. But even eight years later, in *Roe v. Wade*, only one member of *Roe*'s seven-Justice majority, Potter Stewart (a *Griswold* dissenter), was willing to explicitly concede the self-obvious point that *Griswold* of course was and always had been a substantive due process liberty decision.[58] While William O. Douglas, a true child of 1937 if ever there was one, still sought to deny what was self-obviously undeniable,[59] the *Roe* majority simply chose to elude the point.[60]

Hence only two decades later, in 1992's *Planned Parenthood of Southeastern Pennsylvania v. Casey*,[61] did a Supreme Court majority directly and explicitly confront the fundamental doctrinal issue that had been sidestepped in both *Griswold* and *Roe*. The *Casey* "trio" opinion of Justices O'Connor, Kennedy, and Souter—joined also in its major parts by Justices Blackmun and Stevens—indicated no hesitation whatsoever, and no lingering fear of *Lochner*'s ghost, in straightforwardly announcing that "Constitutional protection of the woman's decision to terminate her pregnancy derives from the Due Process Clause of the Fourteenth Amendment." Stressing that "[t]he controlling word in the case before us is 'liberty,'" the *Casey* majority noted that

> [a]lthough a literal reading of the Clause might suggest that it governs only the procedures by which a State may deprive persons of liberty, for at least 105 years, at least since *Mugler v. Kansas*, 123 U.S. 623 (1887), the Clause has been understood to contain a substantive component as well, one "barring certain government actions regardless of the fairness of the procedures used to implement them." *Daniels v. Williams*, 474 U.S. 327, 331 (1986).[62]

Quoting both Louis Brandeis's 1927 concurrence in *Whitney v. Califor-nia*[63] and John M. Harlan's now-famous 1961 dissent in *Poe v. Ullman*[64] in further support of that point, the *Casey* majority went on to explain that

> [i]t is a promise of the Constitution that there is a realm of personal liberty which the government may not enter. We have vindicated this principle before. Marriage is mentioned nowhere in the Bill of Rights and interra-cial marriage was illegal in most States in the 19th century, but the Court was no doubt correct in finding it to be an aspect of liberty protected against state interference by the substantive component of the Due Process Clause in *Loving* v. *Virginia*, 388 U.S. 1 (1967).[65]

Most centrally of all, the *Casey* majority forthrightly held that "[n]either the Bill of Rights nor the specific practices of States at the time of the adoption of the Fourteenth Amendment marks the outer limits of the substantive sphere of liberty which the Fourteenth Amendment protects"[66]—a holding that of course spoke not only to the elusions of *Roe* and *Griswold* but also to the substantive essences of *Brown* and *Bolling* as well. Quoting again twice at some length from the Harlan dissent in *Poe*, the *Casey* majority willingly acknowledged that "[t]he inescapable fact is that adjudication of substantive due process claims may call upon the Court in interpreting the Constitution to exercise that same capacity which by tradition courts always have exercised: reasoned judgment. Its boundaries are not susceptible of expression as a simple rule. That does not mean we are free to invalidate state policy choices with which we disagree; yet neither does it permit us to shrink from the duties of our office." Some of the century's best-known jurists, such as Learned Hand and Felix Frankfurter, no doubt would have advised just such a course.[67]

Led by Justice Souter, the *Casey* majority presented perhaps the Court's most extended discussion of the concept of precedent in this century, review-ing not only how *West Coast Hotel Co.*, by overruling *Adkins v. Children's Hospital*,[68] had "signalled the demise of *Lochner*,"[69] but also the manner in which *Brown* had vanquished *Plessy*. The heart of Souter's analysis, and the heart of *Casey* itself, however, focused upon the institutional and historical grounds as to why *Roe v. Wade* should not and *could not* be overruled. Any such reversal, Souter warned,

> would seriously weaken the Court's capacity to exercise the judicial power and to function as the Supreme Court of a Nation dedicated to the rule of law. To understand why this would be so it is necessary to understand the source of this Court's authority, the conditions necessary for its preserva-tion, and its relationship to the country's understanding of itself as a constitutional Republic.[70]

Alluding to the old saw about how the judiciary commands neither the purse nor the sword, the *Casey* majority reiterated that the Court's actual power lies very largely "in its legitimacy, a product of substance and percep-tion that shows itself in the people's acceptance of the Judiciary as fit to determine what the Nation's law means and to declare what it demands."

The Court must take care to speak and act in ways that allow people to accept its decisions on the terms the Court claims for them, as grounded truly in principle, not as compromises with social and political pressures having, as such, no bearing on the principled choices that the Court is obliged to make. Thus, the Court's legitimacy depends on making legally principled decisions under circumstances in which their principled character is sufficiently plausible to be accepted by the Nation.[71]

Then, in a core section that actually spoke more about *Brown* than *Roe*, Souter and his *Casey* colleagues put forward in five paragraphs the most institutionally important statement made by the Court since *Cooper* and the most substantively significant declaration about the role and function of the U.S. Supreme Court since the time of John Marshall:

Where, in the performance of its judicial duties, the Court decides a case in such a way as to resolve the sort of intensely divisive controversy reflected in *Roe* and those rare, comparable cases, its decision has a dimension that the resolution of the normal case does not carry. It is the dimension present whenever the Court's interpretation of the Constitution calls the contending sides of a national controversy to end their national division by accepting a common mandate rooted in the Constitution.

The Court is not asked to do this very often, having thus addressed the Nation only twice in our lifetime, in the decisions of *Brown* and *Roe*. But when the Court does act in this way, its decision requires an equally rare precedential force to counter the inevitable efforts to overturn it and to thwart its implementation. Some of those efforts may be mere unprincipled emotional reactions; others may proceed from principles worthy of profound respect. But whatever the premises of opposition may be, only the most convincing justification under accepted standards of precedent could suffice to demonstrate that a later decision overruling the first was anything but a surrender to political pressure, and an unjustified repudiation of the principle on which the Court staked its authority in the first instance. So to overrule under fire in the absence of the most compelling reason to reexamine a watershed decision would subvert the Court's legitimacy beyond any serious question. Cf. *Brown* v. *Board of Education*, 349 U.S. 294 (1955) (*Brown II*) . . . .[72]

The *Casey* majority took note of the costs imposed upon those who were closely identified with controversial watershed decisions:

The price may be criticism or ostracism, or it may be violence. An extra price will be paid by those who themselves disapprove of the decision's results when viewed outside of constitutional terms but who nevertheless struggle to accept it, because they respect the rule of law. To all those who will be so tested by following, the Court implicitly undertakes to remain steadfast, lest in the end a price be paid for nothing. The promise of constancy, once given, binds its maker for as long as the power to stand by the decision survives and the understanding of the issue has not changed so fundamentally as to render the commitment obsolete. From the obligation of this promise the Court cannot and should not assume any exemption when duty requires it to decide a case in conformance with the Constitution. A willing breach of it would be nothing less than a breach of faith, and no Court that broke its faith with the people could sensibly expect credit for principle in the decision by which it did that.[73]

"Like the character of an individual," the *Casey* majority warned,

the legitimacy of the Court must be earned over time. So, indeed, must be the character of a Nation of people who aspire to live according to the rule of law. Their belief in themselves as such a people is not readily separable from their understanding of the Court invested with the authority to decide their constitutional cases and speak before all others for their constitutional ideals. If the Court's legitimacy should be undermined, then, so would the country be in its very ability to see itself through its constitutional ideals. The Court's concern with legitimacy is not for the sake of the Court but for the sake of the Nation to which it is responsible.

"The Court's duty in the present case is clear," they concluded.

In 1973, it confronted the already-divisive issue of governmental power to limit personal choice to undergo abortion, for which it provided a new resolution based on the due process guaranteed by the Fourteenth Amendment. Whether or not a new social consensus is developing on that issue, its divisiveness is no less today than in 1973, and pressure to overrule the decision, like pressure to retain it, has grown only more intense. A decision to overrule *Roe*'s essential holding under the existing circumstances would address error, if error there was, at the cost of both profound and unnecessary damage to the Court's legitimacy, and to the Nation's commitment to the rule of law. It is therefore imperative to adhere to the essence of *Roe*'s original decision, and we do so today.[74]

Casey of course vindicated *Roe v. Wade*, committing the Court to constitutional protection for abortion in a manner unlikely ever to be undone. *Casey* also offered an extended and significantly intensified reprise of *Cooper* and the powerful historic legacy of *Marbury*, and went at least a very long way toward fully elevating *Roe* into the tiny pantheon of American constitutional precedents that perhaps otherwise is peopled only by *Marbury*, *Brown*, and possibly *Baker*.

But in elevating *Roe* to *Brown*-like stature, *Casey* also did—or ratified—something even far more significant as well, something that so far, some four years after the event, has received stunningly little attention or discussion. The *Casey* Court formally and explicitly buried *Lochner*'s ghost. Substantive due process *is*—as it *should be*—a fundamental and fully accepted aspect of present-day American constitutional doctrine.

Casey may well represent the culmination (and conclusion) of a constitutional era that began so dramatically with *Brown* and *Bolling*. Although some conservative scholars now seek to make *Brown* into a badly miscast constitutional poster child for their jurisprudence of "original intent,"[75] such efforts to rebut the interpretive (and doctrinal) radicalism of *Brown* (and *Bolling*) is unlikely to win many followers outside of certain narrow precincts. *Brown* heralded not only the Court's explicit freeing of itself from the constraints of historically bounded constitutional "originalism," but also a newly expansive application of the Fourteenth Amendment that energetically encompassed both equal protection and due process. *Brown* opened the institutional door for *Baker* and *Reynold's* revolutionary expansiveness involving equal protection, and *Bolling v. Sharpe* represented the first salvo in a reconstruction of fundamental due process liberty that quietly prepared the doctrinal ground for *Griswold* and for the eventual burial of *Lochner's* ghost in *Roe* and *Casey*.

Brown and *Casey* are hence bookends to the twofold rereading that the Court has accorded the Fourteenth Amendment—both, in *Brown* (and in *Baker*) with regard to the Equal Protection Clause, and, in *Casey* (as in *Griswold* and *Roe* before it) with regard to a new rebirth of the Due Process Clause—over these past forty years. If we justifiably celebrate the political revolution(s) heralded by *Brown* (and *Baker*), and if we further celebrate or at least accede to the way in which the *Brown* Court reached above and beyond the Fourteenth Amendment's historical fetters to blot the stain of *Plessy*, so too does *Casey* call upon us to acknowledge if not applaud the manner in which the modern Court has similarly expanded due process—like equal protection before it—to hasten another revolution as well. As *Brown* and *Casey* both signify, the modern-day meanings of American constitutional protections should not be—and happily are not—fettered by the burdens and limitations of history.

Notes

1. 347 U.S. 483 (1954).

2. For a survey of conceptual distinctions and specifications concerning "intent," see John G. Wofford, "The Blinding Light: The Uses of History in Constitutional Interpretation," 31 *University of Chicago Law Review* (1964), 502, 502–03, Charles A. Miller, *The Supreme Court and the Uses of History* (Cambridge: Harvard University Press, 1969), 20–28, 153–55, 165–66, and William M. Wiecek, "Clio as Hostage: The United States Supreme Court and the Uses of History," 24 *California Western Law Review* (1988), 227, 228–32.

3. See Poe v. Ullman, 367 U.S. 497, 522 (Harlan, J., dissenting) (1961), Griswold v. Connecticut, 381 U.S. 479, 499 (Harlan, J., concurring in the judgment) (1965), and Roe v. Wade, 410 U.S. 113, 167 (Stewart, J., concurring) (1973).

4. 323 U.S. 214 (1944).

5. 478 U.S. 186 (1986).

6. See Harold Cruse, *Plural But Equal* (New York: William Morrow, 1987), and Alex M. Johnson, Jr., "Bid Whist, Tonk, and *United States v. Fordice*: Why Integration Fails African-Americans Again," 81 *California Law Review* (1993), 1401, esp. 1402 ("*Brown* was a mistake."). Cf. David J. Garrow, "A Contrary View of Integration," *Boston Globe*, May 31, 1987, at B14–B16; and Drew S. Days III, "*Brown* Blues: Rethinking the Integrative Ideal," 34 *William & Mary Law Review* (1992), 53. Note as well Pamela J. Smith, "All-Male Black Schools and the Equal Protection Clause: A Step Forward Toward Education," 66 *Tulane Law Review*

(1992), 2003; and Richard Cummings, "All-Male Black Schools: Equal Protection, the New Separatism and *Brown* v. *Board of Education*," 20 *Hastings Constitutional Law Quarterly* (1993), 725. See also especially Missouri v. Jenkins, 63 U.S.L.W. 4486, 4498 (1995) (Thomas, J., concurring); and David J. Garrow, "On Race, It's Thomas v. an Old Ideal," *New York Times*, July 2, 1995, at IV-1, IV-5.

7. 5 U.S. 137 (1803).

8. 300 U.S. 379 (1937).

9. United States v. Carolene Products Co., 304 U.S. 144, 152 n.4 (1938). See also Alpheus T. Mason, *Harlan Fiske Stone: Pillar of the Law* (New York: Viking Press, 1956), 513–14, Louis Lusky, *By What Right? A Commentary on the Supreme Court's Power to Revise the Constitution* (Charlottesville, Va.: Michie Co., 1975), 108–12, and Lusky, *Our Nine Tribunes: The Supreme Court in Modern America* (Westport, Conn.: Praeger, 1993), 119–32, 177–90.

10. 369 U.S. 186 (1962).

11. 381 U.S. 479 (1965).

12. 377 U.S. 533 (1964).

13. 410 U.S. 113 (1973).

14. 358 U.S. 1 (1958).

15. 112 S. Ct. 2791 (1992).

16. See also generally William E. Nelson, *The Fourteenth Amendment: From Political Principle to Judicial Doctrine* (Cambridge: Harvard University Press, 1988), 4–11, Nelson, "The Role of History in Interpreting the Fourteenth Amendment," 25 *Loyola of Los Angeles Law Review* (1992), 1177, Judith A. Baer, "The Fruitless Search for Original Intent," in Michael W. McCann and Gerald L. Houseman eds., *Judging the Constitution* (Glenview, Ill.: Scott, Foresman, 1989), 49, and Mark V. Tushnet, "The Warren Court as History: An Interpretation," in Tushnet ed., *The Warren Court in Historical and Political Perspective* (Charlottesville, Va.: University Press of Virginia, 1994), 1, 17–18.

17. See Brown v. Board of Education, 98 F. Supp. 797 (D. Kan.) (1951); Briggs v. Elliott, 103 F. Supp. 920 (E.D.S.C.) (1952); Davis v. County School Board, 103 F. Supp. 337 (E.D. Va.) (1952); Gebhart v. Belton, 91 A.2d 137 (Del. Sup. Ct.) (1952); cf. Bolling v. Sharpe, 347 U.S. 497 (1954).

18. 345 U.S. 972 (1953). See also Richard Kluger, *Simple Justice: The History of* Brown v. Board of Education *and Black America's Struggle for Equality* (New York: Vintage Books, 1976), 614–16.

19. See Kluger, supra note 18, at 618–41; Mark V. Tushnet, *Making Civil Rights Law* (New York: Oxford University Press, 1994), 196–99; Jack Greenberg, *Crusaders in the Courts* (New York: Basic Books, 1994), 177–88. As Kluger comments, "[T]he historical evidence seemed to demonstrate persuasively that neither the Congress which framed the Fourteenth Amendment nor the state legislatures which adopted it understood that its pledge of equal protection would require the end of segregation in the nation's public schools." Kluger, supra note 18, at 634. See also Alexander M. Bickel, "The Original Understanding and the Segregation Decision," 69 *Harvard Law Review* (1955), 1, Alfred H. Kelly, "The Fourteenth Amendment Reconsidered: The Segregation Question," 59 *Michigan Law Review* (1956), 1049, and Kelly, "The Congressional Controversy Over School Segregation, 1867–1875," 64 *American Historical Review* (1959), 537. Cf. Nelson, *The Fourteenth Amendment* 6–7. Also note Michael W. McConnell's iconoclastic (and generally unpersuasive) argument, "Originalism and the Desegregation Decisions," 81 *Virginia Law Review* (1995), 947, and Michael J. Klarman's rejoinder:

"Brown, Originalism, and Constitutional Theory: A Response to Professor McConnell," 81 *Virginia Law Review* (1995), 1881.

20. Tushnet, supra note 19, at 203–04. See also Alfred H. Kelly, "Clio and the Court: An Illicit Love Affair," 1965 *Supreme Court Review* 119, 142–45, and Kluger, supra note 18, at 653–55, 668–76.

21. See Kluger, supra note 18, at 678–83, and Tushnet, supra note 19, at 209–11.

22. 347 U.S. 483, 489 (1954).

23. Id. at 489, 490.

24. Cf. Robert H. Bork, *The Tempting of America* (New York: Free Press, 1990), 76–77, 81.

25. After David Glasgow ("Damn the torpedoes! Full speed ahead!") Farragut (1801–1870). See Alfred T. Mahan, *Admiral Farragut* (New York: D. Appleton, 1982), and Charles L. Lewis, *David Glasgow Farragut*, 2 vols. (Annapolis, Md.: U.S. Naval Institute, 1941, 1943).

26. Bolling v. Sharpe, 347 U.S. 497, 499 (1954).

27. 347 U.S. 483, 499–500. "In view of our decision that the Constitution prohibits the states from maintaining racially segregated public schools," the *Bolling* opinion added, "it would be unthinkable that the same Constitution would impose a lesser duty on the Federal Government." Id. at 500.

28. 381 U.S. 479 (1965).

29. Cf. Bork, supra note 24, at 83–84.

30. 358 U.S. 1 (1958). See also Daniel A. Farber, "The Supreme Court and the Rule of Law: Cooper v. Aaron Revisited," 1982 *University of Illinois Law Review* 387, and Tony Freyer, *The Little Rock Crisis* (Westport, Conn.: Greenwood Press, 1984).

31. 112 S. Ct. 2791 (1992).

32. 358 U.S. at 17.

33. Id. at 18.

34. Eugene W. Hickok & Gary L. McDowell, *Justice vs. Law* (New York: Free Press, 1993), 165, 167.

35. Id. at 168.

36. 112 S. Ct. 2791.

37. 328 U.S. 549 (1946).

38. 163 U.S. 537 (1896).

39. See William J. Brennan, "Chief Justice Warren," 88 *Harvard Law Review* (1974), 1, 3; Earl Warren, *The Memoirs of Earl Warren* (Garden City: Doubleday, 1977), 306; G. Edward White, *Earl Warren* (New York: Oxford University Press, 1982), 238; and Bernard Schwartz, *Super Chief* (New York: New York University Press, 1983), 410. See also John Hart Ely, "The Chief," 88 *Harvard Law Review* (1974), 11, 12.

40. 369 U.S. 186 (1962).

41. See 377 U.S. 533, at 566 (1964).

42. 377 U.S. 533. See also Gray v. Sanders, 372 U.S. 368 (1963), and Wesberry v. Sanders, 376 U.S. 1 (1964). On *Baker* and *Reynolds*, see especially Richard C. Cortner, *The Apportionment Cases* (Knoxville, Tenn.: University of Tennessee Press, 1970). More generally, also see Robert B. McKay, *Reapportionment: The Law and Politics of Equal Representation* (New York: Twentieth Century Fund, 1965), and Robert G. Dixon, Jr., *Democratic Representation: Reapportionment in Law and Politics* (New York: Oxford University Press, 1968).

43. 377 U.S. at 566.

44. WMCA, Inc. v. Lomenzo, 377 U.S. 633 (1964); Maryland Committee for Fair Representation v. Tawes, 377 U.S. 656 (1964); Davis v. Mann, 377 U.S. 678 (1964); Roman v. Sincock, 377 U.S. 695 (1964); and Lucas v. Forty-Fourth General Assembly of Colorado, 377 U.S. 713 (1964).

45. See 377 U.S. at 572–73.

46. See Kelly, supra note 20, at 135–37, Miller, supra note 2, at 119–48, esp. 128–38, and Robert H. Bork, "Neutral Principles and Some First Amendment Problems," 47 *Indiana Law Journal* (1971), 1, 18: "The principle of one man, one vote . . . runs counter to the text of the fourteenth amendment, the history surrounding its adoption and ratification and the political practice of Americans from colonial times up to the day the Court invented the new formula." See also Bork, supra note 24, at 84–87.

47. See Miller's accurate observation that "the apportionment decisions . . . have been accepted as law in a way that other momentous exercises of judicial review have not been." Miller, supra note 2, at 119. But see Alex Kozinski, "The Warren Court—A Critique," Remarks delivered at the conference "The Warren Court: A Twenty-Five Year Retrospective," University of Tulsa College of Law, October 13, 1994.

48. See David J. Garrow, *Liberty and Sexuality* (New York: Macmillan, 1994, 245–46).

49. 198 U.S. 45 (1905).

50. 323 U.S. 214 (1944).

51. See United States v. E. C. Knight Co., 156 U.S. 1 (1895), and Pollock v. Farmer's Loan and Trust Co., 157 U.S. 429 (1895).

52. See Carter v. Carter Coal Co., 298 U.S. 238 (1936), and Morehead v. New York *Ex rel.* Tipaldo, 298 U.S. 587 (1936).

53. See West Coast Hotel Co. v. Parrish, 300 U.S. 379 (1937), and National Labor Relations Board v. Jones & Laughlin Steel Corp., 301 U.S. 1 (1937).

54. See, e.g., United States v. Darby, 312 U.S. 100 (1941), and Wickard v. Filburn, 317 U.S. 111 (1942).

55. See Helen Garfield, "Privacy, Abortion, and Judicial Review: Haunted By the Ghost of *Lochner*," 61 *Washington Law Review* (1986), 293.

56. 381 U.S. 479, 481–82 (1965).

57. Id. at 482.

58. 410 U.S. 113, 167–69 (1973).

59. Doe v. Bolton, 410 U.S. 179, 212 n.4 (Douglas, J., concurring) (1973).

60. 410 U.S. 113, 153.

61. 112 S. Ct. 2791 (1992).

62. Id. at 2804.

63. 274 U.S. 357, 373 (1927).

64. 367 U.S. 497, 541 (1961).

65. 112 S. Ct. 2791, 2805.

66. Id. at 2805.

67. Id. at 2806. See also Gerald Gunther, *Learned Hand* (New York: Knopf, 1994), and David J. Garrow, "Doing Justice," 260 *The Nation*, Feb. 27, 1995, 278.

68. 261 U.S. 525 (1923).

69. 112 S. Ct. at 2812.

70. Id. at 2814.

71. Id. at 2814. See also Tom R. Tyler & Gregory Mitchell, "Legitimacy and

the Empowerment of Discretionary Legal Authority: The United States Supreme Court and Abortion Rights," 43 *Duke Law Journal* (1994), 703, 796–98, and James Boyd White, *Acts of Hope: Creating Authority in Literature, Law, and Politics* (Chicago: University of Chicago Press, 1994), 168–83.

72. 112 S. Ct. at 2815.
73. Id. at 2815–16.
74. Id. at 2816.
75. See McConnell, supra note 19.

II

RACIAL DISCRIMINATION AND ANTIDISCRIMINATION LAW

4

GEORGE KATEB

Brown and the Harm of Legal Segregation

What is the harm of legal segregation of the races? A better wording of the question is this: What is the harm done when the majority race, convinced of its superiority, arranges for the legal segregation or separation of the majority and minority races, in a nominally democratic society? (I shall not ordinarily distinguish among the various situations and institutions in which legal segregation was in force, but speak of segregation most generally.) My view is that the harm done is of more than one kind. I would like to take up at least two kinds: the harm that consists in the violation of basic rights by a system of legal segregation, and second and secondarily, the harm or injury done to the character of persons, especially but not only the character of persons in the majority race. Concern with these harms is not antiquarian. Although legal segregation is gone, its effects are still with us. Furthermore, to think about it is also to think about other kinds of oppression, actual or past or future possible.

I would like to begin with the case that is at the center of our attention, *Brown v. Board of Education of Topeka*, 347 U.S. 483 (1954). I find the jurisprudence of the Court's opinion minimal, indeed minimalist. It is as if the Court thought that legal segregation was so obviously wrong, nothing much was needed to be said to explain why it was wrong. It would be morally stupid to go on to elaborate on the wrongness; only a few words should be necessary, and those words only a reminder of the obvious. I incline to support the general idea that fundamental moral ideas suffer from the effort to defend them at any length. The ideal audience for moral discussion is not made up of unpersuadable sceptics. To try to persuade them is likely to result in contortions and ingeniousness, which though sometimes creative and productive, as with Plato in *The Republic*, may often have the unhappy result of unpersuading the already persuaded. The idea suffers from the tactics used to defend it. Still, silence or, at best, the brevity of a few sentences, is sometimes institutionally impossible. The Court had to speak; it spoke minimally. But the question is whether it spoke well, in *Brown* or in the companion case, *Bolling v. Sharpe*, 347 U.S. 497 (1954).

I remember that when *Brown* was decided many people seemed dissatisfied with it. Some of them were racist, but not all were. For those who were not racist, the opinion seemed not only rather undeveloped, given its significance, but also weakened by its appeal to the so-called evidence of social science to sustain its holding. In going back to the case now, I feel some dissatisfaction myself; and that dissatisfaction is not lessened by the thought that there may have been good tactical reasons for both the opinion's moral restraint and its use of social science. But so much has happened in the past forty years, that reading *Brown* with unanachronistic eyes is difficult. Oddly, I discover that reading *Brown* is facilitated by reading Justice John Marshall Harlan's solitary dissent in *Plessy v. Ferguson*, 163 U.S. 537 (1896). Closer in time to the abolition of slavery and Reconstruction, the dissent may be closer to the proper spirit of constitutional opposition to legal segregation—at least what I deem the proper spirit—than *Brown*, which is closer in time to us. I think that Harlan's dissent is, on the whole, a more valuable critique of legal segregation than *Brown* is. The dissent helps us to see the very meaning of legal segregation more adequately.[1]

When we look again at Brown, what do we find? In a long footnote that begins on the first page of the actual opinion, Chief Justice Earl Warren goes over the decisions by three-judge federal district courts in Kansas, South Carolina, and Virginia, in which elementary schools or high schools or both were allowed to stay segregated, and the case in Delaware where the state supreme court sided with black children of elementary and high school age who sought to end legal segregation, but "intimated" that the equalization of black schools would permit the lawful reinstatement of segregation (486–88 n. 1). The district court in Kansas suggested that separate schools were somewhat harmful but not constitutionally so, and not in themselves unequal; the courts for South Carolina and Virginia suggested that separate schools were constitutionally valid when equal; and the Delaware court, despite its ruling, seemed to deny that the normal tendency of separate schools was to become unconstitutionally unequal in material resources, and was, additionally, unresponsive to the idea that "segregation itself results in an inferior education for Negro children" (488 n. 1). (I paraphrase all the judicial holdings.) The import of Warren's opinion is to strike down all the court judgments that had upheld legal separation and also to find the reason for invalidating it in Delaware inadequate. Warren's move is to say that the Court will not deal with tangible factors, but with "intangible considerations" (492, 493). The Court is willing to acknowledge that school facilities in the four just-named states were in the process of becoming equal; but "buildings, curricula, qualifications and salaries of teachers, and other 'tangible' factors" are not the heart of the issue

(492). Warren wants to know "the effect of segregation itself on public education" (492). By his move, Warren is beginning to cast constitutional doubt on the mere fact of separation or segregation, and to do so on the basis of "intangible considerations." What are they?

This is where the Warren opinion may fail to give enough satisfaction. Warren asks whether segregation, even with equal tangible factors, deprives "the children of the minority group of equal educational opportunities" (493). Quoting *Sweatt v. Painter*, 339 U.S. 337 (1950), he affirms (or concedes) that the notion of equal educational opportunities includes "qualities which are incapable of objective measurement but which make for greatness in a law school" (493). But then the Court in *McLaurin v. Oklahoma State Regents*, 339 U.S. 637 (1950), had already provided some specificity by giving examples of intangible considerations. These refer to such things as the student's "ability to study, to engage in discussions and exchange views with other students, and, in general, to learn his profession" (493). And Warren is persuaded that "[s]uch considerations apply with added force to children in grade and high schools" (494). Yet when Warren, in the next sentence, unpacks the meaning of equal educational opportunities and hence of the decisive intangible considerations, he does not speak directly of opportunities, but of the psychological consequences of segregation on the young. It is only implied that harmful psychological consequences may impede one's education, but that must mean that students cannot learn as well in a segregated school as in an integrated one. Warren relies on Kenneth Clark's assertion that "[a] sense of inferiority affects the motivation of a child to learn" (494). This strikes me as a questionable assertion; and the Court makes use of it because, to begin with, it has fixed on equal opportunity as the core of the Equal Protection Clause. (The relevant meaning of equal opportunity here is the right to hold or compete for a role or position on the basis of one's talents, unimpeded by discrimination.)

Equal opportunity is all well and good, but it is not a sufficiently weighty moral idea to combat legal segregation, which is institutionalized racism. Nor is denial of equal opportunity a very good way to measure the psychological effects of segregation. That point becomes clear when we look at one of the most famous sentences in the opinion: "To separate them [black students] from others of similar age and qualifications solely because of their race generates a feeling of inferiority as to their status in the community that may affect their hearts and minds in a way unlikely ever to be undone" (494). The psychological effects reach deep into the soul, and indelibly; they affect more than "the motivation of a child to learn." What Warren and the Court are concerned about, and rightly, is the authoritative state-administered effort to inflict intentional social humiliation. Such systematic and authoritative humiliation of an entire group of individuals can never be compatible with the Equal Protection Clause, not to speak at this moment of other provisions of the Constitution. Warren's best sentence is "Separate educational facilities are inherently unequal" (495). This sentence transcends motivation to learn, and reaches to the essence of the meaning of the legal segregation of a minority.

Simply, separation is inherently unequal. The "intangible considerations" that really matter are deliberatley induced negative (harmful) psychological effects, not positive opportunities. The psychological effects of intentional and authoritative humiliation comprise a sufficient reason to invalidate legal segregation within the frame of the Constitution. In not being spared deep and calculated official humiliation, the racial minority is denied equal protection of the laws.

Yet the matter does not end there. Let us ask, If the humiliation is intended but not felt, what would a possible jurisprudential result be? I will address this question in the course of looking at Harlan's dissent in *Plessy*. But I want first to take a more inclusive look at his opinion. I do so because, as I have said, I think that Harlan offers a more searching analysis of intentional and authoritative humiliation and why it is unconstitutional. The harm is in the humiliation, which is an especially acute and systematic violation of basic rights. If there is no going beyond the simple idea found in *Brown* that separate is inherently unequal, there are matters nevertheless that may be adduced to fill out the idea. Harlan does that job as well as it can be done, one is tempted to say.

In thinking about Harlan's dissent, I find that the place to begin is at the end of it. He summarizes his contention that legal segregation (of intrastate railroad transportation) violates the Thirteenth, Fourteenth, and (potentially the Fifteenth) Amendments by saying that the system of segregation (not just segregated trains) "is inconsistent with the guarantee given by the Constitution to each state of a republican form of government, and may be stricken down by Congressional action, or by the courts in the discharge of their solemn duty to maintain the supreme law of the land, anything in the constitution or laws of any State to the contrary notwithstanding" (564). Harlan is referring to Article IV, section 4 of the Constitution. I think that the invocation of this clause is a stunning rhetorical moment; indeed, it is a fitting climax. The invocation is unexpected. But once we ponder Harlan's move, we should feel vindicated in having experienced its power as it were reflexively. By ending his opinion with a reference to the Republican (or Guaranty) Clause, Harlan not only makes vivid the constitutional ideas of freedom and equality that dominate his dissent, he also opens up a number of significant matters, constitutional and extraconstitutional (or apparently extraconstitutional).

I propose that Harlan's use of the Republican Clause achieves three purposes, and I will take up each in turn. First, the clause distills the essence of the harm done to the basic rights of freedom and equality of the minority race. Second, the clause, in the context of the systematic treatment of the minority race by the majority, raises in a drastic way the question of the legitimacy of the state governments in which legal segregation is practiced, and also raises, more subtly perhaps, the legitimacy of the United States government itself, when the practice of legal segregation is ratified by the Court as constitutional. Third, the clause helps to make insistent the question (to which I have already referred), Does the unconstitutionality of legal segregation, when it is finally declared, depend necessarily on whether the authoritative intention to humiliate succeeds, and humiliation is (and has been) actually felt, widely and pervasively, with all the consequent devastations to the average individual and to that individual's capacity to lead a life, that humiliation of such a sort is expected to inflict? Suppose humiliation is intended, but not felt by its recipients. What then?

Allow me a preliminary word about the Republican Clause. In its entirety, it reads: "The United States shall guarantee to every State in this Union a Republican Form of Government, and shall protect each of them against Invasion; and on Application of the Legislature, or of the Executive (when the Legislature cannot be convened) against domestic Violence." The annotation of cases prepared by the Congressional Research Service (1973) says that since *Luther v. Borden*, 48 U.S. 1 (1849), the courts have held that questions arising under this clause are political, not judicial. Except "for a brief period during Reconstruction the authority contained within the confines of the clause has been largely unexplored."[2] A series of cases early in this century "made the clause in effect noncognizable by the courts in any matter."[3] It played no role even in the Court's opinion in *Baker v. Carr*, 369 U.S. 186 (1962). Well before, Congress was given sole guardianship over the clause.

When Harlan invoked it he was doing an uncustomary thing, but a profoundly interesting one—even if uninteresting to courts and maybe even to most of us.

It is well to remember, however, that the Republican Clause figured in some abolitionist arguments and also in some arguments put forth by more radical Republicans during Reconstruction. But the story is one of failure. Hence the leading scholar of the Republican Clause, William M. Wiecek, can say, "Since 1867 the guarantee clause has lingered in a state of desuetude."[4] Yet Harlan uses it. And though Wiecek does not mention his name or his dissent, we should try to see what Harlan is up to.[5]

For Harlan, the Thirteenth, Fourteenth, and Fifteenth Amendments had revolutionized the Constitution. Their purpose was to make the break with slavery complete and irrevocable. In legal segregation Harlan does not quite see the perpetuation of slavery, but he does see a new form of degradation. It is as if segregation were second-best to slavery, a partial victory for the former slave states, a substantial undoing of the three great amendments. "Personal liberty" is one of the stakes (*Plessy*, 557, 563), but even though he says that the "fundamental objection" to segregated trains is the interference with "the personal freedom of citizens" (557), I think that Harlan is less concerned with the ability of blacks to sit where they please, less concerned with free agency as such, whether that of blacks or whites,[6] than he is with the standing or status (to use Warren's word in *Brown*, 494) of blacks under the law. That is, Harlan is concerned, above all, with equality. He says that he does not mean "social equality" (561); and while he quotes from the Fourteenth Amendment, including the Equal Protection Clause, he does not make argumentative use of the phrase, "equal protection," even though it was obvious to him that equal protection includes preservation of equal standing. (He does use the phrase in the *Civil Rights Cases*, 56.) In any case, for Harlan the stake is finally equal standing in the eyes of the law, "equality before the law" (562). If the states do not provide it to all citizens, and Congress seems unwilling or unable to do so, then the Court must. What the amended Constitution requires is the abolition of the minority race's "condition of legal inferiority" (563). The amended Constitution forbids the administered humiliation (or effort to humiliate) that comprises a systematic assault on both freedom and equality; but perhaps more significantly on equality than on freedom.

The energy of Harlan's language of denunciation is supplied, in part, by reaction to the language of the Court's opinion, written by Justice Henry Brown. The Court says:

> The object of the [fourteenth] amendment was undoubtedly to enforce the absolute equality of the two races before the law, but in the nature of things it could not have been intended to abolish distinctions based upon color, or to enforce social, as distinguished from political equality, or a commingling of the two races upon terms unsatisfactory to either. Laws permitting, and even requiring, their separation in places where they are liable to be brought into contact do not necessarily imply the inferiority of either race to the other. . . . The most common instance is connected with the establishment of separate schools for white and colored children.
> (544)

Justice Brown locates the authority for legal segregation in the police power of the state. Against such an invincible disposition not to see humiliation and degradation, Harlan summons great forceful powers of articulation. He delineates the meaning of impermissible inequality; the first use of the Republican Clause is to summarize and heighten that meaning.

Here are some of the noteworthy formulations. Each is a variant on the nature of the harm done to the black minority by legal segregation. Harlan holds that the Fourteenth Amendment contains "a right to exemption from unfriendly legislation . . . from legal discrimination, implying inferiority in civil society, lessening the security of their enjoyment" of rights (556). Toward the end of the opinion, Harlan intensifies the idea of unfriendly legislation by finding that discriminatory legislation is "conceived in hostility to, and enacted for the purpose of humiliating citizens of the United States of a particular race" (563). Legal segregation is more than an *implication* of inferiority, it is an act of hostility meant to assert and maintain subjection. Whereas Warren is fairly reticent on the intention that appears to animate the system of legal segregation, Harlan insists on an unadorned genealogy. Separation therefore is not only inherently unequal, it is inherently degrading, when it is legally established and administered, and reaches to every aspect of life.

The recent past weighs heavily on Harlan's analysis. He sees in legal segregation "a badge of servitude wholly inconsistent with the civil freedom and the equality before the law established by the Constitution" (562). A moment later in the opinion, the badge of servitude becomes a "brand of servitude and degradation upon a large class of our fellow-citizens, our equals before the law" (562). There is thus a continuity between slavery and segregation. By Warren's time, it may have been harder to feel that continuity; but it was always hard to feel it; or if easy to feel it, then even easier to ignore it and fail to act in accordance with its constitutional prompting.

In the first use of the Republican Clause, to distill the essence of the harm done to freedom and equality, Harlan is eloquent on the structural nature of legal segregation. In his most famous passage, he says that under the Constitution "there is in this country no superior, dominant, ruling class of citizens. There is no caste here. Our Constitution is color-blind, and neither knows nor tolerates classes among citizens. . . . The law regards man as man" (559). The mention of caste points to inherited inequality, which is anathema to the amended Constitution. But Harlan is suggesting something even more sinister (a word he in fact uses, 563). Legal segregation makes the blacks pariah, untouchable; "branded as . . . inferior and infected," he says in dissent in the earlier *Civil Rights Cases* (40). He is certain that the "real meaning" of segregation is that "colored citizens are so inferior and degraded that they cannot be allowed to sit in public coaches occupied by white citizens" (560). And then he projects an ever ramifying system of legal segregation because members of the dominant race "affect to be disturbed at the possibility that the integrity of the white race may be corrupted, or that its supremacy will be imperilled, by contact on public highways with black people" (562). With these sentiments, what will stand in the way of, say, separating jurors of both races by partitions and perhaps separating the jurors when the time comes to deliberate? Harlan's moral passion for basic rights elevates his language, and permits him to give real life to the concepts of freedom and equality. Freedom means not to be anything like a slave, and equality means not to endure inherited and arbitrary discrimination. We can say that not every particular denial of freedom or equality is humiliating, and that even authoritarian systems, despite oppressive denials of freedom and equality, may perhaps in some instances be regarded as unhumiliating, in intention and effect. Legal segregation is, however, an especially severe denial of freedom and equality because it creates a general system that is meant not only to curtail the ability to exercise or take positive advantage of the rights of freedom and equality enjoyed by others, but also to entwine that curtailed ability with a continuous humiliated feeling of unworthiness to exercise those rights to any extent whatever. All this constitutes a denial of what Harlan calls in his dissent in the *Civil Rights Cases* (47, 57), "republican citizenship."[7] The oppression of inflicted harm is as it were ontological, as the evil of slavery was. The true pathos of both liberty and equality, the source in history and personal experience of the craving for both or the urge to spread both to those denied them, the return to the reality of both freedom and equality after a sojourn in complacency or hypocrisy or indifference—all these attitudes permeate Harlan's dissent. The jurisprudence is Lincolnian.

There is nothing at all automatic in Harlan's invocation of the Republican Clause. I refer not just to the enfeebled condition in which the clause then languished. Rather, one could imagine that the ideas of freedom and equality did not have to be brought together under the republican rubric. But to think that there was no conceptual necessity may itself be a conceptual mistake. What I mean to suggest is that by invoking the Republican Clause Harlan is not merely bestowing a classical lustre on the grand names of freedom and equality. Actually, classical lustre many would have found unfashionable, not to say obsolete, even if they were wrong to do so. Rather, the point is that invoking the Republican Clause emphasizes the total nature of the harm intended to the minority race's freedom and equality.

Harlan's use of the Republican Clause serves a second function. He is implicitly raising, as I have said, the question of political legitimacy.

In the American context, the main antithesis to republican government is hereditary monarchical government. If one of the original sources of inspiration for the Republican Clause was the wish to prevent the emergence of hereditary monarchies in the several states, the accompanying sense was either that the tendency of hereditary monarchies was to become tyrannical or that the very nature of hereditary monarchies—no matter how informally or prescriptively constrained by constitutional limitation—was tyrannical. Both ideas circulated in the colonies before the Revolution, and after. Tyranny is thus the dread at the center of the defense of republicanism. For a sensibility like Harlan's, the Republican Clause means, among other things, that no state of the Union could become or remain a tyranny, whether hereditary or not. But where is the tyranny in legal segregation? Though the usage is variable, tyrants are usually single rulers, autocrats. But the majority can also be tyrannical: recall Tocqueville's concept from the first volume (chs. 15, 16) of *Democracy in America*. In fact, Tocqueville explicitly characterizes white domination over blacks as a tyranny (ch. 18). And in the *Civil Rights Cases*, Harlan himself speaks of "class tyranny": "there cannot be in this Republic, any class of human beings in practical subjection to another class, with power in the latter to dole out to the former just such privileges as they may choose to grant" (62). In *Plessy*, Harlan does not use the word "tyranny," but he does use words to describe legal segregation that render that complex of institutions and practices as a kind of tyranny—the tyranny of the majority race over the minority one.

All the references to caste, and the fear of corruption through physical proximity, and sinister legislation aiming at humiliation and degradation, are manifestations of Harlan's perception of legal segregation as tyranny, not as odious as slavery, but continuous with it. The idea of tyranny provides a political, a politicized, redescription of legal segregation. The harm of segregation is heightened by conceiving it in the likeness of the monstrosity hated and resisted by Americans in the revolutionary generation. And if the colonists felt humiliated and degraded by the sinister legislation of the British parliament and the conduct of the British king, well, how should the recipients of legally discriminatory treatment feel? And if Americans continue to loathe tyranny, why should they practice it?

Legal segregation is tyrannical imposition. The Republican Clause is introduced by Harlan to suggest that point, among other points. But tyranny—the systematic degradation imposed on a group of people by the political power— is the fully realized antithesis to republican government, to constitutional democracy. It is, therefore, the presence of a fundamental illegitimacy in a supposedly legitimate form of government. Tyranny is lodged within constitutional democracy. The system contains within itself its own practical repudiation. I now wish to make explicit Harlan's latent theory.

We can say first, and most obviously, that confronted with such blatant disregard to their fundamental rights—confronted with such deliberate harm to their human dignity—blacks have no reason but a prudential one to accept the U.S. government as their own. If the U.S. government itself sponsors legal segregation only in the District of Columbia, it is also guilty of a much larger failure: it does not guarantee a republican form of government in and to any state where it does not act to end legal segregation. In that pervasive failure to act, the U.S. government loses or should lose, its moral hold on the black people; it loses its claim to their rightful allegiance, or obligation to obedience. I do not see what milder idea Harlan can be implying when he invokes the Republican Clause. At the least, he is going back to the example set when governments were imposed by the U.S. government on the rebellious slave-holding states in the wake of the Civil War. Legal segregation is a more muted rebellion, which is now directed at the amended Constitution—rebellion as it were legitimated by the Court's opinion in *Plessy*. Harlan is no mere dissenter; he is standing alone for the principle of legitimacy. To the blacks the U.S. government is and should appear illegitimate. How about the whites? They are the ultimate source of the policy that creates a sectoral illegitimacy, which just by being only sectoral, appears to immunize the U.S. government from the charge that it is altogether illegitimate.

Here I wish to extend Harlan's argument, but in a way that I hope is neither alien to his thinking nor arbitrary in itself. To conscientious whites, the idea that the government is theoretically illegitimate for a sector of the population ("a large class of our fellow citizens," 562) should make it illegitimate for them, for everyone. Or, to put the point unsubjectively, the U.S. government, as the sponsor, but especially as the protector, of legal segregation, is illegitimate, simply. It is not merely, for incurable structural reasons— for example, its method of representation rather than direct popular participation—imperfectly legitimate (contra Madison); it is illegitimate. The harm done to some individuals—the violation of rights that reach to their human status and identity—is so great that the U.S. government passes from the acceptable condition of being incurably imperfectly legitimate, deserving of every benefit of the doubt, to being illegitimate. It is a tyranny even though blacks are enfranchised (often only nominally) under it. The affront to the several constitutional criteria of legitimacy, as distinct from the democratic criteria, is intolerable. Legal segregation leaves the thoughtful members of the segregationist race living under an illegitimate government, a government they cannot recognize as their own. As Thoreau said in "Civil Disobedience": "I cannot for an instant recognize that political organization as *my* government which is the *slave's* government also."[8] His idea is extendable to legal segregation, and perhaps to other matters as well.

The protection of their own fundamental rights is—that is to say, should be—insufficient reason for conscientious whites to confer legitimacy on the government that protects them but profoundly harms others. To repeat: I am extending Harlan's argument. My warrant is his extraordinary invocation of a clause in desuetude. The marvel is that a different decision by the Court in *Plessy* would have begun legitimating the U.S. government, which had to wait fifty-eight years to lose its illegitimacy and have its imperfect legitimacy restored for the first time since Reconstruction, which was the first time it had ever been (imperfectly) legitimate at all.

The work achieved or intimated by the Republican Clause includes one more contribution in addition to the two already mentioned (the enhanced conceptualization of the harm done to freedom and equality by legal segregation, and the subsequent shadow cast on the claim of the U.S. government to legitimacy). The third contribution is the doubt it throws on the claimed necessity for showing that blacks actually suffered the humiliation that the system of legal segregation was designed to inflict. I am confident that if somehow it were clear and obvious that all or most blacks gave unmistakable signs of feeling inferior, then a sufficient case for voiding legal segregation would exist. It is unlikely, however, that evidence satisfactory to all observers could be produced. The truth is that we must attribute, and are right to attribute, to blacks the psychological wounds to their human dignity—and the basis for rights is concern for the equal dignity of every individual—that legal segregation was designed to inflict, whether or not blacks felt wounded (humiliated, degraded). Meditation on the Republican Clause may help us to make that point plausible.

Let us speak timelessly. Under a system of legal segregation, the chances are good that there will be a wide variety of psychological responses to it on the part of the segregated. Some will feel perpetually humiliated; some will manage to lead lives in which they seldom come in contact with the occasions of segregation; some will grow inured to segregation and scarcely notice it; some will grow unbitterly resigned to it; some will take it as a test of faith to endure; a few will perhaps enjoy it; and a few will rise above it in the spirit of late Stoicism and control their impressions so as to become inwardly impervious to it, while outwardly conforming and thus leading a double or compartmentalized life. All these mentalities are possible. I am sure they all existed when legal segregation existed. This variety, including as it does (psychological, not merely expedient) acceptance of segregation cannot be taken, however, as jurisprudentially determinative.

To repeat the point, we must attribute to all blacks the humiliation that the system was meant to inflict. Why? There are two main reasons. First, since people can get used to practically any condition of life, no matter how injurious to their dignity, we can receive from that fact no warrant for perpetuating the system that they have grown used to. Victims' acceptance does not make a system innocent. Their own contribution to their own degradation, and by the authority of the law, cannot sanction the system. Second, the law of a constitutional democracy can never rightly expect of people the amount of *civil* courage required to rise Stoically above a system meant to degrade, and having behind it the full authority of the law. The Socratic maxims "it is not allowed that a good man be injured by a worse" and "no evil can happen to a good man,"[9] can never govern public policy. Socrates himself did not think they should, as his episodic dissent and noncompliance in the name of avoiding injustice demonstrated. At the same time, the extent of *political* courage required of blacks to test the system of segregation and challenge it and try to circumvent it was also too much to require by any government that, as a constitutional democracy, claimed to be legitimate. That eventually black resistance to legal segregation came is a heroic fact. But one of the defining traits of constitutional democracy is that political courage—the willingness to risk legal punishment as well as social penalty—is not a daily necessity, is not needed to claim or exercise one's rights.

Along the same lines, we may propose that there is also a wide variety of psychological responses to legal segregation among the majority race, whether they live in segregated states or not. Many will feel keenly the pleasure of knowing that they are members of a race that can force another race "to keep to themselves" (Harlan in *Plessy*, 557). Some will take pleasure in implementing the practice of segregation. Some will become almost unaware that segregation exists because they live lives cut off from regular exposure to the minority race. Some will just find segregation to be the way things are done, or have always been done, and go through the prescribed motions while forgetting or half-forgetting the point of the system. Some may regret the system, but say that they could not imagine dismantling it: the disruption would be too great. Some may think that the blacks are happy enough with the way things are, and may even prefer it.

The plain fact is that once a system is initiated by a will to humiliate, it may, like any system of oppression, accommodate many attitudes and sentiments among the oppressors and oppressed alike. Many people in each group may not recognize themselves as oppressors or oppressed. We need a standard of condemnation that does not depend on variable psychological effects, especially the effects on the minority. As I have suggested, we should attribute to the minority the feelings of profound humiliation. What that means is that we must posit them as unconstitutionally harmed or wronged, even if some or many do not feel harmed or wronged. As Mill said, people can be "degraded, whether aware of it or not."[10] If what I, following Mill, have said sounds like Friedrich Engels' idea of false consciousness, so be it.

But how can we stand by the attribution and allow it to condemn a system of oppression, regardless of the actual feelings of the two races? My initial suggestion is that an answer is found in a simple thought-experiment based on the golden rule. You simply would have asked a white person, whether outspoken and demonstrative in his or her commitment to legal segregation or just going along, how he or she would like it if suddenly they were in the minority (or otherwise powerless) and authoritatively compelled to live under a system of racial segregation. Therefore, the most relevant feelings may be hypothetical, not actual: those of privileged or dominant people asked to step outside themselves and contemplate the possibility of a radical reversal of their fortunes. The idea is that of trading places. Trading places with the disadvantaged is a disorienting thought, a potential cleansing of perception. It is to be assumed that no white person would want to suffer the humiliation of being thought so inferior on racial grounds as to be capable of corrupting or dirtying members of a different race just by "contact on public highways" (Harlan, 562) or in other institutions and social settings. With this standard, it may be possible to establish an indefeasible case against legal segregation, and not content ourselves with an empirically variable one, which would be sufficient only if empirically invariable.

A possible obstacle in the way of the argument from trading places is presented by Justice Brown in the Court's opinion in *Plessy*. In a remarkable moment in an otherwise (fittingly) ineloquent, not to say dreary and sometimes ill-written decision, Brown says:

> We consider the underlying fallacy of the plaintiff's argument to consist in the assumption that the enforced separation of the two races stamps the colored race with a badge of inferiority. If this be so, it is not by reason of anything found in the act, but solely because the colored race chooses to put that construction upon it. The argument necessarily assumes that if, as has been more than once the case, and is not unlikely to be so again, the colored race should become the dominant power in the state legislature, and should enact a law in precisely similar terms, it would thereby relegate the white race to an inferior position. We imagine that the white race, at least, would not acquiesce in this assumption. (551)

What of Brown's thought-experiment? The racism is suave, but do the words contain anything other than racism?

There is no evidence that the blacks wanted to trade places with the whites and treat the whites as the whites had treated them. Dread of vengeance is sometimes only the fantasy of those who know they deserve it. Suppose, however, that whites imagined black-imposed legal segregation. What of the claim that the whites would never have acquiesced in the imputation of inferiority? that they would never have felt humilitaed? that they would never have believed that their basic rights were being violated? (Would the *Plessy* Court uphold black segregation of whites, thinking that whites would prefer separation from blacks on any terms?) What is involved is not a Stoic transcendence of a normally painful condition. Justice Brown is suggesting that no matter what, whites can never be made to feel inferior to blacks. (The proof: blacks could never have succeeded in the effort to enslave whites.) Presumably, if whites can refuse to be humiliated, so can blacks, even though "the colored race chooses to put that construction ['badge of inferiority'] upon" enforced separation (551). Brown is not willing to posit that a system designed to humiliate (whether a majority or minority race) is humiliating, or must be humiliating. Pride in one's race—that is, racism—should supposedly immunize one against feeling racist humiliation.

In answer to Brown and the Court, Harlan says almost everything that can be said. Pervading his dissent is awareness of the recent existence of the enslavement of the blacks and how elements in society are cooperating in the effort to perpetuate the practices and corresponding mentality of inferiority. No other construction is possible upon legal segregation than that it is "a badge of inferiority," a reminder of servitude, and—here I pursue Harlan's intimation—a declaration of regret that slavery was ever ended, and a desire that, short of its restoration, blacks be forever aware both of their previous enslavement and of their impotence to claim genuine freedom and equality.

Grant that if, *per impossibile*, whites were suddenly segregated invidiously, they would not initially feel humiliated or inferior. Justice Brown is right to suggest that racism immunized the whites against the imagination of trading places.[11] Such immunization, however, could survive legal inferiority only for a while. Let some time pass, and the whole range of responses to legal segregation would emerge among the segregated race. Only then would the thought-experiment of trading places be held under the appropriate circumstances. Only then would the masters have to be called to account by the thought experiment. Only then would the postulate that a humiliating system designed to humiliate is or must be humiliating. The temporary immunization given by racism to a now dominant group should not be allowed to defeat the thought-experiment.

But suppose the tactic of the trading places thought-experiment is misconceived, or if not misconceived, still deemed too closely joined to speculative considerations. Suppose we return, instead, to black feelings. We could say that black habituation to, or acceptance of, or resignation to, or reconciliation with, a system designed to humiliate them is rather too much like voluntary slavery. Mill takes up the wrong of voluntary slavery in *On Liberty*. He says:

> But by selling himself for a slave, he abdicates his liberty; he forgoes any future use of it beyond that single act. He therefore defeats, in his case, the very purpose which is the justification of allowing him to dispose of himself. He is no longer free; but is thenceforth in a position which has no longer the presumption in its favour, that would be afforded by his voluntarily remaining in it. The principle of freedom cannot require that he should be free not to be free. It is not freedom to be allowed to alienate his freedom.[12]

Mill sees the matter only from the point of view of the voluntary slave. I would add, however, that no one has the right to treat another like a slave, even if a person wants to be a slave. One cannot degrade those willing to be degraded; one has no right to do so, even if Mill is mistaken, and someone has a right to become a slave. This is a right, if it is a right, that can never properly be given effect. One cannot be the instrument by which another is degraded, even if voluntarily, even if degradation is not felt as degradation, and even if the enslaver takes no pleasure in enslaving another and may deplore the other's readiness to submit.

The whole relationship is impermissible, whatever the mentalities involved. It is impermissible, with a special force, in a constitutional democracy. Whatever people feel or want, they cannot live in a constitutional democracy except on certain terms, explicit and objective. The standard relevant not only to voluntary slavery but also to legal segregation when acquiesced in is the Republican Clause. This clause cuts out all empiricisms and simply states that legally compelled or allowed relationships of caste-like superiority and inferiority are impermissible. Even when the humiliation of violated freedom and equality is not felt by all the segregated and even when their humiliation is not consciously desired by many among the segregationist race, legal segregation is nevertheless a system of humiliation, a system designed to humiliate. The Republican Clause, as it were indifferent to whether inequality and unfreedom are accurately perceived as such, rules out any system designed to humiliate. Such a system is incompatible with constitutional democracy, with the spirit of its laws, and hence the Republican Clause can be used to dismantle the system.

I do not mean to imply that all the serious moral problems disappear when legal segregation is dismantled. The tragedy is that the force of the state can be withdrawn from its perpetuation, and racism still pervade society and inflict humiliation on blacks. The government is (imperfectly) legitimate, but society is still unjust, sometimes seriously so. The question of political legitimacy, major as it is, is only one question to examine. In a democracy, not only can government be indicted, but society, too.[13]

I said at the start that besides my concern with the nature of the harm to basic rights done by legal segregation, I was also interested in the harm or injury done to character by that system, especially the character of the segregationists. Obviously, whenever we pay attention to the possibility that some members of the minority race may not have felt humiliated, especially because they had become inured or docile or exhaustedly resigned, we are taking up the issue of the effects of a system on character. These effects of acceptance are to be understood as theoretically unexpected. More important, the effects may often not be perceived by the persons themselves. The same goes for those who practice segregation. They may not be fully aware of what they are practicing, and be surprised by disclosure. At this point I would like to take up the issue of character—the issue of what happens to people living under a system without their quite knowing it for what it is and without their quite being able to describe it properly—outside the text of the Constitution, and address it directly, if only briefly. The harm I now have in mind is not a wound (real or putative) to the feelings but to the integrity of the person as a democratic individual.

Although, as I have tried to suggest, felt humiliation, when systemically intentional, is an appropriate harm that is to be politically or judicially remedied, and humiliation attributed to a segregated minority must be politically or judicially posited apart from any empirical evidence of humiliation, concern for character is not likely to be thought relevant. Yet I wish to say that as students of legal segregation we should concern ourselves with the frequently unperceived or unarticulated effects of the system on character.

I want to emphasize the effects of the system of legal segregation on the character of the majority race, to their integrity as individuals. Certain feelings and attitudes accompany and pervade the system of legal segregation, and they help to determine conduct, private and public, small-scale and large-scale. The law vindicates these feelings and attitudes, whose effect is obviously much stronger than it would be if segregation were illegal. (These effects are still strong, even though segregation is now illegal.) Racism is in itself a deep fault of character, but we need more specific characterizations. One does not absolutely require Harlan's dissent to identify the feelings and attitudes of the majority race, but he provides a valuable stimulus. In his own time, his words would have led anyone with a conscience to heightened self-examination, and to examination of the prevailing condition.

Let me just mention some main (but often unself-aware or denied) effects on the majority race—that is, on many in the majority, and in varying degrees of intensity. Not every white person suffered these damaging effects to their integrity, but many did. If many did not, there would have been no system of legal segregation. (These effects, though altered, are still with us.) There is, first, racial prejudice, which presumes to judge harshly, if only reflexively or silently or inactively, an entire race. Racism is a specimen of group thinking; it is a refusal to imagine that individuals exist or matter as individuals, especially when they are individuals in the minority race. Common traits are definitive and unappealable: the worst member of the majority race is better for many purposes than the best in the minority. Bottomless ignorance, normally present in group thinking, is especially virulent in race matters. The ignorance is of the merits of individuals; from it, automatic condemnation without a chance for individuals to show themselves. Beyond the question of merits, however, beyond the question of individual worthiness and unworthiness for many of the practical transactions of life, is the fundamental principle that, merits aside, all persons must be thought worthy to have equal standing as citizens and persons under the law. There is such a thing as unearned human dignity, which all human beings have as individuals—or have as members of the human race. Prejudice, prejudgment, in its denial of common humanity, is a terrible disfigurement of character. The refusal to recognize individuality in others impairs the individuality of the racist person. Even now, whites often deny they are prejudiced, and are unaware of the harm their prejudice has done to their integrity of character. The end of legal segregation helps to begin the process of coping with and weakening racist prejudice, and therefore subtracting a little from the sum of thoughtless human vices.

Another effect on character of legal segregation is to fortify the tendency to love exclusiveness. I mean either small-scale exclusiveness, like that found in clubs and fraternities, or large-scale exclusiveness, as legal segregation once was. It is the wish to draw lines and keep others out (not only down). The rights of privacy and freedom of association may be involved here, of course, and their exercise sometimes strains constitutionalism as much as certain kinds of constitutionally protected expression do. But I think that the blatant example of legal segregation should serve a cautionary purpose: to alert us to the often faint moral (if not legal) difference between public systems of invidious categorization and limited, local, private systems designed to humiliate by exclusion.

I would add that the self-segregation of the formerly involuntarily segregated, while humanly understandable, is not to be condoned, just because it is exclusionary. As for those who seek to live in a small world of their own kind, without any experience of having been or now being excluded, they must be tolerated on grounds of the First Amendment. But they themselves could never have invented the idea of toleration, any more than they could have invented modern constitutional democracy as a new form of government. And they could not help to recreate it, should it lapse or fail. Exclusive enclaves are morally parasitic. The spirit of the case against legal segregation is against exclusiveness and group self-segregation, simply. The love of them is a deformation of character because they are groupist, rather than individualist; they have no patience with individual difference. They are also often tinged with insolence or snobbery, two vices that make the health of democracy less certain. Yet how many people who love and practice exclusiveness or group self-segregation would recognize themselves as insolent or snobbish, as affecting superiority? They just think they are only unlike others, and that others are also entitled to be exclusive.

Another fault is living a lie. The lie that the majority race lived when legal segregation was practiced was, as I have said, that the United States was a constitutional democracy and hence had a perfectly legitimate form of government. Questions of political legitimacy are, I know, open to dispute as they are open to subtle perplexities. But surely legal segregation is so blatantly inconsistent with constitutional democracy that even the Court in *Plessy* had to make distinctions, and endorsed an earlier decision that struck down legal segregation in the form of outright exclusion from jury service, *Strauder v. West Virginia*, 100 U.S. 303 (1880). The system of segregation gave the lie to the polity; it encouraged the majority race to live in a lie, but to keep the lie misdescribed so that it preponderantly did not appear as the lie it was. After the end of legal segregation, we should remember how easy it once was to live in or with the lie of perfect legitimacy; and if one cannot accept the theory of imperfect legitimacy, but insists that a form of government is either legitimate or illegitimate, one had better make sure that no practice or pattern of anticonstitutional policy offends against legitimacy as legal segregation once did. One must try to remember legal segregation so that one does not live a lie, as many once did when segregation was legal.

The last effect on character I would mention is adaptation to plain immorality. Members of the white race once regularly made that adaptation. To be party to the denial of basic rights is, to put it otherwise, to be party to wickedness. Yet to hide from the nature of one's adaptation, and from the nature of that to which one is adapting, makes the wickedness worse. Legal segregation implicated the whites in wickedness every day. Yet such wickedness is always possible, and may now even be actual, despite the cultivated inability to see it as it is. But spells can be broken. Harlan's two dissents comprise one of the greatest American examples of demystification.

Notes

For their help in thinking about the matters raised in this paper, I want to thank Kent Greenawalt, Amy Gutmann, Elizabeth Kiss, Austin Sarat, Noel Selegzi, Martha Umphrey, and David Wills.

1. Harlan's also solitary dissent in the *Civil Rights Cases,* 109 U.S. 3 (1883), contains a number of the leading ideas he expounds in his later dissent in *Plessy.* Here and there in this essay, I will quote what he says in the earlier opinion for the sake of reinforcing or amplifying his views in *Plessy.* But I concentrate on the *Plessy* dissent for these reasons: *Plessy,* like *Brown,* deals directly with the amended Constitution, while *Civil Rights Cases* deals, in the first instance (but not solely) with congressional legislation; *Brown* specifically answers and overturns *Plessy;* and Harlan's later dissent is more definitive just by being later, and is also, on balance, more complete and more lastingly suggestive.

All citations in the text are to the Supreme Court case under discussion, unless otherwise indicated.

2. *The Constitution of the United States of America: Analysis and Interpretation* (Washington: U.S. Government Printing Office, 1973), 851.

3. Id. at 852. It is clear that the Supreme Court has shown fright at the possible implications for governmental legitimacy of taking the Republican Clause seriously. Relying on *Luther v. Borden,* the Court in Pacific States Telephone and Telegraph Co. v. Oregon, 223 U.S. 118 (1912), warned that pressing the Clause is to challenge "the State as a State . . . the framework and political character of the government" (150–51). The issue was the validity of an Oregon tax that was imposed not by the state legislature but by a popular initiative. The Court rejected the claim that laws made by initiative rather than by legislation violated the Republican Clause. To accept that claim would affect the validity of every statute passed by the state legislature since the state's adoption of initiative and referendum. Such a result would have "anomalous and destructive" effects upon both the state and the national governments. A court's decision could absolve a state's people from all duty to obey its government, when it has supposedly ceased being republican (141–42). Justice Felix Frankfurter's dissent in *Baker v. Carr* (291–92) quotes from the *Pacific States* opinion (150–51) and adds that the effort to achieve county constituencies of equal population, for the two houses of the Tennessee legislature, is political in nature and therefore out of the range of court jurisdiction. "It is, in effect, a Guarantee Clause claim masquerading under a different label" (297). Writing for the Court in *Baker v. Carr,* Justice William Brennan takes pains to deny that the valid argument for reapportionment can be based on the Guaranty Clause (210, 218–19). In this essay. I will pursue the thought that the governmental policy of legal segregation was so oppressive as to undermine the government's legitimacy, and that a decision that used the Republican Clause to strike down legal segregation could have restored government's (imperfect) legitimacy, by helping to rebut the view that legitimacy already existed. Of course, the Republican Clause is a standing

threat to claims of political legitimacy, but this is not to say that those who objected to the tax imposed by initiative were right to appeal to that Clause for vindication.

4. William M. Wiecek, *The Guarantee Clause of the U.S. Constitution* (Ithaca, N.Y.: Cornell University Press, 1972), 274.

5. The fact that the Republican Clause was part of the original Constitution, which permitted slavery, does not conclusively stamp it as irrelevant to the lesser wrong of legal segregation, once slavery is abolished by amendment. We can say that by permitting slavery, the Constitution had been internally inconsistent, untrue to itself as a permanent aspiration, untrue to the Republican Clause (as well as to the Due Process Clause of the quickly appended fifth amendment). Slavery could never have had a proper place in it, just as, for Harlan, segregation cannot. With the Thirteenth, Fourteenth, and Fifteenth Amendments, the Constitution at last caught up with what was best in itself, and became true to itself. Harlan is committed to the idea that the Republican Clause must now be made to mean what it says. But the *Plessy* majority perpetuates the horrible self-betrayal. The Republican Clause was never compatible with slavery and was not, when *Plessy* was decided, compatible with legal segregation.

6. It makes sense to say that laws against marriage between blacks and whites curtailed the freedom of blacks and whites equally. These laws were aimed at preventing white defection from the cause of white racial purity or "integrity." See the opinion that voided antimiscegenation laws, Loving v. Virginia, 388 U.S. 1 (1967). But other laws mandating racial separation curtailed only whites' freedom to do things they did not want to do.

7. In this dissent, Harlan not only refers to republican citizenship but also calls equal rights of citizens "a principle of republicanism" (49), and says that the absence of racial discrimination is fundamental to citizenship in a "republican government" (56). But he does not cite the Republican Clause. He does, however, explicitly cite the *Slaughter-House Cases*, 83 U.S. 36, 70 (1873), to make the point that legal segregation of blacks "curtailed their rights in the pursuit of life, liberty, and property to such an extent that their freedom was of little value" (37).

8. Jeffrey L. Duncan, *Thoreau: The Major Essays* (New York: Dutton, 1972), 109. I do not suggest that illegitimacy is always a sufficient condition that justifies violent resistance. Illegitimacy, too, has its degrees and kinds. Slavery justified violent resistance to end it. But legal segregation probably did not, though it did justify nonviolent resistance, including civil disobedience.

9. Plato, *The Apology* in *Euthyphro, Apology, Crito*, trans. F. J. Church (New York: Bobbs-Merrill, 1956), 30d:36–37, 41c–d:48.

10. John Stuart Mill, *Considerations on Representative Government*, ed. J. M. Robson, in *Collected Works of John Stuart Mill*, vol. 19 (Toronto: University of Toronto Press, 1977), ch. 8, 470.

11. The only thought-experiment white racists could make was to imagine themselves forced to live under a foreign conqueror who was white and who treated them as the whites now treated the blacks. Justice Brown seems to look on Reconstruction this way. But even if we leave Reconstruction aside, such a thought-experiment is not racial. White racists cannot imagine being humiliated by nonwhite racists. They can imagine all sorts of humiliation, but not this one.

12. John Stuart Mill, *On Liberty*, in J. M. Robson ed., supra note 10, vol. 18, ch. 5, 299–300.

13. It is almost certainly the case that the U.S. political system, operating democratically through elections, would never have abolished legal segregation.

Imperfectly democratic, the system was nevertheless democratic enough to translate popular sentiment into legal segregation. Curing the system of its democratic imperfection by replacing representation with direct participation would have left anticonstitutional evil untouched. To a significant degree, democratic government was a mere tool of the majority race, and a most effective one. Only the judiciary could take the first step to end illegitimacy. The general point is that if popular sentiment is so politically determinative, the question of governmental legitimacy when grave issues are considered, can seem almost beside the point. The condition of society overshadows all specifically political questions. But staying on the political level, we can say that anticonstitutional democracy is illegitimate, just as constitutional nondemocracy is illegitimate (in theory) and often illusorily constitutional (in practice).

5

PAUL GEWIRTZ

The Triumph and Transformation of Antidiscrimination Law

*B*rown both crystallized and launched a revolution in the way our society understands what equality requires, a revolution that is ongoing. I want to discuss two basic aspects of this revolution.

The first is that we have witnessed a triumph of the antidiscrimination model, by which I mean that more and more areas of social life are now viewed as raising a problem of "discrimination"—rather than viewed as raising some other kind of problem, or raising no problem at all.

My second claim is that at the very time that the nondiscrimination idea has been emerging triumphant as a way of addressing matters as diverse as race, gender, age, religion, sexual orientation, and disability, the meaning of nondiscrimination has itself been transformed. Originally, nondiscrimination meant an obligation to treat people the same. But today, nondiscrimination is coming to mean accommodating differences. This transformation has occurred across the board, in all the subject matter areas where nondiscrimination ideas have now come to be applied—and when these changes are seen as a kind of unity, they are really quite striking, and are having a profound impact on American life.

My goal here is not to make particular claims about *Brown* itself, but about the world that *Brown* helped to create. Thus, I am not particularly interested here in establishing a precise causal nexus between *Brown* and these developments. I certainly do not wish to claim that *Brown* made any of this inevitable, or that the road from *Brown* could not have taken other directions. Put another way, I am not suggesting that *Brown* has to be read as so many people came to read it, as a powerful endorsement of a generative principle of nondiscrimination—indeed, *Brown* is written quite narrowly.

But I do see *Brown* as a strong contributing cause of what I will discuss. For example, I think there is a clear link between *Brown* and the 1964 and 1965 civil rights acts that bar various forms of discrimination. In this causal story, *Brown's* constitutional law strengthened a political movement that in turn helped to enact the civil rights acts, which in turn influenced the future direction of constitutional law, of other legislation, and of politics more broadly—all of which influenced the culture and cultural beliefs, and each of which has kept feeding back upon the others to help produce the reality I describe. My main goal here, however, is not to trace out causal links, but to describe and to some extent evaluate our post-*Brown* situation.

The Triumph of Antidiscrimination Law

First, let me explain what I mean by the triumph of antidiscrimination law. I am certainly not claiming that antidiscrimination law has been a triumphant social success. I do think that in the core area of race it has helped change the world for the better in near-revolutionary ways. But coming as I do from New Haven, Connecticut, where the black poor live lives of much misery, despair, and fear, and where the vicious circle of racial disparities, racial anger, and racial apprehension continues unabated, I know that antidiscrimination law has had only limited success in addressing our great national problem of race. What I mean by the triumph of the antidiscrimination idea is that vast areas of social life—not only racial matters but many other areas as well—are now treated as raising problems of "discrimination." Before they came to be seen in this way, these areas were either not seen to raise legal issues at all, or seen to raise legal issues not conceptualized as "discrimination."

Some Examples

Gender   Consider women's rights. Although many people obviously saw the status of women as a major social issue long before *Brown*, and a social issue concerning equality and nondiscrimination, it was not until the post-*Brown* era that the struggle for women's rights produced a general law of sex discrimination. *Brown* and the post-*Brown* black civil rights movement surely helped give new energy to the modern women's rights movement and also helped to shape its identity and some of the terms of its claims (echoing in some ways how the Thirteenth, Fourteenth, and Fifteenth Amendments affected the women's movement in the nineteenth and early twentieth century).[1]

Women's rights lawyers—including those at the NOW Legal Defense Fund, which self-consciously named itself to parallel the NAACP Legal Defense Fund—borrowed legal concepts developed in the racial context, such as the "suspect classification" doctrine. Reflecting *Brown's* influence, they also made a crucial choice among competing strands of feminism. Most significantly, they advocated "formal equality" as the antidiscrimination ideal: nondiscrimination required that women be treated the same as men, and the normative claim to this formal equality rested on the view that women were basically the same as men for the purposes of law. This echoed the basic claim underlying the movement for full civil rights for blacks.[2]

The extension of antidiscrimination principles to women and the conceptual linkage between feminism and black civil rights were solidified in the 1964 Civil Rights Act, which made it unlawful to discriminate against any individual "because of such individual's race, color, religion, sex, or national origin."[3] Opponents of the bill's prohibition of race discrimination were among those pushing most strongly to include "sex" as a forbidden basis of discrimination, believing that would scuttle the entire bill.[4] But the act passed, the modern law of sex discrimination got its statutory footing, and the parallelism the act established between various types of forbidden discrimination assured that concepts developed in one area would be used in others.

It is probably uninteresting, however, to point out that women's rights issues have generally become issues of antidiscrimination law in the post-*Brown* era. What I have called the triumph of the antidiscrimination idea is more nicely revealed by noting how a few particular issues associated with women's interests, but not self-evidently to be characterized as issues of sex discrimination, have become so.

Sexual harassment is one example. Until quite recently, of course, sexual harassment was not a legally cognizable wrong at all. It has now become conceptualized as a matter of sex discrimination, and in fact became legally redressable in a broad way only when it came to be so conceptualized. One could easily imagine that, once society moved to provide remedies for what we now call sexual harassment, it would do so through tort law, treating such harassment as a subcategory of assaults or other wrongs to the person. (To call it discrimination "because of sex," some early judges argued, would immunize people who harassed both men and women, which would make no sense; and how could it be employment discrimination, they said, where the victim did not lose her job or lose compensation?)[5] As matters developed, of course, such harassment came to be seen dominantly through the legal lens of antidiscrimination law, and seen as sex discrimination.[6] Indeed, I would argue that it was *because* harassment was so conceptualized as "discrimination" that it came to be seen so rapidly as a wrong at all, given the broad social consensus that had developed against "discrimination."

Refusing to pay disability benefits for pregnancy leave is another example. Until recently, this was not seen as a legal wrong at all, even where the employer granted disability benefits for other medical conditions. Rather, it was seen as a plausible way for employers to limit expensive fringe benefits and to manage the need for continuity in the workforce. As recently as the 1976 case of *General Electric Co. v. Gilbert*,[7] decided at a time when the law of sex discrimination was already quite developed, the Supreme Court rejected an argument that the exclusion of pregnancy from GE's otherwise comprehensive disability leave program was sex discrimination. The Court concluded, first, that this was not a "gender" distinction at all, since the category of nonpregnant persons includes members of both sexes, and, second, there was no proof that, on average, GE's program was worth less to women than to men even with pregnancy benefits excluded from coverage. Congress ultimately overturned this decision, by amending Title VII to deem rules based on pregnancy the legal equivalent of rules based on sex, and to make it actionable sex discrimination to treat pregnancy benefits less favorably than other benefits.[8]

Lastly, consider the evolution in how abortion rights are understood. In *Roe v. Wade*,[9] laws prohibiting abortion were characterized as interfering with individual rights of "privacy" and "liberty" protected by our constitution. But nowadays, laws prohibiting abortion are commonly characterized as interfering with women's equality, as discriminatory to women—not only because they single out a medical procedure needed by women alone or because they impose on women alone the burden of pursuing a government interest in protecting fetal life, but, more importantly, because laws requiring women to bear children they do not want restrict women's capacity to achieve equality in other spheres of life.[10]

Age   The emergence of age discrimination law is another example. Making distinctions based upon a person's age need not be seen as invidious discrimination, and for much of world history was not seen as such discrimination. There were seasons of a person's life. When we were "minors," certain privileges were withheld from us and certain protections granted. Various privileges came to us, and protections removed, when we "came of age." Then, at a certain point, it was understood that we could no longer have the same obligations and opportunities that we previously had. This was not seen as discrimination in the contemporary sense, both because these fluctuations in the life cycle were widely accepted and also because everyone was pretty much treated the same. The usual form of discrimination involves different treatment of different people—black people treated differently from white people, women differently from men—but the treatment we received when we got older was the treatment everyone would receive when they got older (if they were lucky enough to live so long). If older people were required to retire at a certain age, that was seen as a way of making scarce jobs available to younger people (who would be expected to make way in turn later) and a means of avoiding the awkwardness of making individual late-career determinations about who was capable of high-quality work and who was not; mandatory retirement was not seen as a matter of discrimination.

The elderly, of course, have always faced many problems: they often are poor, are treated as if their lives are already over, are in need of medical care they cannot afford, are often disabled. But to the extent these were historically seen as matters of governmental concern, rather than the concern of families or charities, they were seen as social needs contending with other social needs for their share of limited public resources, not as questions of discrimination. Government responded to these needs area by area, deciding how much of its limited resources would be allocated to particular facets of this problem. Thus, the Social Security System, Medicare, and other programs were established to deal with particular problems that the elderly had. [11]

But in 1967, three years after the 1964 Civil Rights Act and thirteen years after *Brown*, Congress adopted the Age Discrimination in Employment Act. [12] Rather than addressing the problems of the elderly (such as mandatory retirement) solely by improving government benefits, Congress defined many of these problems as private discrimination against the elderly—and authorized legal redress for this discrimination. [13] The antidiscrimination idea thereby decisively extended its reach to certain matters that had either never before been defined as a problem or had been defined as a problem to be addressed through public benefits.

Disability   The emergence of strong antidiscrimination laws for disabled people reflects a similar shift. The government's role in addressing problems faced by disabled people used to be primarily grant-making and benefits programs, and was therefore fundamentally seen as raising issues of resource allocation. [14] To a considerable extent it still is. But beginning with the Rehabilitation Act of 1973, [15] and culminating in the sweeping provisions of the Americans with Disabilities Act of 1990 (ADA), [16] the problems facing disabled people have increasingly been reconceptualized as problems of "discrimination" in the public and private sector—discrimination in employment (ADA, Rehabilitation Act), discrimination in education (ADA, Rehabilitation Act, Individuals with Disabilities Education Act), [17] discrimination in housing (Fair Housing Amendments Act of 1988), [18] discrimination in access to public accommodations (ADA, Architectural Barriers Act, [19] Air Carriers Access Act of 1986), [20] and discrimination in medical treatment (Child Abuse Amendments of 1984). [21]

Religion   The 1964 Civil Rights Act also made "religion" one of the forbidden bases of discrimination. Traditional matters of religious *liberty* thus became redefined as also questions of religious *discrimination and equality*.

Even more interesting is the way in which antidiscrimination principles have also come to influence contemporary interpretation of the religion clauses of our Constitution. It is perhaps coincidental that modern legal doctrines involving the Establishment Clause begin their development just a few years before *Brown*, in the 1947 case of *Everson v. Board of Education*. [22] That case is most famous for its embrace of Jefferson's metaphor that the First Amendment "erect[s] 'a wall of separation between church and State.'"[23] But, in fact, the decision in *Everson* actually permitted a breach of the proclaimed "wall of separation," for it upheld a local school board's policy of reimbursing parents for money paid to have their children transported to parochial schools on public buses. The lasting vision of *Everson*, the one cemented in the post-*Brown* era, is not a principle of unbreachable separation but a principle of nondiscrimination.

Under this approach, the Establishment Clause allows some government action that benefits religious entities, but, in Justice Black's words, it forbids the government from passing laws which "prefer one religion over another" or that "aid all religions" over religious disbelief.[24] As crystallized in later post-*Brown* cases, the government may not prefer one religion over another or prefer religion over nonreligion—a principle of nondiscrimination and neutrality. The old metaphor of a "wall of separation" has largely been displaced by the modern trope of "no discrimination" in favor of or against religion. Under this approach, the government may (as in *Everson*) spend tax money to aid religious groups "as a part of a general program" to help religious and nonreligious students alike, analogous to "such general government services as ordinary police and fire protection."[25]

Other Areas   I could continue with many other examples of the reach of antidiscrimination ideas, ranging from First Amendment law, where the courts have prohibited "above all" government restrictions on speech that discriminate among viewpoints or discriminate based on the content of speech,[26] to a vast range of state and local laws prohibiting many different types of discrimination (including laws prohibiting discrimination against gay people and AIDS patients in certain localities). But I have said enough, I hope, to illustrate how broadly and powerfully the antidiscrimination idea has now swept through American life and law in the post-*Brown* era.

Assessing the Triumph

Why has the antidiscrimination idea triumphed, vastly extending its reach and displacing or broadly supplementing other ways of conceptualizing and addressing many social problems? I have three hypotheses.

First, the civil rights revolution of black Americans, including *Brown*, assumed a centrality as political experience and metaphor. Other marginalized groups borrowed analytic tools and rhetoric from that movement, hoping thereby to repeat its successes. Other decision makers followed suit, as the moral power of the black civil rights movement and the idea of nondiscrimination in that context created a broader social receptivity to the nondiscrimination norm in other contexts.

Second, a politics based on personal self-identity emerged. As part of broader cultural trends in the 1960s, people came to identify themselves more and more as members of social groups based on important personal characteristics rather than abstractions such as "citizen" or "class." This helped to produce a politics in which people's concerns rested more centrally on their conceptions of themselves as black, women, religious, gay, or disabled. Although it is possible to see this development as a product of the triumph of the antidiscrimination idea, rather than one of its causes, at the very least I think these forces were mutually reinforcing.

Third, government itself sought to shift the costs of addressing various social problems to the private sector and away from costly government benefit programs. Antidiscrimination norms gave the government a moral basis for requiring the private sector to carry a greater burden in addressing serious social problems.

But rather than speculate at length about why the antidiscrimination idea has triumphed, let me trace out a few consequences of this legal and cultural turn toward nondiscrimination principles. Most obviously, much irrational social conduct has been delegitimated. The idea that women cannot do this or that job—an idea that was pervasive in our society twenty-five years ago—is utterly irrational. Mandatory retirement rules are irrational for society in many circumstances (among other things, they deprive the workforce of productive workers and individuals of productive work lives, and they increase the social cost of the government programs for the elderly). Antidiscrimination law dismantled these and many other irrational ideas and rules.

In addition, conceptualizing these social practices as "discrimination" immediately presents these matters as issues of justice, not just resource allocation. It underscores that we are talking about moral wrongs, not just competing claims on society's resources. It makes these practices transgressions of the great American ideal of equality—and equality, as a group of America's leading historians recently wrote, is "the most powerful and influential concept in American history."[27] Thus, those who suffer what has been defined as discrimination become linked to a moral value of extraordinary prestige in our culture. Moreover, because the word "discrimination" in American culture is inescapably linked to the racial oppression of black people, all victims of what becomes labeled as "discrimination" become linked, at least by language, to perhaps the greatest moral evil in our country's history.

Deeming more and more conduct "discrimination" also creates legal rights, and that too is very significant. To be sure, rights to nondiscrimination are often less demanding than other rights in certain respects. The right to nondiscrimination is a right that people be treated equally, but they can be treated equally well or equally badly—so conceptualizing some burden as a violation of a right not to be discriminated against does not require that the burden end, only that it be imposed or not imposed more equitably. (This is one difference between conceptualizing some claim as a "liberty" right and an "equality" or "nondiscrimination" right. If constitutional "liberty" bars the imposition of some burden, it may not be imposed at all; if constitutional "equality" bars the imposition of a particular burden, the bar usually disappears if the burden is imposed more evenhandedly and equally.) But still, to conceptualize conduct as a legal wrong is undoubtedly very significant.

Legal rights are empowering even if one never goes to court. That is why so many cases are settled. Legal rights also bring with them the machinery of enforcing the law: courts, lawyers, trials, and so forth. Expanding the reach of antidiscrimination law brings more issues within the courts, with their comparative independence from political pressure—in contrast to the political fights for more resources that groups without legal rights have to make. Being able to go to court to enforce a legal right can be very empowering, even liberating, for those who had previously viewed themselves as powerless. (This is why the "critique of rights" that was fashionable among some on the left a few years ago seems strikingly blind to the actual situation of otherwise quite powerless people.)[28]

Each of these potentially positive consequences of the expansion of non-discrimination rights does have a potentially darker side. Not all "discriminations" among people have the irrationality or invidiousness typically associated with the word "discrimination" today; the expansion of nondiscrimination rights can potentially go "too far." In addition, conceptualizing a social problem as a matter of morality or justice or right can obscure that resource allocation questions really are central, and that the social response actually should rest on a careful assessment of benefits and costs; a reallocation of resources typically is taking place when the government creates antidiscrimination rights, but the reallocation often comes about in a less visible and more decentralized fashion that may make it hard to assess the costs and benefits of what the government has done.

Moreover, legal claims mean litigation, and litigation is often very wasteful. The dynamic of a lawsuit, as is well known, often heightens the plaintiff's sense of grievance and embitters the defendant, turning disputants into enemies, turning a potential route to solve a problem into a war for vindication. Thus, expanding legal rights to nondiscrimination may conceivably heighten social and personal divisions rather than provide a mechanism for overcoming them. Part of this dynamic is that legal claims, surely including discrimination claims, create a rhetoric of wrongdoers, violations, blame, and victimhood. Indeed, widening definitions of discrimination may have contributed to what some have called a growing culture of victimization.[29]

Additionally, expanding the classes of people protected by antidiscrimination laws arguably dilutes the moral force of the antidiscrimination idea. In particular, it arguably weakens the distinctiveness of the moral claim of black Americans, whose history of slavery and oppression have traditionally made them the core group protected by antidiscrimination laws. Although it is rarely discussed, blacks do often resent the fact that other groups are piggy-backing on their moral claims—assimilating nonracial wrongs to the racial paradigm. The practical side of this is that as the classes of people protected by antidiscrimination laws grow, there is a growth in the scope of responsibilities of law enforcement agencies such as the Equal Employment Opportunity Commission (EEOC). And with that, enforcement resources may be spread very thin. Enforcement priorities, moreover, can become skewed in the direction of groups whose members file the most complaints with the agency, which may not be the groups hurting the most from discrimination.[30]

Lastly, there are real limits to what antidiscrimination law can do to address many problems of social inequality; antidiscrimination law is unlikely to provide much help for the black poor in New Haven, for example. As I see my students at Yale Law School being inspired by famous antidiscrimination law cases—indeed, as I try to inspire them—I sometimes wonder whether they are being distracted from other strategies for reform, strategies that may be outside the particular expertise of lawyers.

The Transformation of Antidiscrimination Law

So much, then, for the first aspect of the post-*Brown* revolution—the triumphant emergence of the antidiscrimination idea as a way of addressing matters as diverse as race, gender, age, religion, sexual orientation, and disability. The second aspect of the post-*Brown* revolution is this: at the same time that antidiscrimination ideas have been spreading their subject-matter hegemony, the very meaning of nondiscrimination has itself been transformed.

Originally, nondiscrimination typically meant "formal equality," an obligation to treat people the same. Today, in area after area, nondiscrimination is coming to mean *accommodating differences*. Nondiscrimination used to require that we ignore or deem irrelevant various differences among us that had previously been the basis for treating some people as inferiors. But today, in area after area, "difference" is everywhere emphasized, and nondiscrimination has come to require that explicit account be taken of those differences, that the differences be accommodated,[31] that social practices be adjusted to assure that those differences are supported. This, I believe, represents a major sea-change in American culture.

In one sense, of course, the idea that equal treatment may mean accommodating difference is an ancient one. Aristotle's *Ethics*, the progenitor of many of Western civilization's ideas about distributive justice, articulates an equal treatment principle that has two parts: distributive justice requires that similarly situated people shall be treated the same, but also that differently situated people be treated differently.[32] This second half has been invoked far less often in discussions of equality, but most of us intuitively recognize its plausibility. A five-year-old recognizes that it is not equal treatment to give a person with size 6 feet and a person with size 10 feet the same size shoes (I asked mine); equal treatment sometimes requires different treatment.

To an extent, then, even the original understanding of nondiscrimination allowed for the differently situated to be treated differently. But differences in race, gender, or religion were not adequate reasons for differential treatment. Discrimination meant failing to treat people alike in their common humanity—their common humanity was emphasized, not their differences; and formal equality was required, not accommodating differences. Today, to a large degree, differences-in-fact are emphasized, and accommodation of those differences is the goal. Today, taking account of differences by treating people differently hardly implies discrimination; rather, it is often viewed as discriminatory to treat everyone the same, to fail to accommodate differences. The shift has been within the antidiscrimination paradigm itself, in the very *meaning* of the word discrimination itself. Nondiscrimination once meant insisting that certain characteristics of people be treated as irrelevant in dispensing benefits and burdens, and nondiscrimination has now come to mean an insistence that those same characteristics of people be treated as highly relevant as the basis for requiring accommodations.

Some Examples

Race Consider, most immediately relevant here, how the law has moved beyond requirements of formal equality in the core area of race discrimination. First, in the context closest to *Brown* itself, school desegregation, the notion that racial differences should be accommodated and supported is reflected in a weakened commitment to integration and greater acceptance of racially identified black institutions—a development that occurred in part because blacks themselves often experienced "integration" as a coercive strategy of assimilating them to white norms and devaluing their differences.[33] Within racially integrated settings, there has been a dramatic growth of multicultural perspectives that recognize and take account of racial and cultural differences, and view it as racist or discriminatory to treat certain values as universal or to privilege a Western canon and give a less central place to other cultural traditions.

Second, the idea of accommodating differences has emerged clearly with race-based affirmative action and racial preferences. The type of affirmative action I am speaking of is the explicit taking account of race in order to assure the actual inclusion of members of certain racial minority groups. It means recognizing racial differences and counting them as relevant, and it obviously moves us beyond formal equality. Historically, affirmative action arose out of the gradual recognition that, given the effects of centuries of discrimination against blacks, strict insistence on formal equality would still leave blacks far behind and greatly segregated. As the perception grew that a legal regime of formal equality, along with persistent white racism, perpetuated the exclusion of blacks from the mainstream of American society, pressure developed for affirmative action that would assure fuller inclusion, entailing a shift away from formal equality. However beleaguered affirmative action is in certain respects, it is socially pervasive and deeply entrenched in many of the major institutions of American life, including (perhaps most importantly) American business.

Third, we see the shift away from formal equality in the emergence of the so-called disparate impact concept of discrimination. Nondiscrimination as formal equality in the racial context prohibits decision makers from using criteria that either on their face treat racial groups differently or are used with the motive to disadvantage people because of their race.[34] By contrast, the doctrine treating disparate impact as discrimination holds that a law or employment criterion may be deemed discriminatory when it has a more adverse effect on certain groups than others, even though the law formally treats whites and blacks the same. For example, Title VII of the Civil Rights Act is violated if an employment practice has a disparate impact on racial minorities, unless the employer can demonstrate that the practice is significantly related to effective job performance. Thus an employment requirement (say, requiring a high school diploma) may be found discriminatory because it has a more adverse effect on blacks than other groups, even though the employer has no discriminatory intent, even though the employment requirement formally treats whites and blacks the same, and even though there are actual group "differences" in some sense (say, differences in the percentage of each racial group having a high school diploma). The basic premise here is that employment practices that have the effect of excluding blacks at a higher rate than whites should be deemed discriminatory unless the employer can demonstrate a good reason for using them.[35]

Strictly speaking, this disparate impact standard does not require accommodation of differences. Although the standard requires employers to change facially neutral employment requirements that disparately exclude minorities where those requirements are unjustified, employers are not required to change employment requirements that genuinely relate to job performance, even where such requirements fail to include or accommodate racial minorities. And unlike affirmative action, at least in theory, the standard does not require employers to take explicit account of race to assure that more racial minorities are hired. Nevertheless, the cost and risks of validating those criteria create strong pressures toward deliberate inclusionary efforts that will avoid creating any disparate impact. In any event, employers must at least be attentive to the racial consequences of their practices.[36]

The Supreme Court first interpreted Title VII of the Civil Rights Act as incorporating a disparate impact test in 1971, in *Griggs v. Duke Power Co.*[37] Given its status in between formal equality and accommodating differences, this disparate impact test, perhaps unsurprisingly, was until recently a highly controversial Supreme Court doctrine that Congress had never endorsed with full explicitness—and that the Supreme Court itself had eroded.[38] But in the 1991 Civil Rights Act, Congress determinedly did embrace it, for the first time amending Title VII to use language that made clear that formal equality was not a sufficient measure of discrimination—and underscoring the movement in our political culture away from formal equality as the exclusive meaning of discrimination.

Some might argue that antidiscrimination law never really meant formal equality, that it always reflected a commitment to a results-oriented approach requiring accommodation of differences, a particular racial mix in public schools, proportional representation in the country's workforces, and so forth—in other words, that from the beginning the focus on formal equality was just a public relations strategy that masked very different principles of equality. On this view, there was never really a shift in approach. I do not agree with this view of history. To be sure, in the early post-*Brown* years it was commonly assumed by civil rights advocates that formal equality would eventually produce something like racially proportional outcomes and full integration among the races—and this was something to be hoped for. But the principal moral and legal commitment, even if not the exclusive one, was to the principle of formal equality. Formal equality was the principle that gave civil rights activists the high moral ground. The gradual recognition that formal equality was not producing sufficient inclusion and sufficiently equal results undoubtedly led many people to reconsider whether their moral principle was really formal equality, and led many to move toward a principle of accommodating differences that focused more on results—but that is to agree with my point, not disagree with it.

While much has been written about the shift from color blindness to color consciousness in the area of race, much less attention has been paid to the fact that a parallel norm of accommodating differences is taking hold in virtually all the areas to which nondiscrimination norms are now applied. What is particularly striking, and has received virtually no attention, is that this shift has been occurring in so many areas simultaneously.[39]

Gender   As recently as ten years ago, the women's rights movement was predominantly a movement seeking formal equality—a movement that descriptively emphasized the ways in which women were the same as men, and normatively argued that women should be treated the same as men. This is what Ruth Bader Ginsburg, the leading appellate litigator of the women's movement in the 1960s and 1970s, stood for.[40]

In 1987, when a major case involving pregnancy leaves was being litigated in the Supreme Court of the United States, the feminist movement was sharply divided over a "formal equality" and "accommodating differences" conception of nondiscrimination. The Supreme Court case was *California Federal Savings & Loan Ass'n v. Guerra*,[41] and involved a California statute that required employers to give women up to four months' disability leave for pregnancy, but required no such leaves for people with other medical conditions that might force them to need a disability leave. The legal issue was whether the federal government's requirements of nondiscrimination between men and women permitted California to single out pregnancy for particular legal protections. Leading feminists filed briefs on both sides of the case, one side arguing that the California law was special protectionist legislation that violated federal antidiscrimination norms of formal equality, and the other side arguing that women's unique capacity to become pregnant permitted distinctive measures to accommodate that uniqueness in the workforce.

The Supreme Court upheld the California statute, concluding that accommodating differences between men and women in this context promoted equality. According to the Court, "By 'taking pregnancy into account,' California's pregnancy disability-leave statute allows women, as well as men, to have families without losing their jobs."[42] This case was a watershed.

Although the legal issue involved only the permissibility of accommodation, not whether federal law required it, the case marked the triumph of the "accommodate differences" idea in feminist legal thought and action, and the other side essentially folded its hand. There is now broad support for the view that it is discrimination against women to fail to accommodate pregnancy in the workplace.[43] And there is increasing support for the idea that nondiscrimination for women means accommodating differences in other contexts as well.

Carol Gilligan's basic thesis that men and women tend to have different voices[44] is now widely (if not universally) accepted, and has given new respectability to the idea that these different voices must be valued as such. Among many other things, it has greatly reduced objections to single-sex educational institutions for girls and women. (Much stronger objections to single-sex schools for men persist, not because gender differences are denied but because such institutions are thought to replicate men's current social dominance.) More broadly, it has helped foster challenges to formal equality as an adequate conception of nondiscrimination, on the ground that the norms being applied in formally equal fashion are male norms, norms that reflect the needs of a typical male biography or the values and voice of the typical male. "Difference feminism," as it is sometimes called, stands for the proposition that institutions must take account of women's differences, either by specially accommodating them or by revamping the norms applicable to everyone. And these ideas are gaining strength outside the feminist community. For many purposes, of course, nondiscrimination is still understood to mean that men and women must be treated the same. But for many other purposes nondiscrimination has come to mean something else: different treatment of men and women, accommodation of women's differences, nonsubordination of women, or just plain inclusion of women.

Religion   We also see the notion of accommodating differences playing a role in the area of religion. In fact, in prohibiting discrimination based on religion, the text of Title VII of the Civil Rights Act explicitly requires "accommodation," which it does not do for any of the other categories of prohibited discrimination—race, sex, color, or national origin. Title VII deems it discrimination "because of . . . religion" for an employer to fail "to reasonably accommodate to an employee's . . . religious observance or practice," unless doing so would cause "undue hardship" to the employer.[45] Read literally, this suggests that nondiscrimination requires more than formally equal treatment of religious observers and nonobservers. Formal equality would be satisfied by an employer requiring all employees to work on Saturday; but "reasonable accommodation" might require the employer to accommodate Orthodox Jewish employees whose religious "difference" made it impossible for them to work on Saturday (even though the employer would not have to accommodate employees who wanted Saturday off to be with their families for important secular reasons).

In 1977, however, the Supreme Court essentially gutted this "reasonable accommodation" provision of Title VII by holding, in *Trans World Airlines, Inc. v. Hardison*,[46] that anything more than a "de minimis" burden on the employer was an undue hardship that extinguished any duty to accommodate religious differences. This restrictive construction of the "reasonable accommodation" language of Title VII was consistent with the still-dominant place of formal equality principles in legal thought; indeed, one explanation for the *Hardison* decision is that it reflected the Court's anticipatory uneasiness about the "racial preference/affirmative action" cases that were on the Court's doorstep. (The famous *Bakke* case was decided the following year.)[47] The members of the Court who were the most uneasy with race-based "preferences" were generally the most uneasy about what they saw as religious-based "preferences" in the *Hardison* context.

But accommodation of religion and religious differences—rather than strict neutrality—has had a resurgence in recent years. The permissibility of certain "accommodations" of religion has become a theme of the Supreme Court's Establishment Clause cases since the 1980s.[48] And although the Supreme Court's decision in *Employment Division, Dept. of Human Resources of Oregon v. Smith*,[49] refused to read the Free Exercise Clause to mandate accommodations of religious exercise when government applies a neutral and generally applicable law, Congress promptly embraced that mandate legislatively. The Religious Freedom Restoration Act, passed overwhelmingly by Congress in 1993, broadly prohibits government from burdening religious exercise "even if the burden results from a rule of general applicability," unless doing so is the least restrictive means of furthering a compelling interest.[50] This effectively requires accommodation of religious differences, either by special exceptions from general requirements to avoid interference with religious exercise or by abandonment of the general requirement altogether.

Disability   No statute demonstrates the transformation of antidiscrimination law better than the Americans with Disabilities Act (ADA), enacted in 1990 and now having such a major impact on American society. In the ADA, discrimination means far more than formal equality and far more than refusing to hire or admit disabled people who can meet existing criteria and utilize existing physical structures and arrangements. If that were all that discrimination against the disabled meant, only a fraction of disabled people would be helped. Instead, the act explicitly defines discrimination as the failure to accommodate disabled people—and the text of the statute spells out in extraordinary detail what this means. Nondiscrimination requires restructuring of workplace norms to assure accommodation rather than taking those workplace norms as givens; it requires rebuilding physical structures; it requires that job descriptions be rewritten; it requires modifying (and, yes, even lowering) employment qualifications to assure inclusion of the disabled in the workforce. Formal equality is barely visible in the statute.

Assessing the Transformation

How should we think about this broad and profound shift within anti-discrimination law away from "formal equality" and towards "accommodating differences." Is it a good or bad thing?

There are undoubtedly many good things about the transformation. First, it can help address the fact that some norms that formal equality would have us apply across the board are biased norms. An important contribution of difference feminism, for example, is that it forces us to become more self-conscious about the norms of institutions and to see the way in which institutions can privilege ostensibly neutral practices just because they serve the interests of men. It was the emphasis on women's differences from men that made many people see for the first time what now seems obvious: that the basic reason pregnancy has not been treated as a normal part of the workplace is that workplace norms evolved out of the male biography, and that equal treatment of men and women requires "taking account" of pregnancy in setting leave policies and disability benefits. Equality requires treating pregnancy as a normal event in the workplace.

Second, even if the norms that formal equality would have us apply across the board are not biased, the reality on which they are superimposed may reflect past violations of formal equality—indeed, the effects of past oppression. Formal equality, with its insistence on the same treatment for all, can ignore and therefore perpetuate differences caused by past departures from formal equality. More generally, the idea of accommodating differences encourages us to tailor social policy to current social realities—always a good thing.

Third, accommodating differences in the name of the ideal of equality is actually linked to another powerful American ideal, the ideal of tolerance. Tolerance means accepting a range of ideas and behaviors different from our own—indeed, it has no bite except where there are differences. To the extent that formal equality insists that all people be governed by the same rule, it may sometimes insist upon a conformity to a single norm that is at odds with tolerance. The concept of accommodating differences is tied to an attitude of tolerance that not only accepts differences but allows them to flourish and make their distinctive contribution.

Lastly, and most practically, an approach that "accommodates differences" is simply more likely than "formal equality" to produce a speedy and broad inclusion of previously disadvantaged or subordinated groups in important institutions. That, after all, explains why affirmative action developed, and why "accommodation" is now the centerpiece of disability law. And in some areas—most obviously where religious minorities are involved—the idea of accommodating differences more easily lets us see that allowing opt-outs and separation can sometimes provide as much equal treatment as a guarantee of inclusion.[51]

Nevertheless, I think we need to face more fully the problems that this "accommodate differences" version of nondiscrimination surely raises. First, there is a real risk that good norms will be sacrificed or that the differences that will be accommodated are differences that impose excessive costs. Sometimes people's differences are that they are less skilled or less productive than others—and the costs of accommodation may outweigh the gains even if we view the gains most comprehensively. Similarly, in some circumstances we may find ourselves valorizing differences that in fact are regrettable products of oppression, differences that we should try to change rather than valorize or "accommodate." Indeed, in the effort to promote more equal status among groups, there is the risk that we may lose our moorings about what human qualities are in fact right to value and right to try to develop.

Second, there is individual fairness. Scarcity means that not everyone's "difference" can be accommodated. Since we cannot adjust standards for everyone, when is it fair to adjust them for some people and not for others? This is not just the standard question about race-based affirmative action. Consider disability law. Given that lots of people who are *not* disabled may be turned down for jobs when they cannot do parts of the job as well as others, when is it fair to require that jobs be redefined to accommodate people defined as disabled when *they* cannot do a job as well as others?

Lastly, to view nondiscrimination as "accommodating differences" runs the risk that we will overemphasize people's differences from each other, rather than their commonalities. This can exacerbate social friction and social division—and, in any case, it may *encourage* people to identify themselves and others primarily in terms of group membership rather than as human beings, primarily as factions rather than as Americans with common interests.

Although I have long been a supporter of race-based affirmative action, some of the concerns I have just mentioned about the general approach of "accommodating differences" have made me more troubled by some aspects of affirmative action in recent years. A development that has particularly raised concerns for me is the profound and important shift in the *rationale* for affirmative action.[52] Until quite recently, the prevailing rationale for affirmative action was as a *corrective for past discrimination*, a view that I have endorsed and written about, and still endorse.[53] But the dominant rationale for affirmative action today in universities, business, and government is to promote *diversity*.[54] This shift represents a much more decisive move away from formal equality and toward a policy of accommodating differences than affirmative action based on a corrective rationale.

The "corrective" rationale accepts the centrality of formal equality as the ideal. It does not reject the view that official color-blindness is a worthy ideal. Rather, affirmative action is viewed as a temporary departure from formal equality for one specific overriding reason: to eliminate conditions traceable to past discrimination—indeed, conditions traceable to past departures from the norm of formal equality.

Nor do defenders of corrective affirmative action fault most qualification criteria as biased. Where corrective affirmative action is used because the usual, sensible qualifications criteria were ignored when minorities applied for jobs, affirmative action assures that minorities with equal or better qualifications under the existing criteria are given their due.[55] In other cases, to be sure, corrective affirmative action is used to give preferences to people who may be less qualified than those not preferred under the existing qualifications criteria, typically on the ground that this may be necessary to eliminate an underrepresentation of minorities caused by cumulative effects of past discrimination. But this too does not require faulting existing qualifications criteria as biased. After all, given generations of harmful discrimination it should not be surprising if members of historically victimized groups, on the average, possessed somewhat fewer of the skills and achievements that reasonable "qualification criteria" properly measured. To temporarily supplement and modify these criteria somewhat in order to correct historic exclusionary patterns causally linked to past discrimination may be an approach that accommodates differences, those resulting from past discrimination. But this corrective approach does not permanently embrace race-based policies or repudiate formal equality or the usual qualification criteria. Rather, race-based action is used temporarily with the goal of rectifying past wrongs and then, after a corrective period, applying qualifications criteria in a race-blind way.

The movement away from the corrective rationale has many causes, including complexities in establishing causal linkages between past discrimination and particular current disadvantages, perceived moral problems in imposing the costs of rectifying continuing effects of past discrimination on people who are not themselves wrongdoers or unique beneficiaries of past wrongs, and strains from using a rationale for affirmative action that acknowledges that its beneficiaries are at times less qualified than nonbeneficiaries. While not insurmountable, in my judgment, these problems have helped produce a widespread shift to a diversity rationale for affirmative action that is quite different from the corrective rationale.

The diversity rationale rests entirely upon a premise of racial differences, and insists upon, emphasizes, and typically celebrates those differences. It is asserted differences that produce the diversity, and the equal value of those differences that justifies efforts to establish diversity within a program or institution through self-conscious racial preference policies.

There are several troubling things about this rationale. The first is that it gives up the strong moral predicate of the "corrective" rationale, which is rooted in our country's shameful history of racial wrongs and provides the strongest possible reason for taking account of racial differences in distributing scarce benefits. In its place, it has substituted a weaker and debatable instrumental claim that promoting greater diversity will make various programs and institutions function better.

In addition, racial preference policies justified by diversity typically rest on the doubtful and disturbing assumption that all, or at least most, members of the racial group in fact share or should share some distinctive characteristic, outlook, or voice. The empirical claim of difference is often unproven, and, beyond that, the diversity rationale signals to everyone an expectation that they will speak or act differently from members of other racial groups. This can be both unfair and unwise, creating pressures to conform one's ideas and actions to some diversity-producing stereotype of one's racial group and to emphasize differences even where they do not exist or are minor, and reinforcing ideas of difference rather than commonalities. The diversity rationale also creates pressure for continued division of groups into subgroups, each claiming to be different from the larger group in certain respects and therefore to add an additional dimension of diversity that deserves separate consideration. Moreover, in at least some of its forms, race-based diversity policies can wind up catering to and entrenching people's racial prejudices, as when an employer says, "I want a racially diverse workforce to appeal to the preferences of my racially diverse customers." We heard the "customer preference" argument from southern whites thirty years ago, and it does not sound any prettier now.

There is also something troubling in the way that diversity theory makes race definitionally a qualification and an aspect of merit. This can obscure the degree of some of the real trade-offs regarding other qualifications that affirmative action sometimes does require. I appreciate that this is precisely one appeal of diversity theory: by defining away the question of whether affirmative action leads to any "lowering" of qualifications, it sidesteps a difficult and divisive debate over qualifications and merit. But the trade-offs involved in instituting affirmative action should be faced. That is the only way to separate any real trade-offs from imagined ones, and, to the extent real trade-offs do exist, the only way to find the right balance among possibly contending values that each deserve our respect—as promoting racial inclusiveness and fostering meritocratic decision making both do.

Diversity theory also seems to permit a ceiling to be placed on the representation of some groups (say, Asians or Jews) on the ground that "too many" representatives of that group are inconsistent with achieving diversity from other groups. This problem arises because the diversity rationale makes the simple absence of diversity a basis for race-conscious measures, rather than requiring that the absence of diversity be causally linked to past discrimination, as the corrective theory does.[56]

Lastly, the diversity rationale would seem to invite and justify race-conscious policies permanently. For those of us who have not given up the view that our ideal is that government should distribute benefits and burdens without regard to race, it is important to insist that race-conscious measures are temporary and transitional—that they are not permanent and not our ideal. The corrective rationale does this, even if it accepts that the transition may prove to be quite long.

In short, to the extent we have abandoned the corrective rationale for racial preferences and now embraced the diversity rationale, I think we have taken a wrong turn. I underscore that I certainly am not arguing that diversity is a bad thing—only that promoting this diversity by using race-based policies is a wrong turn in light of the distinctive dangers of such policies. In addition, I confess that I am less firm about this conclusion in the context of educational institutions than in other settings such as government contracting or employment. The dangers of race-based diversity policies generally do seem as great in the education context as elsewhere. On the other hand, education is centrally about exposing students to people with ideas and life experiences different from their own; and, in a multiracial society, where learning to understand and interact with people of all races is essential, I acknowledge that there are some distinctive arguments for allowing educational institutions to use race-based policies to foster a more racially diverse student body. Most importantly, I underscore that my argument here is limited to the diversity rationale. It is one thing to criticize the diversity rationale for race-based affirmative action, quite another to criticize all race-based affirmative action.

I should also add that I do not find it particularly helpful in the present debates to point to statements by Thurgood Marshall and other civil rights advocates in the *Brown* period to the effect that color blindness or formal equality, not racial preference, was the policy that they wanted.[57] True enough. But whatever one thinks is the right way to deal with our racial dilemmas, we surely see more clearly now than forty years ago the various consequences of insisting upon color blindedness after long centuries of racial oppression—just as we now see more clearly than twenty years ago some of the consequences of affirmative action. Experience has taught us things, and it taught Thurgood Marshall things after the *Brown* era. As I have written elsewhere about Thurgood Marshall (for whom I was a law clerk):

> [W]hen affirmative action issues first started to emerge in bold relief [on the Supreme Court], he was very uneasy with race-conscious hiring, admissions, and set-asides as a corrective for past discrimination. In time, he became their most passionate defender on the Court. He came to that position, I think, in much the same way many others did: reluctantly, through a gradually developed judgment that, against the backdrop of centuries of oppression, colorblind measures would not work, or at least not work fast enough, to achieve a significantly greater inclusion of minorities in mainstream American life. Those who have tried to quote back at the Justice his endorsement of colorblind remedies at the time of *Brown* ignore the fact that judges continue to change while in office, and that the life revealed in cases continues a judge's education.[58]

In a similar way, of course, one's views about race-conscious remedies may continue to evolve over time as experience and reflection continue to teach us about their benefits and costs. The views about the diversity rationale for affirmative action contained in this essay certainly represent that sort of evolution for me. And as I have already suggested, I have come to see both benefits and risks in some of our other policies that make accommodating differences the antidiscrimination approach.

This is not the place to spell out what I consider to be the precise boundaries of the concept of accommodating differences. All of us who see some merit to the approach, as I do, need to think more about where the limits are, and where we should still insist on formal equality. It is right, I think, to reexamine the norms of institutions to make sure they are not irrationally or self-interestedly promoting the norms of their current occupants; but it goes too far to say all general norms that disparately exclude members of certain groups are discriminatory norms. It is right to recognize that racial integration completely on white terms can itself be insulting and a form of cultural domination; but it goes too far to accept uncritically the valorizations of all cultural differences. It is right to conclude that workplaces must accommodate pregnancy if there is to be gender equality; but we should be much more cautious about assuming that women inherently have different voices from men. It is right to insist that employers take steps to accommodate the disabled, but it goes too far to be indifferent to costs. It is right to recognize that many claims to neutrality and evenhandedness really reflect a self-interested privileging of certain values; but it goes too far to insist reflexively that privileging of certain values is always a bad thing.

The transformation from "formal equality" to "accommodating differences" is occurring across a broad spectrum of American law and American life. Like *Brown*, this development is changing the way our society understands what equality and nondiscrimination require. And just as we could say of *Brown*, the very moment of triumph of antidiscrimination ideas has opened up a new range of difficult issues for our society.

Notes

1. See Reva B. Siegel, "Home as Work: The First Woman's Rights Claims Concerning Wives' Household Labor, 1850–1880," 103 *Yale Law Journal* (1994), 1073, 1146–52.

2. This choice for "formal equality" was not inevitable, nor, as we know, was it irreversible. See text accompanying notes 40–44 infra. Feminism had long had another strand that insisted upon women's differences from men, and made those differences the normative basis for either rights to inclusion or rights to special protection. For example, the women's suffrage movement had two main strands: the first strand argued that women should have the right to vote because women were basically the same as men and therefore deserved the same civic role as men. But there was an alternative strand that argued that women were different from men, among other things having a different perspective on public issues. It was this valuably different perspective, many women argued, that made it right for women to have the vote; difference, in other words, was what entitled women to inclusion. See Nancy F. Cott, "Feminist Theory and Feminist Movements: The Past Before Us," in *What is Feminism?*, Juliet Mitchell & Ann Oakley eds. (New York: Pantheon Books, 1986), 49–62; William H. Chafe, *The American Woman: Her Changing Social, Economic, and Political Roles, 1920–1970* (New York: Oxford University Press, 1972), 13.

3. 42 U.S.C. § 2000e-2(a)(1) (Supp. 1995).

4. "Note, Developments in the Law—Employment Discrimination and Title VII of the Civil Rights Act of 1964," 84 *Harvard Law Review* (1971), 1109, 1167.

5. See, e.g., Corne v. Bausch and Lomb, Inc., 390 F. Supp. 161, 163 (D. Ariz. 1975), vacated on procedural grounds, 562 F.2d 55 (9th Cir. 1977); Neeley v. American Fidelity Assurance Co., Civ. Act. No. 77-0151-B, 1978 Westlaw 65, at 5 (W.D. Okla. Feb. 21, 1978).

6. For the pathbreaking analysis, see Catharine A. MacKinnon, *Sexual Harassment of Working Women* (New Haven: Yale University Press, 1979). The leading Supreme Court case is Meritor Savings Bank, FSB v. Vinson, 477 U.S. 57 (1987).

7. 429 U.S. 125 (1976).

8. Pregnancy Discrimination Amendments of 1978, 42 U.S.C. § 2000e(k) (Supp. 1995).

9. 410 U.S. 113 (1973).

10. In contrast to *Roe*, the more recent decision in Planned Parenthood of Southeastern Pennsylvania v. Casey, 505 U.S. 833 (1992), placed greater emphasis on the equality perspective. See id. at 856, 912, 927. On the equality basis of abortion rights more generally, see Reva Siegel, "Reasoning from the Body: A Historical Perspective on Abortion Regulation and Questions of Equal Protection," 44 *Stanford Law Review* (1992), 261, 263; Sylvia A. Law, "Rethinking Sex and the Constitution," 132 *University of Pennsylvania Law Review* (1984), 955, 1013–28.

11. Social Security Act of 1935, Pub. L. No. 74-271, 49 Stat. 620 (1936), codified as amended 42 U.S.C. § 301 et seq. (Supp. 1995); Health Insurance for the Aged Act of 1965, Pub. L. No. 89-97, 79 Stat. 286 (1966), codified throughout 42 U.S.C.

12. 29 U.S.C. §§ 621–34 (Supp. 1992). The act has been amended several times to expand its coverage: Age Discrimination in Employment Act Amendments of 1978, Pub. L. No. 95-256, 92 Stat. 189 (1980), 29 U.S.C. § 623(f)(2) (1985); Age Discrimination in Employment Amendments of 1986, Pub. L. No. 99-592, 100 Stat. 3342 (1989), recodified throughout 29 U.S.C. §§ 621–34 (1994).

13. See Peter H. Schuck, "The Graying of Civil Rights Law: The Age Discrimination Act of 1975," 89 *Yale Law Journal* (1979), 27 (distinguishing between allocative and nondiscrimination models of legislation involving the elderly).

14. E.g., Vocational Rehabilitation Act of 1918, Pub. L. No. 65-178, 40 Stat. 617 (1919) (amended 1919, Pub. L. No. 66-11, 41 Stat. 158 (1921)) (providing for vocational rehabilitation of disabled veterans); Act of June 2, 1920, Pub. L. No. 66-236, 41 Stat. 735 (1921) (providing for the vocational rehabilitation of persons disabled in their occupations, and also authorizing limited services to those whose disability, whether congenital or caused by injury or disease, leads them to be incapacitated for remunerative occupation); Randolph-Sheppard Act, Pub. L. No. 74-732, 49 Stat. 1559 (1936) (aiding blind people in employment). On the transformation of approaches to the disabled due to the models provided by civil rights law, see Jonathan C. Drimmer, "Cripples, Overcomers, and Civil Rights: Tracing the Evolution of Federal Legislation and Social Policy for People with Disabilities," 40 *U.C.L.A. Law Review* (1993), 1341.

15. Pub. L. No. 93-112, 87 Stat. 355 (1974), codified as amended, 29 U.S.C. §§ 701 et seq. (Supp. 1992).

16. 42 U.S.C. §§ 12101–213 (1995).

17. 20 U.S.C. §§ 1400–85 (Supp. 1995).

18. 42 U.S.C. §§ 3601–31 (1994).

19. 42 U.S.C. §§ 4151–57 (1994).

20. 49 U.S.C. § 1374(b) (Supp. 1995) (repealed).

21. Pub. L. No. 98-457, 98 Stat. 1749 (1986), codified throughout 42 U.S.C.

22. 330 U.S. 1 (1947).

23. Id. at 16.

24. Id. at 15.

25. Id. at 17. On the requirement of government neutrality as a central element of what the Establishment Clause has been interpreted to mean, see also Rosenberger v. Rectors and Visitors of the University of Virginia, 115 S. Ct. 2510, 2521 (1995); Lee v. Weisman, 505 U.S. 577, 610, 612 (1992) (Souter, J., concurring); Mueller v. Allen, 463 U.S. 388, 398–400 (1983); Gillette v. United States, 401 U.S. 437, 454 (1971); Walz v. Tax Commission of the City of New York, 397 U.S. 664, 668–69 (1970); Larson v. Valente, 456 U.S. 228, 246 (1982). This principle of neutrality has prohibited government action that favors religion over nonreligion, see, e.g., *Lee*, 505 U.S. at 610–12 (Souter, J., concurring) (reviewing history and precedents), as well as government action that favors some religious sects over others. This requirement of neutrality has been interpreted in various contexts to permit the government to grant certain benefits to religious entities and persons if the benefit is granted on a "neutral basis to a wide spectrum" of entities or individuals, so that it cannot be said that the government is discriminating against some sects in favor of others, or against nonreligion in favor of religion. E.g., *Rosenberger*, supra (access to university funding); *Muller*, supra (tax deductions for costs of sending children to parochial schools); *Walz*, supra (exemption from property tax for religious organizations).

In interpreting the scope of the Free Exercise Clause, the Court has also used a principle of nondiscrimination to uphold the constitutionality of government action that may burden religion. "[T]he right of free exercise does not relieve an individual of the obligation to comply with a 'valid and neutral law of general applicability on the ground that the law proscribes (or prescribes) conduct that his religion prescribes (or proscribes).'" Employment Division, Dept. of Human Resources of Oregon v. Smith, 494 U.S. 872, 879 (1990), quoting United States v. Lee, 455 U.S. 252, 263n.3 (1982) (Stevens, J., concurring in the judgment). And when it invalidated a local regulation as violative of the Free Exercise Clause after *Smith*, it explicitly invoked principles familiar from Equal Protection law in holding that "[o]fficial action that targets religious conduct for distinctive treatment cannot be shielded by mere compliance with the requirement of facial neutrality. The Free Exercise Clause protects against government hostility which is masked, as well as overt." Church of the Lukumi Babalu Aye, Inc. v. City of Hialeah, 113 S. Ct. 2217, 2227 (1993).

26. E.g., Police Department of Chicago v. Mosley, 408 U.S. 92, 95–96 (1972) ("[A]bove all else, the First Amendment means that government has no power to restrict expression because of its message. . . . There is 'an equality of status in the field of ideas,' and government must afford all points of view an equal opportunity to be heard."); R.A.V. v. City of St. Paul, 112 S. Ct. 2538, 2545–46 (1992); id. at 2568–69 (Stevens, J., concurring in the judgment) (discussing impermissibility of "viewpoint discrimination"); Perry Educ. Assn. v. Perry Local Educators' Ass'n., 460 U.S. 37, 62 (1983) (Brennan, J., dissenting) ("Viewpoint discrimination is censorship in its purest form.").

27. Bernard Bailyn et al., *The Great Republic: A History of the American People*, 4th ed., vol. 1 (Lexington, Mass.: D. C. Heath, 1992), 277.

28. For an overview of the legal literature critiquing rights, see "Symposium: A Critique of Rights," 62 *Texas Law Review* (1984), 1363–1599; see also Mark Tushnet, "The Critique of Rights," 47 *Southern Methodist University Law Review* (1993), 23. Influential responses to this literature include Patricia J. Williams, "Alchemical Notes: Reconstructing Ideals from Deconstructed Rights," 22 *Harvard Civil Rights–Civil Liberties Law Review* (1987), 401, and Randall L. Kennedy,

"Racial Critiques of Legal Academia," 102 *Harvard Law Review* (1989), 1745, 1785–86.

29. E.g., Robert Elias, *The Politics of Victimization* (New York: Oxford University Press, 1986). On victimization culture among blacks, see Shelby Steele, *The Content of Our Character: A New Vision of Race in America* (New York: St. Martin's Press, 1990); Glenn C. Loury, *One by One from the Inside Out: Essays and Reviews on Race and Responsibility in America* (New York: Free Press, 1995). Of course, believing oneself or one's group or community to be victimized is not necessarily bad. If more and more people over time are hurt by environmental hazards, we do not become exercised over the fact that more people view themselves as victims. The finger of blame, we would say, should be pointed at those who are causing more harm, not those who are suffering it.

The recent criticism of a so-called culture of victimhood in the discrimination context reflects several things, I think. Some critics believe that many people falsely claim or exaggerate claims that they have been hurt by discrimination. Others are concerned that the laws now define victims too broadly, or that the concept of victim is now interpreted so broadly that virtually all members of society can see themselves as victims. For others, the concern about "victimization" reflects not a view about the actuality or seriousness or scope of harm, but rather a view about how the harms are best ameliorated. On this view, people who view themselves as victims and seek redress from those who have caused their victimhood are unlikely to assume enough responsibility themselves for changing their situation. They will await redress from others, rather than develop their strengths and capabilities to change their lot themselves. The latter, many people think, is the only truly effective way to reverse social disadvantage. As with so much else today, even though the distemper we hear about a so-called culture of victims is usually phrased generally, a lot of the distemper probably rests on views about black Americans in particular—a view that too many blacks feel an anger and resentment that is self-destructive and unproductive, or that too much conduct is being labeled as "racism" and "discrimination" that is really innocent or just the jostles of life that other people put up with.

30. These are not hypothetical concerns. Peter T. Kilborn, "Backlog of Cases Is Overwhelming Jobs-Bias Agency," *New York Times*, Nov. 26, 1994 at A1, col. 6.

31. I use the term "accommodation" throughout this essay because it already has a place in statutes and case law, but it is imperfect. To say that some "difference" must be "accommodated" may suggest that something other than the "difference" will remain the benchmark, and that the difference will be "accommodated" without achieving equal status. Those who today view nondiscrimination as requiring the "accommodation of differences" obviously seek to assure equal status for those differences.

32. Aristotle, *Nicomachean Ethics*, Terence Irwin trans. (Indianapolis: Hackett Pub., 1985), bk. 5, ch. 3.

33. See, e.g., Derrick A. Bell, *And We Are Not Saved: The Elusive Quest for Racial Justice* (New York: Basic Books, 1987), 102–22. Cf. Missouri v. Jenkins, 115 S. Ct. 2038, 2064 (1995) (Thomas, J., concurring) (objecting to integration remedies as "rest[ing] upon the idea that any school that is black is inferior, and that blacks cannot succeed without the benefit of the company of whites").

34. See, e.g., Washington v. Davis, 426 U.S. 229 (1976).

35. This approach has also been extended to employment practices disparately affecting women. Dothard v. Rawlinson, 433 U.S. 321 (1977).

36. See generally Paul Gewirtz, "Discrimination Endgame," *New Republic*, Aug. 12, 1991, 18–23.

37. 401 U.S. 424 (1971).

38. See, e.g., New York City Transit Authority v. Beazer, 440 U.S. 568 (1979); Wards Cove Packing Co. v. Atonio, 490 U.S. 642 (1989).

39. The fact that I have joined together and identified some common themes in the various subject matter areas of antidiscrimination law should not obscure some real differences in just how readily accommodation ideas are being accepted in the law. Compare, for example, disability and race. In the disability area, legislation *mandates* inclusionary accommodation and requires departures from formal equality. Where race is involved, however, the Supreme Court is still wavering on when it is even *permissible* to depart from formal equality and use affirmative action, and it has mandated affirmative action only for certain proven violations of law. In the area of disability, the ADA requires that job qualifications be redefined in order to achieve inclusion of the disabled, but where racial minorities are involved, the mere suggestion of changing the existing definition of qualifications to achieve greater inclusion of minorities is often explosive. The ADA with its sweeping accommodation requirements for the disabled achieved broad bipartisan support in Congress; but recent civil rights legislation that would codify the disparate impact test for racial minorities and women produced a protracted and bitter political struggle before its passage. In short, accommodation ideas have met with easier acceptance on some fronts than on others.

40. Ruth Bader Ginsburg & Barbara Flagg, "Some Reflections on the Feminist Legal Thought of the 1970's," 1989 *University of Chicago Legal Forum* (1989), 9 (fundamental premise of 1970s litigation was gender neutrality).

41. 479 U.S. 272 (1987).

42. Id. at 289.

43. This particular legal issue is now less significant, since Congress has now legislatively required that employers accommodate all medical conditions, not just pregnancy, by allowing up to twelve weeks of unpaid leave. Family and Medical Leave Act of 1993, Pub. L. No. 103-3, 107 Stat. 6 (1994), codified in scattered sections of 2 U.S.C., 5 U.S.C., and 29 U.S.C.

44. Carol Gilligan, *In a Different Voice* (Cambridge, Mass.: Harvard University Press, 1982).

45. 42 U.S.C. §§ 2000e(j), 2000e-2(a) (1994).

46. 432 U.S. 63 (1977).

47. Regents of the University of California v. Bakke, 438 U.S. 265 (1978).

48. See, e.g., Lynch v. Donnelly, 465 U.S. 668, 673 (1984); Corporation of Presiding Bishop of the Church of Jesus Christ of Latter-Day Saints v. Amos, 483 U.S. 327, 334–35 (1987); Board of Education of Kiryas Joel Village School District v. Grumet, 114 S. Ct. 2481, 2495–500 (1994) (O'Connor, J., concurring in part and concurring in judgment).

49. 494 U.S. 872 (1990).

50. 42 U.S.C. § 2000bb-1 (1994).

51. I have in mind particularly the practice of accommodating religious differences by allowing religious students to opt out of certain school programs or activities—a practice sometimes required by the Free Exercise Clause of the Constitution, see Spence v. Bailey, 465 F.2d 797 (6th Cir. 1972) (allowing opt-out from ROTC); but see Mozert v. Hawkins County Board of Education, 827 F.2d 1058 (6th Cir. 1987) (holding that requirement that public school students study basic

reader series did not create unconstitutional burden on Free Exercise Clause), cert. denied 484 U.S. 1066 (1988), and more frequently simply permitted by local school policy. Sometimes accommodating religious differences allows a form of opt-out that itself permits a broader inclusion. For example, when Sabbath observers are accommodated by being given a different day off from other employees, they are allowed a form of opt-out—but this opt-out allows them to remain included in the employer's workforce rather than have to look for work elsewhere.

52. The scholarly literature on affirmative action is vast, of course. The legal literature is usefully summarized in John H. Garvey & T. Alexander Aleinikoff, *Modern Constitutional Theory: A Reader*, 3rd ed. (St. Paul: West Publishing Co., 1994), 559–617.

53. See, e.g., Paul Gewirtz, "Choice in the Transition: School Desegregation and the Corrective Ideal," 86 *Columbia Law Review* (1986), 728. The Supreme Court's fullest debate about the corrective rationale for affirmative action appears in City of Richmond v. J. A. Croson Co., 488 U.S. 469 (1989) (especially the opinion of Justice O'Connor and Justice Marshall's dissent).

54. The diversity rationale is debated in the various opinions in Metro Broadcasting, Inc. v. FCC, 497 U.S. 547 (1990) (see especially Justice Brennan's defense in the opinion of the Court and Justice O'Connor's criticism in her dissent). See also T. Alexander Aleinikoff, "A Case for Race-Consciousness," 91 *Col. L. Rev.* (1991), 1060, 1064–65, 1108–10 (supporting diversity rationale); Kathleen M. Sullivan, "Sins of Discrimination: Last Term's Affirmative Action Cases," 100 *Harvard Law Review* (1986), 78 (criticizing corrective argument and supporting diversity rationale); Patricia J. Williams, "Metro Broadcasting, Inc. v. FCC: Regrouping in Singular Times," 104 *Harvard Law Review* (1990), 525 (supporting diversity rationale).

55. See, e.g., United States v. Paradise, 480 U.S. 149 (1987).

56. The problem is illustrated by Justice Powell's opinion in the *Bakke* case, which concluded that using race as a "plus" to promote a more racially diverse student body in a university medical school would be constitutional. 438 U.S. 265, 311–15 (1978). Justice Powell concluded that giving this race-based plus for diversity purposes would be upheld as constitutional because it satisfies the most demanding constitutional test that exists: it is necessary to promote a compelling interest. Precisely the same constitutional arguments that Justice Powell used would lead to the validation of a university admissions policy that gave a race-based plus for non-Asians to achieve greater diversity. The problem with Justice Powell's reasoning, and a problem with the diversity rationale more generally, is that it does not require a causal link between the absence of diversity being addressed and a history of discrimination. This is precisely what the corrective approach requires, and what would usually furnish an easy distinction between a "plus" for blacks and a "plus" for non-Asians.

57. See, e.g., Charles Fried, *Order and Law: Arguing the Reagan Revolution* (Simon & Schuster: New York, 1991), 112–13; Andrew Kull, *The Color-Blind Constitution* (Cambridge: Harvard University Press, 1992), 146, 148, 156–57, 166–67, 173. Professor (now Justice) Fried elaborated on this point in a paper that was presented at the conference resulting in this volume, but does not appear here.

58. Paul Gewirtz, "Thurgood Marshall," 101 *Yale Law Journal* (1991), 13, 16.

READING THE "REALITIES" OF RACE

DAVID B. WILKINS

Social Engineers or Corporate Tools?

Brown v. Board of Education *and the Conscience of the Black Corporate Bar*

If Thurgood Marshall were alive today, he would tell us that 1995 and not 1994, the fortieth anniversary of *Brown v. Board of Education*, was the most important anniversary associated with the civil rights movement. That year marked the centennial of the birth of Marshall's former dean and mentor Charles Hamilton Houston. As Marshall frequently acknowledged, Houston was the architect of the legal strategy that produced *Brown*. More important, Houston created the educational and organizational strategy that produced Marshall and the other black lawyers whose hard work, skill, and determination resulted in the landmark victory we celebrate today.

Houston believed that the campaign against the separate-but-equal doctrine must be led by an elite core of black lawyers specially trained as "social engineers" for black rights.[1] To that end, Houston ruthlessly transformed Howard Law School from a part-time country club for the aspiring black bourgeoisie into a rigorous training ground for black lawyers committed to eradicating the existing system of de jure segregation.[2] As special counsel to the NAACP, Houston continued his campaign to create a black legal elite on two fronts: first, by making law schools his first target in challenging *Plessy v. Ferguson*;[3] and second, by recruiting the best and brightest black lawyers in the country to join as either full or part-time participants in his legal campaign for black equality.[4] By the time the Supreme Court decided *Brown*, Houston and Marshall (who succeeded Houston in 1938) had created a new model for pursuing social justice through law and the nation's first public interest law firm with the skill and commitment to put that strategy into action.[5] As of 1954, the black lawyers associated with the NAACP's Legal Defense and

Education Fund were, without question, the best educated, best trained, and best known black lawyers who had ever lived.

For the next generation, Houston's social engineers dominated the black bar. In the coming decades, these men and women assumed leading roles in the judiciary, government, academia, and the private bar.[6] Although their roles may have changed from their days at the Legal Defense Fund, their basic commitment to Houston's vision did not. Whether one looks at Thurgood Marshall's jurisprudence, Derrick Bell's scholarship, or William Coleman's testimony against the nomination of Robert Bork to the Supreme Court, it is clear that this pioneer generation of elite black lawyers never wavered from their commitment to use their positions of authority to further the cause of racial justice.

Today, these veterans of the civil rights movement are slowly being replaced by a new generation of elite black lawyers. Born after *Brown*, these lawyers are the products of integrated colleges and law schools, with the largest number coming from the country's most elite educational institutions.[7] Although some have chosen to devote their legal talents to serving the needs of black clients, either through full-time civil rights work or by working in public or private organizations that provide services to blacks, most have followed their white classmates into large corporate law firms or the legal departments of Fortune 500 corporations.[8]

In this essay, I wish to explore the continuing relevance of Houston's vision for this new generation of elite black lawyers. Will black corporate lawyers heed Houston's call to become social engineers who contribute, in unique but important ways, to the struggle for racial justice? Or will they become, to borrow a phase that is popular among some law students, "corporate tools" who slavishly pursue the interests of their powerful clients in a manner that further entrenches existing inequalities?[9]

My interest in this topic stems from a larger work in progress on the ideals and practices of black corporate lawyers.[10] One of the claims I make there is that these lawyers have moral obligations to advance the cause of racial justice that must be balanced against other legitimate professional commitments and personal goals when deciding how to act in particular cases, and more generally, in constructing a morally appropriate life plan.[11] I call this assertion the obligation thesis. Houston, as I have suggested, had a similar view about the elite black lawyers of his day. By studying how Houston's vision was translated into reality, both in the twenty years leading up to *Brown* and in the forty years thereafter, we can begin to get a sense of what it might mean to recognize this kind of race-based moral obligation in our contemporary environment.

Specifically, I believe that a careful review of this history should lead us to reject, or at least to qualify, several arguments that are often raised against the obligation thesis. These objections can be grouped into three general categories. The first asserts that race-based obligations are counterproductive, either because they reinforce a false essentialism about racial identity or because they shift the focus away from the obligations of whites.[12] The second claims that placing obligations on black *lawyers* is either unnecessary, because the law is no longer the primary obstacle to black advancement, or futile, because lawyers (particularly corporate lawyers) will never challenge the fundamental distribution of wealth and power in society.[13] Finally, critics of the obligation thesis assert that whatever this position's abstract merits, it is impossible to make meaningful judgments about what this commitment would actually require in particular cases.[14]

Each of these objections highlights important dangers inherent in any attempt to place status and occupation based obligations on the relatively advantaged members of an otherwise oppressed group. Indeed, in the forty years since *Brown*, it is all too easy to find examples that underscore the importance of these concerns. Nevertheless, just like many of the recent criticisms of the *Brown* decision itself, to which these objections are closely connected, the assertion that Houston's vision has no relevance for today's elite black lawyers is misguided.

All three of these objections to the obligation thesis could have been raised—and indeed *were* raised—in response to Houston's initial plans to create black legal social engineers. Yet not even the most ardent critics of the obligation thesis (or of *Brown*) assert that we would be better off today if Houston had heeded these doubting voices. By examining how Houston avoided the pitfalls inherent in his theory of race-based obligations for black lawyers we can gain valuable insight into how similar dangers can be circumvented in our own time even as we acknowledge the limits of Houston's strategy and of the *Brown* decision itself. As we pause to celebrate Houston and Marshall's crowning achievement, we should ask ourselves how much more there might be to celebrate forty years from today if the current generation of elite black lawyers were to adopt something like Houston's vision.

I. The Critique of Race

The first group of objections to the obligation thesis underscore the paradoxical nature of any attempt to hold the victims of discrimination responsible for struggling against their own oppression. Why should *black* lawyers, who after all are themselves victims of America's racism, have special obligations to remedy a situation that they did not create? Shouldn't white lawyers (or white society more generally) bear the burden of dismantling the structure of racist oppression constructed by their ancestors and through which they continue to reap unjustified advantage? Won't any talk of the "obligations" of black professionals deflect attention from what surely must be white society's more pressing duty? Even worse, won't any discussion of "black" obligations further entrench the racist ideology that all black lawyers share an innate common viewpoint that prevents them from doing anything other than "civil rights work"?

Initial attempts to integrate law schools after *Brown* demonstrate that even well-intentioned efforts to implement Houston's ideas can run afoul of these dangers. Despite Houston and Marshall's many victories, by 1960, the number of black lawyers in the United States remained pitifully small.[15] In the mid-1960s, several law schools, including Harvard, Columbia, Duke, Michigan, and UCLA, instituted affirmative action programs designed to increase black enrollment in these institutions.[16] These early programs shared a distinctly Houstonian set of justifications and goals. In the words of Professors Carl and Callahan speaking in 1965, "[I]n the light of a Negro population of upwards of 20,000,000," the need to increase the number of black lawyers rests on two factors: "(1) adequate legal representation for Negroes and (2) responsible, effective Negro leadership."[17] Whether by providing direct service to poor blacks or continuing Thurgood Marshall's fight to achieve equal justice through law, proponents of these early efforts assumed that many (if not most) of the black students they recruited would become the next generation of Houston's social engineers.[18]

The immediate effect of these early affirmative action efforts was to dramatically increase the size of the black bar. The number of black students enrolled in traditionally white law schools rose from a few hundred in the mid-1960s to more than 2,000 in 1970.[19] By 1976–1977, there were 5,500 black students enrolled in law schools accredited by the American Bar Association, with elite schools such as Harvard and Georgetown graduating almost as many black lawyers every year as Howard and Texas Southern.[20]

The long-term effects of the placement goals of these programs, however, are decidedly more mixed. In a seminal article, former University of Michigan law professor (now United States circuit court judge) Harry Edwards exposed the dangers inherent in the wholesale transplantation of Houston's policies at Howard in the 1930s to this new setting. In 1971, Edwards surveyed the career goals of black second- and third-year law students at the University of Michigan. He found that 71 percent of these students planned to join either government law offices or private firms specializing in civil rights, criminal law, or poverty work.[21] Rather than viewing this as a positive development, Edwards argued these preferences reflected continuing racism in the legal profession that limited the opportunities available to black lawyers. By "nudg[ing], or forc[ing]," black students to "return to their communities," Edwards argued, law schools both falsely imply that racial justice is solely a "black" concern and perpetuate the existing exclusion of black lawyers from the most lucrative and influential sectors of the bar.[22]

There is ample evidence to support Judge Edwards's accusations. As Edwards himself demonstrated by way of a survey of the seventy largest corporate law firms in the Midwest, there were virtually no black corporate lawyers prior to 1970.[23] With the exception of those black lawyers who had gone into full-time civil rights work or who had gained employment with one of the newly emerging government agencies providing services to the poor, the great majority of black lawyers in the 1960s continued to do what their predecessors did in the 1930s: solo practice on behalf of black individuals and small businesses. As a result, black lawyers earned significantly less than their white counterparts and were foreclosed altogether from wielding the kind of political and social power exercised by elite corporate lawyers.[24] Even if one does not believe, as Judge Edwards and I do, that giving black lawyers access to the professional, economic, and political capital embedded in corporate law practice may improve the status of the black community as a whole,[25] one should still recognize that desegregating the corporate sphere is itself a civil rights issue. To the extent that the initial wave of affirmative action programs deflected attention from this question, and instead implied that black students bear the entire weight of remedying the effects of past injustices, they put forward a narrow and distorted vision of why it was important to increase the number of black lawyers that, ironically, was inconsistent with the integrationist vision embedded in *Brown*.

Recognizing the deficiency of these programs does not mean that we ought to abandon altogether the Houstonian impetus underlying these post-*Brown* attempts to create black legal social engineers. Houston's vision was never as limited or as absolute as these programs might lead one to suspect. Instead, when we look at the manner in which Houston and Marshall actually carried out their goal of creating an elite group of black social engineers, it is apparent that these two men steered clear of the twin dangers of reinforcing racial stereotypes and of absolving whites of moral responsibility to work for racial justice.

There was nothing remotely essentialist about Houston's intense commitment to transforming the elite black bar into social engineers for justice. Houston clearly did not believe that white lawyers were incapable of fighting for black rights. Houston self-consciously molded his strategy for undermining *Plessy v. Ferguson* on a memo written by Robert Margold, one of several white lawyers who spearheaded the NAACP's early campaign against legal segregation.[26] Nor did Houston or Marshall's commitment to producing black social engineers prevent them from forming profitable and enduring relations with white lawyers. From its inception, the NAACP legal team included several white lawyers, and, in a move that angered many of his black supporters, Marshall, upon his appointment to the Second Circuit, handed the reigns at the Legal Defense Fund to Jack Greenberg.[27] Finally, Houston and Marshall's entire campaign was designed to force white society to take responsibility for the evils of racism.

And yet, it cannot be denied that Houston's mission was expressly racialist in both its tone and operation. While Houston's legal strategy may have relied on the principle of color blindness,[28] his litigation strategy clearly did not. Houston passionately believed that *black* lawyers should take the leading role in fighting racial injustice. For Houston, the justification for this commitment sounded in both practicality and principle. Despite their clear moral responsibility for eliminating racism, Houston knew that few white lawyers would be willing to make the sacrifices necessary to see the long and painful battle against de jure segregation through to its conclusion. Moreover, Houston understood that if blacks deferred to whites to wage this campaign, many whites and blacks would interpret this as a sign that black lawyers were incapable of taking responsibility for their own liberation. It was only by actively struggling against the bonds of racial oppression, Houston believed, that blacks could achieve true self-determination in the American polity.[29]

Although Houston undoubtedly thought that many black lawyers would sympathize with these arguments, he clearly realized that there was nothing inevitable about this fact. That is why he set about creating a special school to train the black lawyers who would lead this legal campaign. As Marshall and his classmates repeatedly affirmed, a central component of their education was Houston's insistence that as black lawyers they had an obligation "to give something back" to their community.[30] Houston understood that assuming this burden would require sacrifices on the part of these vulnerable women and men.[31] Indeed, by closing Howard's night division, dramatically raising admission standards, and replacing almost the entire faculty, Houston demonstrated that he was willing to sacrifice the careers of many aspiring black lawyers in order to produce social engineers with the quality and commitment to put his ideas into practice.[32]

Few today would deny that the results of Houston's policies have proven to be worth the price. Perhaps it is possible to imagine that *Brown* would have eventually occurred without Houston's black social engineers, but it hardly seems worth the effort. Moreover, although Houston undoubtedly envisioned a world in which black lawyers fought primarily for the rights of the black community, it is clear that the actual results of the strategy he put in motion have turned out to be substantially more inclusive. Not only did white lawyers participate in the NAACP's efforts, but white society has both shouldered an important measure of the costs of dismantling Jim Crow as well as received (along with other disadvantaged groups) many of the benefits of living in a world in which it is clear that law can sometimes act as a vehicle for social change.[33] Similarly, rather than limiting the opportunities available for black lawyers, the fact that Houston was able to convince Marshall and his peers that they did have an obligation to assist their community has opened up a universe of possibilities for the black bar that, but for the efforts of these pioneers, could scarcely have been imagined. Today's black corporate lawyers are, of course, the very embodiment of this post-*Brown* legacy.

Of course, one can accept all of this and still deny that something like Houston's vision has any continuing relevance for contemporary practitioners. On this view, the campaign to defeat legal segregation was just that—a war that called for extraordinary efforts to defeat a clearly defined common enemy. Given the success of that campaign, the argument continues, such extraordinary measures are no longer either necessary or desirable. This leads us to the second objection to the obligation thesis.

II. The Critique of Law

The argument that we should no longer encourage elite black lawyers to think of themselves as social engineers in the struggle for black progress rests on some combination of the following two premises. First, some argue that

Brown and its progeny render such tactics unnecessary in the modern world. At the opposite pole, other critics assert that law and lawyers are a poor medium through which to pursue social justice.

The first of these assertions is easily refuted. Even if one concedes that *Brown* and the series of judicial and legislative enactments that quickly followed this landmark decision provided blacks with all of the "law" that they need to fight discrimination,[34] these provisions are not self-executing. Blacks still must have access to lawyers who will press for their rights under the law. Despite the twelvefold increase in the number of black lawyers since 1960,[35] and the private and public efforts to serve black clients by the bar as a whole, blacks continue to have significantly less access to legal services on average than whites.[36] Standing alone, the existence of this racial gap underscores the continuing need for the kind of committed black lawyers Houston sought to develop.

Nevertheless, there is evidence that Houston and Marshall's long shadow may lead blacks to overemphasize litigation as a vehicle for achieving social change. The undeniable success of the carefully crafted campaign to overturn America's apartheid in the courts has created a strong presumption in favor of litigation-based strategies in the minds of many contemporary social reformers.[37] The courts, however, have frequently proved hostile to black interests.[38] Moreover, as Girardeau Spann argues—*Brown* and other legal victories notwithstanding—courts are unlikely to vindicate claims of racial injustice that substantially destabilize existing distributions of wealth and power.[39] Finally, even if the courts were considerably more open to claims by blacks than they now are, it is not at all clear that these institutions are in a very good position to address the complex and subtle institutional policies and practices that constitute the most important roadblocks to black economic, political, and social advancement.[40] By urging black lawyers to adopt Houston's moral philosophy, are we also pushing this new black legal elite to embrace a legal strategy that has already produced all of the gains that the courts are likely to yield—at least in our lifetimes?[41]

Despite its power, this objection assumes too narrow a role for black legal social engineers. Lawyers do more than simply litigate cases or otherwise work to create or enforce formal legal rules. Lawyers also assist their clients in structuring transactions, forming long-term goals, interpreting ambiguous public policies, lobbying legislative and administrative decision makers, and perform a host of other counseling functions that importantly affect the functioning of our economic, political and social order.[42] Because they represent the largest and most influential entities in our society, the manner in which corporate lawyers discharge these duties is likely to be especially important.[43] It is because of this potential influence that Judge Edwards argued more than two decades ago that, from the perspective of social justice, it was a mistake to discourage the new generation of elite black lawyers from going into corporate law practice.[44] A large percentage of black Americans continue to live in poverty, oppression, and despair.[45] Precisely because the struggle for racial justice in the 1990s and beyond will focus on achieving economic (as opposed to formal legal) parity, there is a pressing need for black social engineers who will carry the fight for black progress to the boardrooms and back rooms where important economic decisions are most likely to be made. In today's hyperlegal environment, lawyers—particularly corporate lawyers—are almost always present in these arenas.

It is at this point that critics of the continuing relevance of Houston's vision are likely to invoke the second pillar of their argument. Even if one believes that black corporate lawyers are in a position to promote the interests of the black community, there is little reason to suspect that they will actually do so. Two insights undergird this suspicion. First, lawyers (especially corporate lawyers) are inherently conservative. Studies of their attitudes and practices reveal that they rarely disagree with the objectives or tactics of their powerful clients.[46] And why should they? The income and status of the corporate bar is directly tied to how diligently these lawyers promote their clients' interests. Moreover, the skeptics conclude, even if they were somehow able to liberate themselves from their clients, corporate lawyers (and lawyers in general) would still be enmeshed in a discipline that preaches incrementalism and the creation of rights at the expense of broad-based political or economic action.[47]

Second, *black* corporate lawyers are likely to be in an even more vulnerable position than their white counterparts vis-à-vis corporate clients. Despite their small toehold in the ranks of the elite bar, blacks continue to be marginalized along virtually every dimension. Blacks are substantially more likely to be associates than partners, work in low visibility/low prestige areas of practice, and labor under the deadly combination of diminished expectations and increased scrutiny.[48] Given these circumstances, it is pointless to ask these few beleaguered black lawyers to use their supposed power to push their clients in a more progressive direction.

Both of these objections to the modern-day application of the obligation thesis are powerful. Nevertheless, if Houston had been deterred by similar concerns, we might not be gathered here today to celebrate his handiwork.

Houston was well aware of the claim that law and lawyers would never produce any real change in the status of black Americans. To quote Houston's skeptical colleague Ralph Bunche, many black intellectuals believed that a legal campaign designed to turn the "instruments of the state" in opposition to the "political and economic ideology of the dominant group" was doomed to failure.[49] No doubt, Houston would have been even more mindful of these dangers if his social engineers had been employed by organizations beholden to powerful clients whose interests were frequently at odds with the black community's demands for justice.[50]

History shows that Houston's critics were at least partially correct. As others have documented, *Brown* and its progeny have not resulted in the elimination of segregated schools.[51] Moreover, a good argument can be made that civil rights victories in the courts may have unintentionally sapped the energy of nascent social movements that might have produced even more wide ranging change.[52] Indeed, there is good reason to believe that even Thurgood

Marshall was blinded by the law's seductive power to declare "rights" that seemed to render other social action unnecessary or counterproductive. Thus, Marshall told his biographer Carl Rowan that blacks in Montgomery, Alabama, could have saved themselves all of the aggravation associated with their bus boycott if they had just waited for the Legal Defense Fund to have the transit company's discriminatory policies struck down in court.[53] As Randall Kennedy eloquently demonstrates, this assessment misses the essential point that the boycott's collective action and sacrifice galvanized the Montgomery black community, and the nation, in ways that could never have been achieved through the passive and abstract language of the law.[54]

From the contemporary vantage point, it is almost superfluous to note that these admitted shortcomings, either singly or in combination, do not come close to demonstrating that black America would be better off if Houston and Marshall had abandoned their legal crusade. At most, these qualifications help us to see that the civil rights movement was a necessary, but by no means sufficient, step on the road to full equality for black Americans. Although Houston's social engineers could not by themselves lift blacks out of poverty and degradation, they could and did reform the rules that made this fate appear neutral and just as opposed to the naked oppression that it was and continues to be.[55]

Moreover, as Robert Cover persuasively argued more than a decade ago, judicial intervention to undo the structure of American apartheid was not ultimately inconsistent with the development of meaningful black political activity.[56] Indeed, Houston and Marshall's early efforts were expressly designed to nurture just such a connection. Houston was acutely aware of the need to build a political base of support for his legal crusade against *Plessy*. He therefore urged that cases be filed in small communities, preferably in state courts.[57] Meetings were held at local churches and social halls to explain the goals of the litigation and to report on its progress. Black residents were encouraged to attend court hearings. Although these measures certainly did not guarantee meaningful participation by black citizens,[58] they nevertheless allowed the Legal Defense Fund to pursue its legal strategy while at the same time contributing to the creation of a new brand of black politics.[59]

A similar line of argument underlies the claim that an updated version of Houston's obligation thesis for today's black corporate lawyers would produce some (though only some) improvement in the status of black Americans. Notwithstanding their close ties to their clients, elite corporate lawyers have on occasion used their considerable influence to press social reforms that were not (or at least not obviously) in their clients' best interests.[60] Although many of the factors that allowed them to exert this kind of influence in the past are on the decline,[61] it would be a mistake to conclude that these lawyers no longer play an important role in shaping their clients' interests, objectives, or strategy.[62]

To be sure, the reforms proposed by corporate lawyers have rarely been revolutionary. At best, these proposals generally take the form of "creative" win-win solutions to apparently intractable disputes or technical legal reforms designed to rationalize existing institutions. A good argument can also be made that many of these "reforms" effectively derailed political movements that might have produced more radically egalitarian results.[63] Nevertheless, ordinary citizens have received real benefits from these counseling and law reform projects.[64] Like the NAACP's legal victories, the progressive actions of corporate lawyers, both inside and outside the arena of client representation, can contribute to an overall strategy for achieving racial justice.

This is particularly true in light of the fact that black corporate lawyers, notwithstanding their privileged status as members of the emerging black middle class, are probably more likely than their white counterparts to be suspicious of their corporate clients' views about the appropriate distribution of wealth and power in American society. Beginning with William Julius Wilson's pioneering work, social scientists have marshaled an impressive array of data calling attention to the growing class divisions within the black community.[65] Given their income, status, and educational credentials, black corporate lawyers stand at or near the top of this class structure. Nevertheless, as Michael Dawson has recently demonstrated, the range of opinion on many important issues within the black community is much more narrow than traditional theories about the effect of class structure on political participation would predict.[66] Dawson argues that there are several reasons for this phenomenon, including the widespread economic dependence of all blacks on an activist government, the black middle class's tenuous grip on its newly acquired elite status, the link between group progress and individual progress, and the tendency of institutions and familial support structures within the black community to emphasize a strong racialist orientation. Collectively, these factors reinforce what Dawson calls a "black utility heuristic" in which individual blacks evaluate policies, parties, and practices in terms of their effect on the well-being of the black community as a whole.

The experience of blacks in corporate law practice gives us good reasons to suspect that Dawson's black utility heuristic will lead them to be, on average, more skeptical of existing hierarchies than whites, and therefore, more likely to see the need for reform projects that curb corporate power. Notwithstanding the fact that, unlike members of the traditional black middle class, the incomes of black corporate lawyers are not directly tied to the black community, the fate of these professionals is still closely linked to the kind of government policies that have traditionally enjoyed broad support among blacks. For example, black lawyers have been most successful in those areas of corporate practice where the federal government is either a client or (through federal regulation, including affirmative action guidelines) exerts a strong influence over the purchasing decisions of private parties.[67] Similarly, black corporate lawyers prospered when Harold Washington was elected mayor of Chicago, just as their fortunes waned after his death and replacement by a white.[68] Moreover, black corporate lawyers suffer from the same forms of group stereotyping and statistical discrimination that Dawson persuasively demonstrates gives middle-class blacks a stake in improving the mean achievement levels of poor blacks.[69]

None of this means that black corporate lawyers will *inevitably* see it in their interest to work toward improving the status of the black community as a whole. To the contrary, Dawson's research suggests that as the economic, institutional, and familial ties that presently link the individual and group interests of most blacks begin to fray, we should expect to see members of the black elite begin to hold views that are more similar to those of their white peers. But this caveat only restates the need for something like the obligation thesis. By instructing black corporate lawyers to pay attention to the ways in which their clients' actions affect the black community, this modern incarnation of Houston's vision attempts to provide additional reinforcement against the natural tendency on the part of all corporate lawyers to gradually adopt their clients' world view. The fact that this tendency is likely to become more pronounced as black lawyers become more entrenched in the corporate sector only underscores the need for a return to Houston's understanding.[70]

Finally, it is not fair to conclude that the admittedly marginal position of most black corporate lawyers prevents them from exerting any meaningful influence over their clients or their firms. Once again, Houston's example is instructive. Certainly, the current crop of black corporate lawyers are no more marginal than Houston's original band of black social engineers. The idea that this ragtag group of black lawyers could bring down an overtly racist system that had stood in one form or fashion for more than two hundred years must have sounded as far-fetched to Houston's contemporaries as the claim that today's black corporate lawyers might precipitate an important redirection in corporate power.[71] And yet, as we stand here today, it is clear that these lawyers, at great personal risk, were able to change at least some important aspects of the existing legal and social order.

Given this background, the prospects for success by this new generation of elite black lawyers seems less daunting. To be sure, the new target—let us call it American capital—is arguably even better financed and more entrenched than the Jim Crow south of a generation ago. But if the enemy is better prepared, so are the social engineers. With the exception of Houston and Hastie,[72] virtually the entire new black legal elite is better educated than its 1930s counterpart. Some of these lawyers have already achieved positions of power and influence in the corporate world.[73] Notwithstanding the fact that these positions do not always confer the same authority on blacks as they do on whites,[74] those who occupy these roles have access to the kind of money, information, and clout that opens doors and influences opinions.

Even black associates have some limited power to shape decisions that affect the fight for racial justice. Typically, associates sit on hiring committees, evaluate (or perhaps even hire) support staff, and comment on firm policies. These lawyers often are quite knowledgeable about the facts surrounding a particular controversy or client practice, and are given the responsibility for reporting those facts up the chain of command. Associates also generally have some flexibility to choose the projects they work on, and more generally, the types of firms in which they will work.

Without question, exercising any or all of these options carries a certain amount of risk. Although one is tempted to say that these risks could never equal those faced by Marshall and his peers, the fact that these dangers are rarely life-threatening does not mean that they should be dismissed as unimportant. By the same token, one should not automatically assume that any attempt to shift the balance of corporate power toward more socially desirable goals will automatically end one's career. Paradoxically, by virtue of their scarcity and visibility, black lawyers may have somewhat greater space than other lawyers to press their particular version of social justice through law. Even if they do not, however, the multiple and overlapping centers of power that exist within any given corporate law environment provide avenues for skillful social engineers to search for powerful institutional allies who can offer protection from what might otherwise be the retaliatory responses of colleagues or clients.[75]

To be sure, even when taken as a whole, these measures seem unlikely to place today's black corporate lawyers in the kind of leadership roles occupied by Houston's social engineers. This, however, may not be an altogether negative development. Although some veterans of the civil rights movement continue to long for a new generation of legal leaders,[76] the "lawyer-as-crusader . . . prototype of lone heroism and lawyer-centered decisionmaking" is increasingly criticized by many scholars and activists interested in using law as a tool for improving the status of subordinated groups.[77] By working to reform institutions from the inside out, forming contingent and context specific alliances with others interested in social justice, and pushing for a diverse array of localized, incremental solutions to concrete problems, this new generation of social engineers might avoid some of the problems of rigidity and domination that plagued the undeniably heroic efforts of their predecessors.

In the last analysis, however, the merits of this kind of strategy depend on the actions that a given black lawyer intends to take to further the goals of the obligation thesis. It is at this point that critics of obligation theory raise their final objection.

III. The Critique of Judgment

Notwithstanding the barriers described above, many black corporate lawyers subscribe to some version of the obligation thesis—at least in theory. Whether one looks at statements by black law students,[78] the substantial contributions made by black corporate lawyers to civil rights related pro bono and law reform activity,[79] or the plethora of programs pushed by black lawyers to open up opportunities for blacks in the corporate sector,[80] one is inescapably led to the conclusion that a substantial percentage of this new generation of elite black lawyers is committed to using their position in the corporate mainstream to press for some version of social justice.

This conclusion is hardly surprising.[81] Houston and Marshall continue to cast a long shadow over the black bar. At the most basic level, today's practitioners know that were it not for the efforts of these pioneers, there would be no black corporate lawyers. Moreover, because Houston and Marshall indelibly stamped the civil rights movement as a *legal* campaign, many blacks went to law school in order to pursue the promise of social justice through law.[82] Unlike Marshall's experience at Howard, many of the express and implicit messages these lawyers receive in law school work to undermine this commitment.[83] Nevertheless, there are enough countervailing messages, both inside and outside the legal profession, to insure that the idea that black lawyers ought to be social engineers for justice remains a prominent part of the culture of the black bar.

The question remains, however, whether the actions black corporate lawyers have taken in the name of this ideal honor its purposes.[84] At best, a black corporate lawyer's contribution to the cause of racial justice will be both partial and indirect. Unlike Houston's original social engineers, these lawyers are not engaged in the full-time struggle for black rights. Indeed, one might reasonably argue that corporate law practice will inevitably place black lawyers in situations where the interests of their powerful clients will conflict—sometimes quite directly—with the black community's efforts to achieve substantive equality.[85] Moreover, even a cursory examination of the list of programs undertaken by black lawyers in this area reveals the danger that the obligation thesis can be used as an attractive cover for self-interest. To the extent that corporate lawyers act in ways that simply promote their own interests, or the interests of the tiny number of blacks who will ever have the opportunity to become corporate lawyers, is it really fair for them to assert that they are following in Houston and Marshall's footsteps?

In order to answer these troubling questions, we must first confront the skeptic's charge that judgments of this kind are either impossible or unwise. According to this line of argument, there are no acceptable criteria for determining what actions are likely to further the cause of racial justice. The 25 million blacks in the United States have a multiplicity of "interests," many of which conflict with the "interests" of other blacks. In addition, the argument goes, there is no standard by which to choose which of these conflicting goals are entitled to priority. Indeed, skeptics often assert that even if we could select among these diverse goals, there would still be no reliable way to determine whether any particular action is likely to promote or retard our preferred ends. In the face of this uncertainty, the argument concludes, any effort to evaluate the actions of black corporate lawyers (or any other black person) will inevitably degenerate into an enforced political orthodoxy or the tyranny of the black elite.

Once again, Houston's example highlights both the partial wisdom and the ultimate fallacy of this position. At first blush, it might appear that Houston did not face the problems of definition and strategy that give rise to this last critique. After all, Jim Crow laws burdened every black American from the least advantaged to the most powerful. It was obviously in the "interest" of every black citizen to remove these unjustified barriers. This truth about America in the 1930s, however, understates the problems Houston faced. Although all blacks suffered under the yoke of Jim Crow oppression, they did not all suffer in the same way and to the same extent. Whatever strategy Houston employed to combat legal segregation would necessarily entail making choices about which kinds of suffering would be addressed and how. By examining the manner in which Houston pursued his campaign to dismantle *Plessy*, we can see how these differential benefits and burdens were distributed. The long-term consequences of this distribution are still being felt today.

Houston's strategy was expressly elitist. Like Du Bois, he believed that there needed to be a "talented tenth" capable of leading the "masses" of blacks out of the darkness of American apartheid.[86] To create this elite cadre, Houston was willing to sacrifice the interests of certain ordinary blacks. Thus, as I have noted above, Houston closed Howard's night division, raised admissions standards, and replaced virtually the entire law school faculty.[87] As a consequence, many blacks both inside and outside the university branded Houston as an elitist who was insensitive to the plight of the significant number of blacks who could no longer attend Howard.[88]

Moreover, the legal strategy that Houston proposed was itself elitist, or at least less designed to provide immediate relief to poor blacks than others that might have been pursued. As Ralph Bunche and his supporters argued, a campaign to link black and white workers in a common struggle to shake the stranglehold of American capital was arguably better designed to provide tangible benefits to blacks at the lower end of the economic spectrum than an attack on legal segregation in public education.[89] Moreover, assuming that education was the proper target, one would be hard pressed to argue that discrimination in *graduate* schools (not to mention *law* schools) was or should have been at the top of most black people's list of problems in the educational system. Yet, it was almost fifteen years before Houston and Marshall challenged the separate-but-equal doctrine in the context of primary or secondary schools. Indeed, in an argument that prefigures one of the sharpest disputes of our own time, some black leaders considered Houston's entire desegregation campaign misguided on the ground that blacks would be better off concentrating their efforts on improving their own educational institutions.[90]

In the eyes of many contemporary critics, these elitist overtones of Houston's strategy ultimately resulted in a movement that benefited the black middle class to the exclusion, and some might contend even at the expense, of poor blacks.[91] According to this line of argument, the removal of de jure barriers in education, housing, and employment allowed a small number of blacks to flee the poverty and limited horizons of the inner city and rural areas where blacks had traditionally been confined. While those who were able to make this transition prospered, the rest of the black community sunk even deeper into poverty, isolation, and despair.[92] Once thriving black institutions and neighborhoods were destroyed as black purchasing power was disbursed throughout the mainstream economy while whites continued to refuse to patronize black businesses or live in black neighborhoods. Worse yet, the visible success of some blacks in post-*Brown* American society is often used as an indication that the race problem has been solved and that those black who continue to suffer in poverty are responsible for their own predicament.[93] The net result, these critics conclude, is a world in which black America is divided into two camps: a small number of middle-class blacks, who with each new generation are able to participate more fully in the fruits of American society, and the vast majority of poor blacks locked in a downward spiral caused by joblessness, poor housing, hopelessly inadequate (though formally "desegregated") schools, drug addiction, and crime.[94]

Moreover, one can also make the case that Houston's strategic choices also contributed to a certain ideological intransigence among his Legal Defense Fund successors. For example, Derrick Bell, who started his career at the Legal Defense Fund, has argued that his former employer's ideological commitment to integration prevented the organization from taking seriously the views of black residents in Atlanta and Detroit who believed that greater local control and increased funding for inner city schools would be a more effective remedy than forced busing in the post-*Brown* era.[95] Bell locates the roots of this problem in the manner in which the NAACP recruits potential plaintiffs and makes all major litigation decisions in its central office. As Justice Harlan argued in his 1963 dissent in NAACP *v. Button*,[96] which Bell cites with approval, these policies have been an integral part of the NAACP's legal strategy since the 1930s. Indeed, one can see Justice Marshall's well-documented antipathy to the tactics used by the Student Nonviolent Coordinating Committee (SNCC) and Martin Luther King as a poignant example of the danger of being too wedded to a particular view about how to achieve social justice.[97]

Nevertheless, each of these criticisms is overblown. Notwithstanding the problems with the "lawyer-as-crusader" image discussed above, lawyers who refuse to push their clients toward socially constructive political ends may do as much harm as those who seek to dominate the struggles in which they are engaged.[98] Similarly, it is hard to imagine a successful political campaign without advocacy organizations that forcefully pursue their vision of social justice even in the face of internal dissent.[99] Finally, Dawson's research suggests that class divisions within the black community are not nearly as deep or as thoroughgoing as the critics of the civil rights movement sometimes seem to suggest.

Moreover, even if one accepts some version of all of these criticisms, one would still be hard pressed to deny that Houston's successful campaign against legal segregation in public education was in the "best interest" of the black community.[100] The grounds that support this conclusion provide important clues about how we might reach similar evaluative judgments about the programs proposed by today's elite black lawyers.

Three features of Houston's strategy support the conclusion that his efforts were in the interests of the black community *as a whole*, notwithstanding the fact that some blacks benefited disproportionately and that others disagreed with either his tactics or his goals. First, although Houston's policies were elitist, they were connected to an overall strategy that was both intended to, and plausibly would, benefit non-elite blacks. As I argued above, Houston was undoubtedly correct when he concluded that only a specially trained group of elite black lawyers would have the capability and the resolve to successfully dismantle legal segregation. Although his decision to close Howard's night division shut off opportunities for some aspiring black lawyers, his victories in *Murray* and *Gaines* quickly opened up others. Similarly, although most blacks will never attend graduate school, initially targeting these elite institutions was a plausible method for improving the educational opportunities available to all black children.[101] The fact that today, some inner-city schools are as segregated, and virtually as inferior,[102] as those that existed in the pre-*Brown* era can hardly be taken as an indictment of this premise.

Second, Houston was self-conscious, open, and adaptive about the choices he made. From the outset, Houston recognized that he would inevitably be called upon to make difficult decisions that would effectively favor the interests of some blacks over others. He made these decisions in a manner that protected as much as possible the legitimate competing interests on both sides. For example, Houston and Marshall couched all of their early attacks on *Plessy* in the alternative, requesting either "equal" or "desegregated" educational opportunities for blacks. Some have criticized this approach as timid and short sighted.[103] Other scholars have responded by pointing out that arguing "within" *Plessy*'s structure was prudent advocacy under the circumstances.[104] Although this response undoubtedly is correct, it misses the point that giving courts the option to strengthen black schools also helped to mitigate the adverse distributional effects of the NAACP's campaign on low- and moderate-income blacks who would not be able to attend white universities even if they were given the chance.[105] The historically black law school associated with the University of Texas, which now appropriately bears Thurgood Marshall's name, as well as several other existing black institutions, were established as a direct result of this strategy.[106]

Houston also spoke out on a wide range of issues affecting the interests of blacks. As indicated above, both he and Marshall traveled extensively to black communities throughout the country to both observe firsthand the conditions under which black people lived and to explain their strategy and their goals to those whose fate they sought to improve. In addition, both men spoke out on a wide range of topics going beyond their campaign to end discrimination in public education, including antilynching legislation, voting rights, and the rights of criminal defendants. Even in circumstances where they could not act directly, neither man missed an opportunity to educate the powerful people he encountered about the dismal conditions under which most blacks lived and to remind white Americans of their obligation to do something to remedy these conditions.[107]

Third, Houston and Marshall's legal strategy did not preclude other blacks from pressing their own competing views about how to achieve racial justice. To be sure, both men believed passionately in their own approach and worked tirelessly to persuade others of its merits. Moreover, as the controversy over busing in Atlanta and Detroit demonstrates, those who did not agree with the NAACP's strategy often had a difficult time making their voices heard. Nevertheless, the legal campaign for social justice did not cut off political

activity within the black community. To the contrary, the NAACP's successful dismantling of de jure segregation, along with its legal victories in the areas
of free speech and associational rights,[108] paved the way for the subsequent
protest movements by Martin Luther King—as well as by organizations such
as SNCC and the Black Panthers who were openly critical of the NAACP's
legal strategy.[109]

Collectively, these three characteristics provide a sound basis for concluding that the legal campaign to end the separate-but-equal doctrine was, despite
its controversial premises and admitted limitations, in the "best interest" of the
black community. When we examine the new black legal elite's claims against
these criteria, it is apparent that some, but by no means all, of their efforts to
implement the obligation thesis can be similarly justified.

Black corporate lawyers have sought to participate in the struggle for racial
justice in one or more of the following three ways: pro bono or law reform
activity directed at improving the status of blacks; efforts to influence the views
or policies of corporate clients; and programs designed to increase the size or
the profitability of the black corporate bar. The first of these actions is the most
closely connected to Houston's legacy and is therefore the easiest to justify.
When black corporate lawyers are loaned out to neighborhood legal services
offices,[110] work on pro bono insitutional reform litigation challenging discrimination and overcrowding in prisons,[111] or financially contribute (or get
their firms to contribute) to civil rights organizations,[112] they press the power
and prestige of their employers into the service of social justice. Of course, the
goals of these pro bono or law reform efforts may be controversial.[113] Nevertheless, so long as these efforts are plausibly connected to a reasonable theory
for alleviating the unjustified suffering of a substantial number of blacks without unduly restricting opportunities for others who are less well off, and are
reflectively undertaken in a manner that does not stifle the expression of
dissenting views, they easily fit within the model for social action endorsed by
Houston and Marshall.[114]

The second strategy also fits comfortably within a Houstonian model. As I
argued above, injecting, in Judge Edwards's words, "the black perspective"
into the corridors of corporate decision making could produce important gains
for the black community. This is clearly true if black lawyers are able to
dissuade corporations from taking actions that unnecessarily harm black communities or interests, such as locating a hazardous waste facility in a black
neighborhood or perpetuating employment practices that disproportionately
burden black employees.[115] Houston and Marshall's consistent efforts to speak
out on issues of concern to the black community, however, should also
remind us of the important role played by those who witness and report on
injustice.[116] Even in circumstances where they cannot affect the outcome of
corporate decision making, black corporate lawyers can still serve the interests
of justice by making their clients aware of how their actions are likely to affect
blacks or by revealing their clients' wrongs to others.

Fulfilling this role will undoubtedly be difficult in many settings. Corporate clients will often not wish to be reminded of the consequences of their

actions. Moreover, reporting on issues relating to client representation impli-
cates important confidentiality concerns, not to mention pragmatic fears of
retribution. Nevertheless, the profession's own codes of conduct recognize
that lawyers should give their clients moral as well as legal advice,[117] and there
is a long tradition of lawyers speaking out (albeit in veiled ways) about abuses
practiced by their clients.[118] At a minimum, these traditions suggest that the
efforts by some black corporate lawyers to deny the tension between their
clients' goals and the interests of the black community not only undermine the
obligation thesis, but are antithetical to the kind of reflective judgment that
must support any effort to pursue social justice in the real world.[119]

The final strategy—increasing the size and strength of the black corporate
bar—is both the most common and the most complex in Houstonian terms.
Since the first blacks started arriving at corporate law firms in the 1970s, black
lawyers have worked tirelessly to increase black recruitment and retention, not
only in their own firms, but throughout the corporate sector. Recently, these
efforts have been formalized in a series of goals and timetables established by
leading corporate law firms in New York, San Francisco, Washington, D.C.,
and Chicago, committing these firms to hire and promote a certain number of
minority lawyers by a specified date.[120] In addition, black lawyers both in law
firms and in corporate general counsels' offices, have long struggled to develop
a network of referral relationships whereby black lawyers would gain access to
corporate business. These efforts culminated in the American Bar Association's Minority Counsel Demonstration Program.[121] This program, which
was the brainchild of a small group of black lawyers, encourages major corporations to give some of their work to minority lawyers.[122] Several local and
state bar associations have instituted similar programs.

All of these programs are unabashedly elitist, in the sense that they are
designed to create opportunities for the small number of blacks who either are,
or might conceivably become, corporate lawyers. Houston's example demonstrates, however, that this fact is not necessarily fatal if it can be shown that
improving opportunities for this group of elite practitioners is linked to a more
general program for achieving racial justice. As I argued above, the fact that in
the absence of these efforts, blacks would continue to be even more excluded
from this sector of the bar than they are today provides a powerful justification
for those programs designed to break the many glass ceilings that retard black
progress. Integrating the corporate sector—and ensuring that black lawyers are
not unfairly deprived of their fair share of corporate business—is therefore a
part of an overall campaign to ensure black equality.[123] Moreover, to the
extent that those black lawyers who are assisted by these efforts use their
positions of influence to press their clients on issues of concern to the black
community as a whole, these programs reinforce the benefits discussed above
of having a black presence in corporate America.

These truths, however, do not imply that everything that might promote
the parochial interests of the black corporate bar is justified by the obligation
thesis. To the extent that creating opportunities for black corporate lawyers
will, all things considered, worsen the situation of blacks who are less well off,

the Houstonian analogy begins to break down. Unfortunately, there is some evidence that this may be true in some settings.

Consider, for example, the Minority Counsel Demonstration Program. This program was initially designed to give small minority law firms access to lucrative corporate work. Studies had repeatedly shown that lawyers in these firms made substantially less money than their white counterparts in firms of similar size primarily because they received very little work from white businesses or individuals. By urging corporations to spin off some of their work to those lawyers, the program hoped to erase this disparity. Shortly after the program got under way, however, black partners in large corporate law firms asked to be included. These lawyers made the plausible claim that they too needed to gain access to new corporate business if they were going to survive in the increasingly competitive world of the large law firm. [124] The problem with this assertion, however, is that *relative to the programs initial beneficiaries*, the needs of blacks partners in large law firms are somewhat less compelling. Indeed, as the blacks in small firms forcefully argued, to the extent that corporate work goes to black partners in major law firms, it will simply follow the same channels—and end up primarily in the same hands—that it did before.

On a more general level, one can argue that increasing the number of talented lawyers of all races that work for large corporations only serves to entrench the existing maldistribution of legal resources in this country. Corporations already have a near monopoly on elite legal talent.[125] Moreover, one of the reasons that corporations have been willing to increase their use of black lawyers is because they see the potential for exploiting racial sympathies to promote their cause. Thus, it is not a coincidence that the Minority Counsel Demonstration Program's efforts to increase corporate hiring of black lawyers has been most successful with insurance companies who have significantly increased their use of black lawyers to defend product liability cases before inner city juries. Given all of these factors, if programs like this were to become the primary focus of the black corporate bar's social justice activity, one might very well conclude that the benefits discussed above were outweighed by the costs.

Of course, it may be that these conflicts between promoting the interests of black corporate lawyers and a general campaign for social justice are more apparent than real. Black partners in major firms may be competing for different work than the kind that would be given to black lawyers in small firms.[126] Similarly, the black lawyers who litigate product liability cases may conduct themselves in a way that reduces or eliminates the unjustified racial advantage that their new clients may seek to obtain. In addition, there may be other considerations, including professional duties and personal commitments, that may bear on our all things considered judgement about these and other similar programs promoting the interests of black corporate lawyers.[127] Nevertheless, to the extent that the obligation thesis is invoked to justify these programs, this claim must be supported, as was Houston's, by a plausible connection between the particular method for advancing the interests of the elite black bar and the general struggle for racial equality.

IV. Conclusion: Toward a Living Legacy

Collections of essays such as this volume underscore the extent to which Marshall (and, unfortunately to a lesser degree, Houston) continue to dominate the conscience of the American legal profession. The splendid story of how this small group of lawyers dismantled one of the most glaring atrocities in our collective history stands as an enduring monument to our best aspirations for law. Unfortunately, by highlighting the magnitude of these accomplishments, we also tend to relegate their significance to the past.

In many important respects, this tendency is correct. The legal campaign against de jure segregation took place during an era quite different from our own. The enemy, after all, was ever present and unambiguous. Moreover, by the time *Brown* was decided, America was in the grip of postwar optimism, intent on protecting its image as leader of the free world. And, perhaps most important, people still believed (whether naively or not) that it was possible to talk comprehensibly and impartially about morality and justice, and believed that social institutions such as courts should and could act according to the dictates that these truths required.

Just because we live in a very different world, however, does not mean that there is nothing about Houston and Marshall's marvelous crusade that we can seek to emulate. In this essay, I have tried to demonstrate that by carefully examining their decisions and goals, we can gain a better understanding about what it might mean to be a social engineer for justice in our own time. I do not mean to suggest that anything like Houston's campaign would be plausible, or perhaps even desirable, in the context of our present situation. I do contend, however, that the basic principles that motivated his efforts—particularly, his passionate commitment to use his position and skill to fight the unjustified oppression of black Americans—are still very much needed today.

Of course, even if every black corporate lawyer (or every black lawyer) were to wholeheartedly embrace the obligation thesis, there would be no guarantee that this ideological commitment would be translated into actions that would actually benefit the black community. The actions that any particular black corporate lawyer is likely to take in a given circumstance will undoubtedly be shaped by a variety of incentives, structures, and constraints that transcend his or her normative ideals. As Dawson points out in a related context, without the reinforcement of supporting institutions and ties, the obligation thesis might become nothing more than the lip service that the vice of class interest pays to the virtue of solidarity.[128]

Nevertheless, ideals are important in their own right. It is through the lens of their normative commitments that today's black corporate lawyers will judge the legitimacy of the institutional policies and practices utilized by their powerful clients. Although the legal profession's history is littered with examples where noble ideals have been consciously or unconsciously sacrificed on the altar of self-interest, there are also important counterexamples where ideals have had a positive and transforming effect on practice.[129] Certainly, the opposite is likely to be true: a world in which race-based normative obligations are condemned is likely to provide few brakes on the otherwise natural tendency for middle-class blacks to exploit their individual success at the expense of the group.

Not surprisingly, the best exposition of my position comes from Thurgood Marshall. In 1987, Marshall refused to allow America to celebrate the two-hundredth anniversary of the Consitution without expressly acknowledging the more pernicious aspects of that document's formation and history.[130] Nevertheless, Marshall made it clear that he intended to celebrate the consitution, not as a dead monument to some past greatness, but "as a *living document*, including the Bill of Rights and the other amendments protecting individual freedoms and human rights."[131] We should take this same attitude, I submit, to Houston and Marshall's legacy. Today's black corporate lawyers are quite literally the living progeny of Houston and Marshall's genius. We should honor these men not by treating them as relics of their past greatness, but as living examples of what we might accomplish in our own time.

Notes

I am grateful to Susan Koniak for invaluable comments on an earlier draft of this essay. Erin Edmonds provided valuable editorial assistance.

1. See Jack Greenberg, *Crusaders in the Courts: How a Dedicated Band of Lawyers Fought for the Civil Rights Revolution* (New York: Basic Books, 1994); Gena Rae McNeil, *Groundwork: Charles Hamilton Houston and the Struggle for Civil Rights* (Philadelphia: University of Pennsylvania Press, 1983).

2. Richard Kluger, *Simple Justice: The History of* Brown v. *Board of Education and Black America's Struggle for Equality* (New York: Vintage Books, 1975), 126–31. Kluger reports that prior to Houston's deanship, Howard was known among black intellectuals as "Dummies' Retreat." Id. at 123.

3. See Murray v. Maryland, 182 A.2d 590 (1936), *aff'd* 169 Md. 478 (1937) (challenging segregation at the University of Maryland Law School); Missouri *Ex rel.* Gaines v. Canada, 305 U.S. 337 (1938) (challenging segregation at the University of Missouri Law School); Sweat v. Painter, 339 U.S. 629 (1950) (challenging segregation at the University of Texas Law School). *Murray* was particularly significant for Marshall, who, in 1930 had reluctantly decided not to apply to his home state's law school because of that institution's longstanding all-white admissions policy. See Michael D. Davis and Hunter R. Clark, *Thurgood Marshall: Warrior at the Bar, Rebel on the Bench* (New York: Carol Publishing Group, 1992). On his retirement from the bench, Marshall stated that Houston's and his victory in *Murray* was sweet revenge. I am indebted to J. Clay Smith for correcting my initial impression, reported by Davis & Clark (id.) among others, that Marshall actually applied to Maryland Law School.

4. Indeed, as Paul Finkelman notes in his excellent review of J. Clay Smith's *Emancipation*, even those black lawyers who did not go into full time civil rights work during this period were, in an important respect, social engineers who "ushered in many types of social change simply by doing their jobs well." Paul Finkelman, "Not Only the Judge's Robes Were Black: African-American Lawyers as

Social Engineers," 47 *Stanford Law Review* (1994), 161, 180. Black lawyers in the pre-*Brown* period contributed to social justice by, among other things, providing legal services to black clients who would otherwise have gone unrepresented, challenging racist stereotypes about black intellectual inferiority, and assuming leadership roles within the black community.

5. See Mark Tushnet, *The NAACP's Legal Strategy Against Segregated Education, 1925–1950* (Chapel Hill: University of North Carolina Press, 1987), 144–45 (crediting the NAACP's campaign in *Brown* as the forerunner of modern public interest practice).

6. See Randall Kennedy, "A Reply to Philip Elman," 100 *Harvard Law Review* (1987), 1938. Among the black lawyers involved in the fight against segregation, William Hastie, Jr., Spottswood W. Robinson, III, Constance Baker Motely, Robert Carter, and of course Marshall himself all became federal judges. James Nabrith (president, Howard University) and Derrick Bell (professor, Harvard and N.Y.U. Law Schools), both went on to distinguished careers in academics. William Coleman, who served as secretary of transportation in the Ford administration, is now the managing partner of the Washington, D.C., office of O'Melveny and Meyers. For an exhaustive list of the subsequent accomplishments of the Legal Defense Fund's alumni, see Greenberg, supra note 1, appendix.

7. See Reynolds Farley, *Blacks and Whites: Narrowing the Gap?* (Cambridge, Mass.: Harvard University Press, 1984), 198–99.

8. It is important not to exaggerate this trend. To my knowledge, there is no accurate count of the number of black lawyers presently in corporate law practice. Surveys indicate that blacks constitute less than 2 percent of the lawyers employed in the nation's 250 largest law firms, and, more importantly, only 1 percent of the partners in these institutions. See Claudia Maclachlan & Rita Henley Jensen, "Progress Glacial for Women, Minorities," *National Law Journal* January 27, 1992, at 1. This would put the total number at roughly 600. See Marc Galanter & Thomas Palay, *Tournament of Lawyers: The Transformation of the Big Law Firm* (Chicago: University of Chicago Press, 1991) (reporting that the total number of lawyers in large corporate firms is approximately 30,000). There are undoubtedly more blacks in the next tier of corporate firms. See Richard L. Abel, *American Lawyers* (New York: Oxford University Press, 1989), 106 (reporting that in 1980, the percentage of blacks in private firms of between 25–90 lawyers was slightly lower than at the largest firms). But see Lewis A. Kornhauser & Richard L. Revesz, "Legal Education and Entry into the Legal Profession: The Role of Race, Gender, and Educational Debt," 70 *New York University Law Review* (1995), 70 (reporting that blacks are most underrepresented in small private firms). Even less is known about the number of blacks employed by corporate legal departments. Given this sector's growth during the 1980s and the natural tendency for lawyers from large firms to migrate into corporate legal departments, it is plausible that there are at least as many black lawyers in general counsel's offices as there are in private firms. See Robert I. Townsend, "Chairman's Message: The Economics of Inclusion," ACCA Docket, Summer 1992, 2 (urging corporate general counsel to hire more minority lawyers); Galanter & Palay, supra (documenting the growth of corporate legal departments in the 1980s). As I discuss below, there are also a small but growing number of black (or minority-owned) firms specializing in corporate practice. Finally, for every black lawyer currently in corporate law practice, there are at least as many who have spent some time in this area before transferring to another sector of professional practice. See Fred Bates & Gregory Whitehead, "Do Something Dif-

ferent: Making a Commitment to Minority Lawyers," ABA *Journal* (Oct. 1990), 78, 82 (reporting the "extraordinary high turnover rates for minorities in large firms"). For a general discussion about the weakness of the data surrounding black participation in the corporate sector, see David B. Wilkins & G. Mitu Gulati, "Why Are There So Few Black Lawyers in Corporate Law Firms? An Institutional Analysis," 84 *California Law Review* (forthcoming 1996).

9. See Robert Granfield, *Making Elite Lawyers: Visions of Law at Harvard Law and Beyond* (New York: Routledge, 1992) (noting that the term "corporate tool" is used by Harvard law students who are planning to go into public interest practice to describe their classmates who will join corporate law firms).

10. See David B. Wilkins, "Race, Ethics, and the First Amendment: Should a Black Lawyer Represent the Ku Klux Klan?" 63 *George Washington Law Review* (1995), 1030; Wilkins, "Two Paths to the Mountaintop? The Role of Legal Education in Shaping the Values of Black Corporate Lawyers," 45 *Stanford Law Review* (1993), 1981; Wilkins & Gulati, supra note 8.

11. For a preliminary defense of this surprisingly difficult to defend proposition, see Wilkins, "Two Paths to the Mountaintop," supra note 10.

12. See generally Stephen L. Carter, *Reflections of an Affirmative Action Baby*; (New York: Basic Books, 1991); Randall Kennedy, "Racial Critiques of Legal Academia," 102 *Harvard Law Review* (1989), 1745; Shelby Steele, *The Content of Our Character* (New York: HarperPerennial, 1990).

13. See generally Derrick A. Bell, "Remembrance of Racism Past: Getting Beyond the Civil Rights Decline," in *Race in America: The Struggle for Equality*, Herbert Hill & James E. Jones eds. (Madison: University of Wisconsin Press, 1993); Derrick A. Bell, "An Expository Exploration for a Thurgood Marshall Biography," 6 *Blackletter Law Journal* (1989), 51.

14. See Stephen L. Carter, "The Black Table, the Empty Seat, and the Tie" in *Lure and Loathing: Essays on Race, Identity, and the Ambivalence of Assimilation*, Gerald Early ed. (New York: Penguin Press, 1993), 55.

15. See Kenneth S. Tollett, "Black Lawyers, Their Education, and the Black Community," 17 *Howard Law Journal* (1972), 326, 333 (reporting that there were 1,175 black lawyers in 1930); J. Clay Smith, Jr., *Emancipation: The Making of the Black Lawyer 1844–1944* (Philadelphia: University of Pennsylvania Press, 1993) (reporting a similar figure and that the number of black lawyers had only increased to 1,450 in 1950 and 2,200 in 1960).

16. See Ernest Gelhorn, "The Law Schools and the Negro," 1968 *Duke Law Journal* 1069; Louis Toepfer, "Harvard's Special Summer Program," 18 *Journal of Legal Education* (1966), 443.

17. Earl T. Carl & Kenneth R. Callahan, "Negroes and the Law," 17 *Journal of Legal Education* (1965), 250, 251.

18. See, e.g. Toepfer, supra note 16, at 443 (justifying "special efforts," such as Harvard's 1965 summer program, to attract Negro students to law school on the ground that the need to provide "equal rights and opportunities for Negro citizens . . . can best be met by a Bar which includes Negro lawyers in significant numbers, for it is those lawyers who most clearly understand the problems and difficulties faced by members of the Negro community."); Charles A. Pinderhughes, "Increasing Minority Group Students in Law Schools: The Rationale and the Critical Issues," 20 *Buffalo Law Review* (1970), 447, 453 (urging law schools to institute programs that make it more likely that the black students who are admitted will provide legal services to disadvantaged blacks).

19. *See* Derrick A. Bell, "In Defense of Minority Admissions Programs: A Response to Professor Graglia," 119 *University of Pennsylvania Law Review* (1970), 364, 365–66 and n. 5.

20. See Abel, supra note 8, at 102, 288 (Table 30). Harry T. Edwards, "A New Role for the Black Graduate—A Reality or an Illusion," 69 *Michigan Law Review* (1971), 1407, 1424 (reporting that in 1971–72, ten elite law schools enrolled almost as many black students as the four traditionally black law schools). As Abel (supra) goes on to document, once one adjusts for population growth in the black community, black law school enrollment has declined in real terms since 1976–1977.

21. Edwards, supra note 20, at 1429. A survey of the class of 1974 at U.C.L.A. Law School revealed a similar percentage of black students intending to practice civil rights or poverty law in either the public or the private sector. See Michael D. Rappaport, "The Legal Educational Opportunity Program at UCLA: Eight Years of Experience," 4 *Black Law Journal* (1974), 506.

22. Edwards, supra note 20, at 1416. Edwards goes on to contend: "This is a deceitful scheme if the true goal is a modicum of Black power in society as a whole. . . . Providing legal services for the poor is a necessary and important task to be discharged by the entire profession as a fundamental duty and responsibility of the calling. The responsibility must not be transmitted as the foreordained role of the newly increasing number of Black graduates." Id.

23. Edwards, supra note 20, at 1425–27 (reporting one black partner and twelve black associates out of a total population of lawyers in these firms of almost 2,300). Undoubtedly most of the black lawyers had been hired in the years immediately proceeding the survey. See e.g., Geraldine Segal, *Blacks in the Law: Philadelphia and the Nation* (Philadelphia: University of Pennsylvania Press, 1983) (reporting that there were *no* black lawyers in white law firms in Philadelphia until 1920, and no significant number until the 1970s); Paul Hoffman, *Lions in the Street: The Inside Story of the Great Wall Street Firms* (New York: New American Library, 1973), 126 (reporting that only sixty-five white law firms in New York had any black lawyers as of 1963, and that by 1973 there were only twenty-five black associates and one black partner among New York's largest corporate law firms); Erwin Smigel, *The Wall Street Lawyer: Professional Organizational Man* (Bloomington: Indiana University Press, 1969), 45 (reporting that in eighteen months spent interviewing in Wall Street Firms "I heard of only three Negroes who have been hired by large law firms").

24. See Abel, supra note 8, at 107 (noting that before blacks gained admission to the "desirable positions" within the legal profession, there was a significant disparity between the incomes of black and white lawyers); Robert Nelson, *Partners with Powers: Social Transformation of the Large Law Firm* (Berkeley: University of California Press, 1988) (discussing the power wielded by corporate lawyers).

25. For Edwards's argument that integrating corporate law practice is "profitable" both to individual blacks and to "Black society," see Edwards, supra note 20, at 1416. I return to this part of Edwards's argument later in this essay.

26. Kluger, supra note 2, at 135–37.

27. Id. For Greenberg's account of the controversy surrounding that decision, see Greenberg, supra note 1, at 502–04.

28. Charles Fried, "*Brown v. Board of Education*: The Orginal Meaning," unpublished manuscript. Paper delivered at the conference "*Brown at Forty*" at Amherst College (Dec. 2–3, 1994).

29. McNeil, supra note 1. As Robert Cover subsequently argued, "Without

vigorous Black protest politics—a claim to be essential participants in the public choices of the day—American race politics might have become like the European Jewish question: politics about the victim group." Robert M. Cover, "Origins of Judicial Activism in the Protection of Minorities," in *Narrative, Violence, and the Law: The Essays of Robert Cover*, Martha Minow, Michael Ryan, & Austin Sarat eds. (Ann Arbor: University of Michigan Press, 1992), 44.

30. Carl Rowan, *Dream Makers, Dream Breakers: The World of Justice Thurgood Marshall* (Boston: Little, Brown, 1993).

31. For a description of the risks—including life-threatening risks—encountered by Marshall and the other NAACP lawyers on the road to *Brown*, see Rowan, id.; Kluger, supra note 2.

32. See Kluger, supra note 2, at 106. Houston closed the night division even though it constituted the largest part of Howard's enrollment and in spite of the fact that his own father had attended law school at night while working full-time to support his family. As a result, enrollment plummeted from a peak of 58 graduates in 1922 to a low of 11 by the third year of Houston's deanship in 1933. Id., 126. I return to this series of decisions below.

33. For example, Professor Gewirtz's contribution to this volume chronicles the many ways in which "[t]he civil rights revolution of black Americans, including *Brown*, assumed a centrality as political experience and metaphor, making other marginal groups wish to use the analytic tools and rhetoric of that movement and thus hope for its successes." Paul Gewirtz, "The Triumph and Transformation of Antidiscrimination Law," ch. 5 in this volume. See also Derrick A. Bell, *And We Are Not Saved: The Elusive Quest for Racial Justice* (New York: Basic Books, 1987) (arguing that whites gained as much or more from the civil rights revolution as blacks).

34. See Thomas Sowell, *Affirmative Action Reconsidered: Was It Necessary in Academia?* (Washington, D.C.: American Enterprise Institute for Public Policy Research, 1975) (arguing that the antidiscrimination laws of the 1950s and 1960s, as opposed to the affirmative action policies of the 1970s, are responsible for black advances). For the record, there are plenty of reasons to doubt Sowell's conclusion that affirmative action programs have not played an important role in black economic advancement during the last twenty years. See e.g., Michael Dawson, *Behind the Mule: Race and Class in African American Politics* (Princeton: Princeton University Press, 1994), 33 (arguing that government policies, including "enforcement of antidiscrimination statutes [and] support for affirmative action remedies" play a pivotal role in black economic advancement); Carter, supra note 12 (conceding the value of affirmative action even while noting its unreported costs). I return to the relationship between Houston's policies and affirmative action below. However one resolves this specific debate, it is doubtful, as Marc Galanter noted in a more neutral context, that the biggest obstacle facing society's "have-nots" is a shortage of formal legal rules. See Marc Galanter "Why the 'Haves' Come Out Ahead: Speculation on the Limits of Legal Change," 9 *Law and Society Review* (1974), 95.

35. There are now more than 30,000 black lawyers in the United States, compared with fewer than 2,500 in 1960. See Andrew Hacker, *Two Nations: Black and White, Separate, Hostile, and Unequal* (New York: Charles Scribner's Sons, 1992), 113.

36. See 4 Report of the New York State Judicial Commission on Minorities, Legal Professions, Nonjudicial Officers, Employees and Minority Contractors

(1991), 33–34 (noting that black heads of households in New York report significantly more unmet legal needs than whites and that 83 percent of black housing court litigants are unrepresented).

37. See Louise G. Trubek, "Embedded Practices: Lawyers, Clients, and Social Change," 31 *Harvard Civil Rights Civil Liberties Law Review* (Summer 1996), 415; Bell, supra note 13. As I have argued elsewhere, the tendency among black law students and lawyers to equate litigation with law's tranformative potential helps to explain the overrepresentation of black lawyers in this area, even in corporate law firms. See Wilkins and Gulati, supra note 8.

38. See Robert L. Carter, "Thirty-Five Years Later: New Perspectives on Brown," in *Race in America*, Hill & Jones eds., supra note 13.

39. See Girardeau Spann, *Race Against the Court: The Supreme Court and Minorities in Contemporary America* (New York: New York University Press, 1993), 3 (arguing that "because racial minorities in the United States are disadvantaged by the socioeconomic status quo, the Court's inherent conservatism impairs minority efforts to achieve racial justice"). Indeed, Spann claims that even *Brown* itself can be criticized on these grounds because the decision "lur[ed] racial minorities into a dependency relationship with the Court that has impeded minority efforts to acquire political power." Id. I return to this claim below.

40. For example, as I argue elsewhere, antidiscrimination litigation is a very blunt instrument with which to try to remedy the myriad ways in which subjective evaluation procedures, informal mentoring relationships, and background stereotypes impede the hiring and promotion prospects of black corporate lawyers. See Wilkins & Gulati, supra note 8.

41. For an example of an effort to link the philosophy with the strategy, see Jack Greenberg, supra note 1, at 516.

42. Indeed, given that most of what takes place in litigated cases occurs outside the courtroom, lawyers exercise substantial discretionary power in this arena as well. See William Simon, "Ethical Discretion in Lawyering," 101 *Harvard Law Review* (1988), 1083.

43. See Robert W. Gordon, "The Independence of Lawyers" 68 *Boston University Law Review* (1988), 1.

44. *See* Edwards, supra note 20, at 1417–18: "It is surely possible that one way to direct the interests of 'the establishment' to the plight of the Black and to cause that establishment to move, albeit slowly, to eliminate the onerous oppressiveness of racism is to inject significant numbers of Black lawyers into the role of corporate legal adviser, for example. Opening the world of the lawyer in the boardroom to the Black input, the Black perspective, and the Black goal is one essential way in which the pith of racial disease may be extirpated from society. . . . [Whatever we do to address the effects of discrimination, there] is also a need to direct Black-thinking Black lawyers into the heart of the cauldron of causes (corporations, banks, brokerage firms, regulatory agencies, and large corporate law firms)." Although one might read Edwards's reference to "Black-thinking" lawyers as evidencing a commitment to black essentialism, I think within the context of his argument, he means only to point out the benefits that might accrue if black lawyers who believe in the obligation thesis were to occupy these roles. In any event, I only intend to defend this latter claim.

45. See generally Hacker, supra note 35.

46. See Nelson, supra note 24, at 231–70.

47. See Richard Delgado & Jean Stefancic, *Failed Revolutions: Social Reform and the Limits of Legal Imagination* (Boulder, Colo: Westview Press, 1994).

48. These ideas are developed at some length in Wilkins & Gulati, supra note 8. See also N.Y. Commission on Minorities, supra note 36; Abel, supra note 8.

49. Kluger, supra note 2, at 130 (quoting a statement by Ralph Bunche in the late 1920s).

50. I return to the tension between the interests of corporate clients and the justice claims of poor blacks below. See also Wilkins, "Two Paths to the Mountaintop," supra note 10.

51. Gerald N. Rosenberg, *The Hollow Hope: Can Courts Bring About Social Change?* (Chicago: University of Chicago Press, 1991) 107–55 (arguing that *Brown* had virtually no effect on school segregation for over two decades).

52. As Professor Seidman has recently argued, "Brown can be understood as the culmination of a process whereby, under the pressure of litigation, the contradictory and intractable requirements of liberal individualism were concretized and reduced to a judicially administrable test that robbed them of their destabilizing potential. . . . [T]he sense of closure resulting from [this] resolution of the contradictions has deprived liberal advocates of their best weapon for combating the status quo." Louis Michael Seidman, "*Brown* and *Miranda*," 80 *California Law Review* (1992), 673, 717.

53. Rowan, supra note 30.

54. See Randall Kennedy, "Martin Luther King's Constitution: A Legal History of the Montgomery Bus Boycott" 98 *Yale Law Journal* (1989), 999, 1066 ("The boycott made black Montgomerians aware of themselves as a community with obligations and capacities to which they and others had previously been blind.").

55. As Randall Kennedy argues in defending the importance of Marshall's victory in *Gayle v. Browder* (the Supreme Court decision striking down Montgomery's segregated bus system): "By winning in court and forcing segregationists to go outside the law to maintain their power, the Movement's litigators helped to erode the facade of inevitability that surrounded the segregation regime and to create the perception of a gap between right and reality, authority and force." Id. at 1065. In Kennedy's view, "[E]xtra-legal protest and litigation" played a symbiotic role in producing the dramatic results achieved in Montgomery. Id.

56. See Cover, supra note 29, at 44.

57. See Kluger, supra note 2. The hostility of most state judges forced Houston to modify this latter aspect of his strategy.

58. See Derrick A. Bell, "Serving Two Masters: Integration Ideals and Client Interests in School Desegregation Litigation," 85 *Yale Law Journal* (1976), 470 (criticizing the Legal Defense Fund for ignoring the interests of black residents despite engaging in the kind of political activity described in text). I return to Bell's important criticism below.

59. See Dawson, supra note 34.

60. See Robert W. Gordon, "The Ideal and the Actual in the Law: Fantasies and Practices of New York City Lawyers, 1870–1970," in *The New High Priests of Law: Lawyers in Post-Civil War America*, Gerald Gawalt ed. (Westport, Conn.: Greenwood Press, 1984); Gordon, supra note 43.

61. See Ronald Gilson, "The Devolution of the Legal Profession: A Demand Side Perspective," 49 *Maryland Law Review* (1990), 869; Gordon, supra note 43.

62. I develop this point at somewhat greater length in Wilkins, "Practical Wisdom for Practicing Lawyers: Separating Ideals from Ideology in Legal Ethics," 108 *Harvard Law Review* (1994), 458.

63. See Delgado and Stefancic, supra note 47.

64. Consider, for example, the organized bar's successful defeat of the Reagan administration's attempts to eliminate the legal services corporation. See Gordon, supra note 43.

65. See William J. Wilson, *The Declining Significance of Race* (Chicago: University of Chicago Press, 1978); Wilson, *The Truly Disadvantaged: The Inner City, the Underclass, and Public Policy* (Chicago: University of Chicago Press, 1987); See also Thomas D. Boston, *Race, Class and Conservatism* (Boston: Unwin Hyman, 1988); Bart Landry, *The New Black Middle Class* (Berkeley: University of California Press, 1987).

66. See Dawson, supra note 34; See also, Jennifer L. Hochschild & Monica Herk, "'Yes, But . . .': Principles and Caveats in American Racial Attitudes," in *Majorities and Minorities*, no. 32, John W. Chapman & Alan Wertheimer eds. (New York: New York University Press, 1990) (noting that the range of views on racial justice issues among blacks is both narrower than and readily distinguishable from the range of views among whites); Howard Schuman, Charlotte Steeh, & Lawrence Bobo, *Racial Attitudes in America: Trends and Interpretations* (Cambridge, Mass.: Harvard University Press, 1988) (documenting differing attitudes among blacks and whites of similar incomes). For an account of the traditional view that class divisions within a given community should produce heterogeneous political opinion, see Robert A. Dahl, *Who Governs: Democracy and Power in an American City* (New Haven, Conn.: Yale University Press, 1961).

67. See Elizabeth Chambliss, "The New Partners with Power? Organizational Determinants of Law Firm Integration" (Ph.D. dissertation, University of Wisconsin, 1992) (documenting the relationship between government practice and racial integration at elite law firms). See also Jose O. Seda, "Hiring of Women and Minority Lawyers for Bank and Thrift Bailout Is the Law," *Bank and Thrift Law Bulletin* (1992) (arguing that affirmative action provisions in the Financial Institutions Reform, Recovery, and Enforcement Act of 1989 create important opportunities for minority lawyers).

68. See Wilkins & Gulati, supra note 8.

69. Id. On the effect of conscious and unconscious racial sterotyping, see Charles R. Lawrence, "The Id, the Ego, and Equal Protection: Reckoning with Unconscious Racism," 39 *Stanford Law Review* (1987), 317. On statistical discrimination, see Glenn Loury, *One by One from the Inside Out* (New York: Free Press, 1995).

70. Whether the obligation thesis, or any other call for moral responsibility, will *in fact* affect the attitudes or actions of black corporate lawyers remains an open question. I return to this issue later in this essay.

71. See Kluger, supra note 2, at 169 (reporting that a 1935 article in the *Journal of Negro Education* argued that a legal attack on segregated education was virtually impossible, having failed already in 113 litigated challenges).

72. It is worth briefly recounting Charles Hamilton Houston's extraordinary credentials. Born in 1895 to prominent black Washingtonians, Houston graduated Phi Beta Kappa from Amherst College in 1915. After two years in the army, he enrolled in Harvard Law School in the fall of 1919, where he became the first black elected to the *Harvard Law Review* and a protégé of Felix Frankfurter, before

graduating in the top 5 percent of his class in 1922. The next year he obtained a doctorate in juridical science from Harvard and was awarded a traveling fellowship, which he used the following year to collect an additional doctorate in civil law from the University of Madrid. In 1924, he returned to Washington, D.C., and joined his father's law firm. By the time he took over the reins at Howard five years later, Houston was, without question, "the best-educated black American ever to study the law." Kluger, supra note 2, at 116. Hastie's credentials were similarly impressive, including magna cum laude degrees from both Amherst College and Harvard Law School where, like Houston, he was an editor of the *Harvard Law Review*.

73. By my rough count, there are three black managing partners in major corporate law firms, William Coleman at O'Melveny in Washington, D.C., David R. Andrews at McCutchen, Doyle in San Francisco, and Harry Daniels in Boston at Hale and Dorr; a handful of black general counsel at major Fortune 500 corporations, including Leroy Ritche at Chrysler; and probably something in the neighborhood of fifty to seventy-five black partners. In addition, a few black lawyers, such as the late Reginald Lewis (president and CEO of Beatrice International) and Richard Parsons (president of Time Warner), have risen to the top ranks of corporate management.

74. See Steven Keeva, "Unequal Partners: It's Tough at the Top for Minority Lawyers," *ABA Journal*, Feb. 1993 (reporting on the problems encountered by black partners).

75. See Robert W. Gordon and William H. Simon, "The Redemption of Professionalism?," in *Lawyers' Ideals/Lawyers' Practices: Transformations in the American Legal Profession* (Ithaca: Cornell University Press, 1992), 248–57 (describing how corporate lawyers can deploy various resources at their disposal to improve corporate compliance with legal norms).

76. See Greenberg, supra note 1, at 516.

77. Margaret M. Russell, "De Jure Revolution?" 93 *Michigan Law Review* (1995), 1173, 1185. See also Gerald P. Lopez, *Rebellious Lawyering: One Chicano's Vision of Progressive Law Practice* (Boulder, Colo.: Westview Press, 1992); Lucie E. White, "Subordination, Rhetorical Survival Skills and Sunday Shoes: Notes on the Hearing of Mrs. G.," 38 *Buffalo Law Review* (1990), 1.

78. For example, in 1993, the title of the black students' annual alumni conference at Harvard Law School was "Many Paths, One Goal: Reconciling Various Strategies to Our Common Struggle."

79. See Carrie Menkel-Meadow, "Culture Clash in the Quality of Life in the Law: Changes in the Economics, Diversification and Organization of Lawyering," 44 *Case Western Reserve Law Review* (1994), 621 (describing the changes that women and minorities have made in practices of corporate law firms). For example, in a small survey of black Harvard law school graduates working in large firms, I found that pro bono rates among these lawyers far exceeded the national average. See Wilkins & Gulati, supra note 8.

80. See, American Bar Association Commission on Minorities in the Profession, Into the Mainstream: Report of the Minority Counsel Demonstration Program 1988–1991 (1991).

81. For example, Kilson reports that over 80 percent of middle-class blacks still feel racial obligations. See Martin Kilson, "The Black Bourgeoisie Revisited," *Dissent* 85 (1983).

82. See Granfield, supra note 9 (noting that many entering black and white

Harvard law students state that they chose law as a career because of its perceived connection to social justice). I count myself among this group.

83. See Wilkins, "Two Paths to the Mountaintop?" supra note 10, at 2013–19. As I indicate below, the early affirmative action programs described above, however narrow and exaggerated, may have provided an important counterweight to the natural tendency in legal education to undermine a student's commitment to pursuing social justice through law.

84. By posing the question in this way, I mean to limit my analysis to those black corporate lawyers who accept some version of the obligation thesis and who have taken actions at least partially in its name. I therefore leave for another day the more difficult question of what to do about those black lawyers who reject the idea that they have any special obligation to serve the cause of racial justice. For a preliminary examination of this broader proposition, see id.

85. I develop this argument in id.

86. See W.E.B. Du Bois "The Talented Tenth," in *The Negro Problem: A Series of Articles by Representative American Negroes of To-Day* (Miami: Mnemosyne, 1969), 33. It is perhaps significant that Houston and Du Bois were contemporaries and were both active in the NAACP. The two men, however, were apparently not close. See Kluger, supra note 2.

87. See Kluger, supra note 2, at 106.

88. See McNeil, supra note 1.

89. See Richard Kluger, supra note 2, at 132–33 (describing the views of Ralph Bunche and ACLU president Roger Baldwin). Needless to say, the idea of using trade unions as a vehicle for social advancement was a much more plausible concept in the early 1930s than it might appear today. Whether this strategy could have been successful, of course, remains an open question. See Dawson, supra note 34, at 49 (reporting that the "radical movements of the first three decades of the twentieth century [did not seriously break] the system of domination under which the great majority of African Americans in the south lived"). I return to the effectiveness question below.

90. See Kluger, supra note 2, at 157 (describing the opposition of the black president of North Carolina College for Negroes to Houston's attempt to desegregate the University of North Carolina). The most famous proponent of this philosophy, of course, was Booker T. Washington. See generally, Booker T. Washington, "Industrial Education for the Negro," in *The Negro Problem*, supra note 86. Even Du Bois toward the end of his life was concerned that the NAACP's all-out desegregation strategy would unduly undermine confidence in black institutions. See Kluger, supra note 2, at 170. The NAACP board censored Du Bois for making these remarks, precipitating Du Bois's resignation from the organization he helped to create.

91. See Robert Staples, "The Illusion of Race Equality: The Black American Dilemma," in *Lure and Loathing: Essays on Race, Identity, and the Ambivalence of Assimilation*, Gerald Early ed. (New York: Allen Lane/Penguin Books, 1993), 231–33; Derrick A. Bell, supra note 33, at 44–50.

92. See Robert L. Allen, *Black Awakening in America* (Garden City, N.Y.: Doubleday, 1969), 27 (arguing that the civil rights movement was a middle-class affair that did "absolutely nothing to alleviate the grim plight of the poorest segments of the black population").

93. As Derrick Bell argues: "[T]here seems little doubt that the abandonment of overtly discriminatory policies has lowered racial barriers for some talented and

skilled blacks seeking access to opportunity and advancement. Even their upward movement is, however pointed to by much of the society as the final proof that racism is dead." Bell, supra note 33, at 48–49.

94. See Wilson, *Declining Significance of Race,* supra note 65.

95. See Derrick A. Bell, supra note 58. For raising this argument, Bell was himself ostracized by his former Defense Fund colleagues. Ironically, a decade later, Bell contributed to an attempt to ostracize his and my Harvard colleague Randall Kennedy for writing an article critical of the positions taken by certain leading minority scholars.

96. 371 U.S. 415 (1963) (Harlan, J., dissenting).

97. Derrick Bell describes an incident during his tenure at the Legal Defense Fund in which Marshall initially refused to allow that organization to defend the first wave of lunch counter protesters. In Marshall's view, these young women and men were jeopardizing the movement's goals by breaking the law and acting outside of normal channels. See Bell "An Expository Exploration," supra note 13.

98. See William Simon, "The Dark Secret of Progressive Lawyering: A Comment on Poverty Law Scholarship in the Post-Reagan Era," 48 *Miami Law Review* (1994), 1099 (criticizing much of the new poverty law scholarship on this ground).

99. See Wilkins, "Race, Ethics, and the First Amendment," supra note 10 (arguing that advocacy organizations like the NAACP have a right to demand that lawyers who represent them refrain from advocating "positions" that the group's leadership believes undermines the organization's goals even in circumstances where no formal conflict of interest exists).

100. Even Derrick Bell, who has been one of the harshest critics on both of the counts described above, does not dispute this basic conclusion. See Derrick A. Bell, supra note 33 (conceding that the elimination of de jure segregation was a necessary step); Derrick A. Bell, supra note 58 (conceding that the kind of group representation approved in *NAACP v. Button* is necessary evil).

101. See Richard Kluger, supra note 2, at 137 (explaining Houston's view that a frontal assault on primary and secondary school education in the 1930s would have been doomed to failure).

102. It is doubtful that any public schools are as underfunded, understaffed, and marginalized as those that existed before *Brown.*

103. See Philip Elman & Norman Silber, "The Solicitor General's Office, Justice Frankfurter, and Civil Rights Litigation," 100 *Harvard Law Review* (1987), 817.

104. See Randall Kennedy, supra note 6, at 1941.

105. See Richard Kluger, supra note 2, at 137 (noting that Houston believed that "at the very least" his dual strategy would "result in improved all-black facilities").

106. See Kenneth S. Tollet, "Black Lawyers, Their Education, and the Black Community," 17 *Howard Law Journal* (1972), 326.

107. See, e.g., Richard Kluger, supra note 2, at 159.

108. See, e.g., NAACP v. Alabama, 375 U.S. 810 (1963); NAACP v. Button, 371 U.S. 415 (1963).

109. See Kennedy, supra note 54, at 1065–1067 (on King's reliance on the NAACP's legal victories); Clayborne Carson, *In Struggle: SNCC and the Black Awakening of the 1960s* (Cambridge, Mass.: Harvard University Press, 1981) (on SNCC and other radical black activists' grudging debt to the NAACP).

110. Six prominent Washington, D.C., firms allow associates to spend three months working full-time in a neighborhood legal services clinic. Anecdotal evidence suggests that many black lawyers have taken advantage of this opportunity.

111. A black senior associate at Arnold & Porter spearheaded this project.

112. This is one of the most common ways in which black corporate lawyers seek to discharge their obligation.

113. For example, not everyone will agree that prison reform will improve the status of black Americans. Similarly, a contribution to the Legal Defense Fund (or, to take an opposite example, to a conservative organization committed to ending teenage pregnancy) may seem to some like a waste of resources, or worse, promoting interests that will damage the black community in the long run.

114. Not every pro bono or law reform project will satisfy this test. Thus, a proposal to repeal all antidiscrimination laws would arguably fail the first prong, while support for a group that seeks to prevent conservative blacks from being appointed to university faculties would probably flunk the second. But see Richard Epstein, *Forbidden Grounds: The Case Against Employment Discrimination Law* (Cambridge, Mass: Harvard University Press, 1992) (urging the repeal of all antidiscrimination laws on the ground that they actually harm their intended beneficiaries). Given the data that Dawson marshals in support of his contention that the economic status of all blacks is tied to the vigorous enforcement of existing antidiscrimination laws, Epstein's proposal must overcome a heavy presumption against its viability. See Michael C. Dawson, supra note 59.

115. Again, there is some evidence to suggest that black lawyers have been active on both of these fronts.

116. See Austin Sarat, "Between (the Presence of) Violence and (the Possibility of) Justice: Lawyering Against Capital Punishment," in *Cause Lawyering: Political Commitments and Professional Responsibilities*, Austin Sarat & Stuart Scheingold eds. (Oxford: Oxford University Press, forthcoming 1997) (describing the importance of lawyers "bearing witness [and] writing history" in the context of the administration of capital punishment).

117. See American Bar Association, *Model Rules of Professional Conduct*, Rule 1.2 (stating that lawyers can give both moral and legal advice).

118. See Gordon, surpa note 60.

119. See Robert Granfield, supra note 9 (reporting that Harvard Law students submerge the tension between their political ideals and their work as corporate lawyers by denying that most of what they do will have any effect on social justice).

120. See, e.g., "Major Effort Launched to Increase Opportunity for Minority Lawyers," *Bar Reporter*, June/July 1992 (discussing Washington, D.C. program); Monica Bay, "BASF Approves Voluntary Minority Quotas," *Recorder*, June 15, 1989 (discussing San Francisco program).

121. See American Bar Association, supra note 80.

122. For example, the program sends letters to general counsels of leading corporations asking them how much of their business is going to minority lawyers.

123. Indeed, it was only when blacks gained access to this sector that the large disparity between the incomes of black and white lawyers began to dissipate. See Abel, supra note 8, at 107.

124. On the growing need for partners to bring in business, *see* Galanter & Palay, supra note 8.

125. See Jack Heinz & Edward Laumann, *Chicago Lawyers: The Social Struc-*

ture of the Bar (New York, N.Y., and Chicago, Ill.: Russell Sage Foundation and American Bar Foundation, 1982).

126. Although black partners frequently make this claim, the growing number of black specialty firms that are staffed primarily by former associates and partners from leading firms casts some doubt on its continuing validity. On the other hand, to the extent that these new black firms are nothing more than a collection of big firm refugees who have made a strategic decision to maximize their personal gain by practicing in this new setting, the historical disparity that gave rise to the initial concern over the presence of black partners in the ABA's program may cease to be a relevant cause for concern.

127. For one attempt to work through these factors in a somewhat different context, see Wilkins, "Race, Ethics and the First Amendment," supra note 10 (examining the case of a black lawyer representing the Ku Klux Klan).

128. See Dawson, supra note 59.

129. See Gordon & Simon, supra note 75; Gordon, supra note 60. For example, there is some evidence that pro bono activity among lawyers increased when bar leaders made it clear that they were serious about this often invoked but rarely enforced professional obligation.

130. See Thurgood Marshall, "Reflections on the Bicentennial of the United States Constitution," 101 *Harvard Law Review* (1987), 1.

131. Id. at 5 (emphasis in original).

7

CAROL J. GREENHOUSE

A Federal Life

Brown *and the Nationalization of the Life Story*

L ives do not make their own stories. How people's lives are wrestled into particular narrative forms is always a complex question of genres, genders, and, especially in the present case, generations. In this essay, I suggest that one element of the cultural impact of *Brown* was the definition of an iconic life story for a particular generation of African Americans. My focus is on the ways federal powers lent their "signs" to public narratives of personal life. I should stress that this essay frames a question—not an ethnographic argument as such.

If *Brown* defined a canonical life story for the children of the civil rights era, it also periodized the timetable of the benefits of civil rights in that generation. It also gave African American citizens of that generation a double life story. The Supreme Court's decision in *Brown* invites readers to weigh two alternative scenarios: in one, the citizen is productive, in the other, the citizen is unproductive and dangerous. Both of the central figures of *Brown* (the good citizen and the dangerous citizen) were essentially literary tropes—tropes borrowed from a literature that exposed the real and epidemic emergencies in the life conditions of African Americans. Accordingly, this essay considers *Brown*'s legacy as a form for biographical narrative, a fictional life story drawn from a current American novel and a "real" life story drawn from a judicial confirmation hearing in the United States Senate.

As for *Brown*'s periodization of the civil rights "era," there is considerable evidence—for example, the 1994 elections—to suggest that the civil rights era is now over. While the causes of this epochal closure are complex and reach well beyond *Brown*'s efficacy as rhetoric or enforceable law, conservatives draw on "the life" in asserting their claims that the need for civil rights is now gone. This aspect of the iconic life—as a rhetorical counter to rights discourses—is also illustrated in this essay, in a brief examination of Justice Clarence Thomas's life story, as it was featured by him and his supporters in the course of the Senate confirmation hearings in 1991.

I also explore the double, or "but for," aspect of the iconic African American life story, and conclude with some reflections on what the end of the civil rights era might mean for the ways identities are constructed and construed in the contemporary United States. I will suggest that what was the icon of the *federal* civil rights powers has now (also) become the icon of *local* criminal law enforcement and prosecutorial powers in a *national* discourse of difference. I do not claim that the present importance of "law and order" programs in electoral politics is due to the *Brown* decision.[1] My suggestion is that *Brown's* icons are currently in circulation among opposed forces on the right and the left—and that the possibility of this complication is part of *Brown's* legacy. It is also part of *Brown's* history, as other essays in this volume make clear.

Brown as Biography

Brown's discourse was biographical. The Supreme Court's wistful anticipation of African American and white children going to school together was not a prescription for a means of achieving equality, but for a means of achieving society itself. Specifically, the Court envisioned equality as the means of African American children becoming *themselves*, future adults. There is no arithmetic of citizenship in *Brown*, only the yardstick of children's vulnerability and well-being, realized—in the *Brown* text—as the anticipatory narrative of an individual's life over time, a life enabled or disabled by its wants.[2]

At each level of litigation, the plaintiffs emphasized the need for a new standard to replace *Plessy v. Ferguson's* "separate but equal" doctrine. They stressed the relationship among public education, cultural values, and citizenship; the negative psychological impact of inequality on children, including pathology and criminality; and the general importance of intangible factors in assessing equality. Each of these claims drew on a range of social science evidence, including the testimony of academics and experimental findings.[3] From these, the Supreme Court concluded:

> To separate [African American children] from others of similar age and qualifications solely because of their race generates a feeling of inferiority as to their status in the community that may affect their hearts and minds in a way unlikely ever to be undone. . . . We conclude that in the field of public education the doctrine of "separate but equal" has no place. Separate educational facilities are inherently unequal.[4]

In this way, through an evocation of children's vulnerability to harm, African American children's lives were drawn into the court's vision of the nation's "life."

Brown's particular equality required federal power as its agent. Accordingly, in the hypothetical life story of *Brown's* children, the federal government became—at least in its self-constitution in *Brown*—the very agent of the children's futures. The life that *Brown* envisioned for African Americans made them a metonymy of federal power; a reference to "Negroes" became, among other things, an evocation of federal power.[5] This is a curious kind of "belonging." After *Brown*, whatever their own sense of belonging as individuals, African American lives were assigned to the semiotics of federal power and, through federal agency, to the nation as a whole.[6] To be more accurate, African Americans are accorded *no particular locale* in the national discourse *in the present*. In place of place and the present stands the federal government; and, sometimes, in place of the government stands its metonym, the life story, conventionalized in particular terms (as we shall see). The discourse of individualism makes the metonymy

individual life = national life

available, in the sense of envisioning the nation as composed of equal citizens. But *Brown* is distinctly not about individual citizens building the nation. It is about the federal power to create the conditions under which individuals can become citizens in this sense. In this sense, *Brown's* vision of "the nation" (that is, the social counterpart of the state) positions African Americans and whites differently: whites constitute the nation directly through their *individual* agency, but African Americans require the intervention of federal power before they are enabled to constitute the nation *from their situation as a social class*.

The rhetorical future in *Brown* is complex. The plaintiffs' strategy required that inequality have both tangible and intangible measures. Equal school facilities as measured by school budgets and infrastructures, or the quality of the teaching staff, were necessary but not sufficient to meet an equality standard in their view, since the experience of segregation itself was deemed to be harmful. The rhetorical and social science arguments in favor of this point focused on the vulnerability of children, and emphasized the trauma and risk intrinsic to the experience of inequality. Experts connected the psychological trauma of discrimination to a risk of abnormal personality development, a risk that a child thus damaged might become an unproductive and even criminally dangerous adult.

In the context of the *Brown* opinion, it is clear that the purpose of these arguments is to encompass both personal and societal health within the concept of equality. At no point did the testimony address the hypothesis that social pathology was a normal or even likely condition for African American children; the text of the opinion refers simply to risk. However, some current rights critics seem to have turned this aspect of *Brown* into an idiom of collective latent deviance, defective lifestyle choices, and societal vulnerability. In hindsight, part of *Brown's* legacy appears to be the rhetorical fusion of the normal life of the citizen and what I call the "but for" version of that life.

In offering these formulations, I hope it is already clear that I am not undertaking to assess the promise of *Brown* as having been fulfilled or defeated. Rather, I am interested in an admittedly hindsighted assessment of *Brown* as a source of contemporary icons in the semiotics of federal power. Today, a generation after *Brown*, some people consider its vision of opportunity and its "but for" double and use these as a yardstick of quality to criminalize difference. Some people consider the span of the generation, and claim that *Brown*'s equality has now been achieved, since *Brown*'s children are grown. Any attempt to justify those readings at *Brown*'s doorstep would be an error, I think, but in considering the cultural impact of *Brown*, I do want to include these current uses of "the life" *Brown* evoked to broaden the "American Dream."

Brown's plaintiffs did not invent the images of the child or the figure of the future adult that played so importantly in the litigation and the Supreme Court's opinion. Beyond the law, the African American life story was already a powerful literary trope, with important sources in fiction (e.g., Richard Wright's *Native Son*)[7] and sociology (e.g., Davis and Dollard's *Children of Bondage*).[8] The crossovers among these genres were important, too; they reinforced both the novelists' and sociologists' claims to authority and authenticity (e.g., Wright's introduction to the original edition of Drake and Cayton's *Black Metropolis*).[9] There were also crossovers with the law: Allison Davis, the Chicago sociologist, was the brother of John A. Davis, who marshalled the social science evidence for the *Brown* brief.[10] The litigation itself was an interdisciplinary curriculum of the social sciences, humanities and law, and the themes of the child within the person, the violence of inequality and the pathology of social harm emerged powerfully from these sources.

In retrospect, the *Brown* court's appropriation of the trope of "the life" from literature and social science into the language of the law itself was a paradoxical act of nation building. Clearly, the intent of the Court was to draw African American children into the national story *in fact*. Today, though, the rhetorical tactic that made the invocation of national interest germane to the issue of children's access to school has become double edged. Does "difference" derive from "the nation" at its points of deepest contradiction? Those would appear to be the very points where cultural notions of biography, time, and power converge to create powerful public symbols that simultaneously qualify and disqualify difference in relation to the civic life. By raising this as a paradox, I do not mean to suggest that the paradox could have been avoided. The paradox is not in *Brown*, but in the experiences of race and class that are its context—as the following modern examples illustrate.

Fictional Lives: *High Cotton*

Darryl Pinckney's *High Cotton* is a fictional memoir, narrated by an unnamed African American man reflecting on his life up to the fictional present in mid-1980s, when he is about forty-five, or perhaps younger.[11] The story is narrated in a conventional autobiographical mode; the chapters are first-person narratives that are entirely convincing in terms of their frames of reference, the authority of their memories, and the disjunctures that signal the narrator's growth—and growing alienation. The characters and their context are a middle-class family in Indianapolis, initially, in the early 1950s.

Pinckney's narrator acquires his racial education in the course of the novel. Some of the novel's power is in the way Pinckney uses narrative to evoke—rather than describe—thresholds of understanding. In the childhood narratives, Pinckney emphasizes his narrator's mystified and resistant distance from his parents and grandparents as the framing for the surreal shock of discovering "race" in the world. An an adult, the narrator is pushed in a variety of ways to enacting a "black man's" life; this then becomes his life, until close to the novel's end. The resolution of the novel comes after the grandfather's death.

The book begins this way:

> No one sat me down and told me I was a Negro. That was something I figured out on the sly, late in my childhood career as a snoop, like discovering that babies didn't come from an exchange of spinach during a kiss. . . . There was nothing to be afraid of as long as we were polite and made good grades. After all, the future, back then, assembled as we were on the glossy edge of the New Frontier, belonged to us, the Also Chosen. The future was something my parents were either earning or keeping for my two sisters and me, like the token checks that came on birthdays from grandparents, great-uncles, great-aunts.[12]

Pinckney develops the theme of difference with a series of plays alternating high national (federal) rhetoric and popular culture icons:

> *All men were created equal*, but even so, lots of mixed messages with sharp teeth waited under my Roy Rogers pillow. . . . You had *nothing to fear*, though every time you left the house for a Spelling Bee or a Music Memory Contest the future of the future hung in the balance. . . . Those who dwelled in the great beyond out there could not stop *His truth from marching on*, but until His truth made it as far as restricted Broadripple Park, you did not go swimming.[13]

The narrator seeks some meaning of difference that is not generic; the ambivalence of difference is the irony of the American duty to "act as though you belonged":

> You were not an immigrant, there were no foreign accents, weird holidays, or funny food to live down, but still you did not belong to the great beyond out there; yet though you did not belong it was your duty as the Also Chosen to get up and act as though you belonged, especially when no one wanted you to.[14]

The central relationship in the book is the one between the narrator and his grandfather. Throughout the book, his grandfather is present from another time: for example, "Grandfather Eustace was the emperor of out-of-it."[15]

Early in the book, Pinckney indexes the generations of grandfather and grandson with legal decisions that identify the narrator's lifespan with the *Brown* generation. The identification occurs in a passage in which the narrator is remembering a "phase" in his childhood when he played at being a dog, but the game is made more complex by the grandfather's reaction:

> Grandfather looked at me, a severe expression I was to see again years later when I had to confess in person that I'd flunked a course. . . .
> "Come here, and on two feet, if you please, *Plessy vs. Ferguson* contemplated *Brown vs. Board of Education.* . . . Your daddy has no right to make you live here. He has no right to turn you into a dog."
> Grandfather, as ever, was true to his word. He didn't come to see us again until we invaded the white suburbs.[16]

Pinckney develops the intergenerational theme—generations divided by *Brown* and the civil rights movement. Time is knowledge. The "old country" in the following passage is Alabama, where the narrator's aunts live, and, initially, the old country is a place of special knowledge. But private knowledge is overtaken by public significance. Having marked the generations with legal decisions, the passage piles additional national referents (television, the Smithsonian) as harbingers of the means by which the narrator's life will be drawn into the space the nation leaves for him:

> The Old Country . . . was a place of secrets, of what black people knew and what white people didn't. No old-timer said openly that Rosa Parks had been secretary of her NAACP branch and a student of interstate commerce rulings and the Equal Accommodations Law of 1948 before she decided she was too tired to move.
> The old-timers fell silent whenever I entered the room . . . and then went back to the possibility that Roy Wilkins of the NAACP hated Martin Luther King of the SCLC because there was not enough real estate in the social-studies textbooks to house them both. Meanwhile, television passed on its pictures. . . . The representations survived the subject and eventually overtook my own images, which were less durable than waxwork figures in an exhibition of Black Life at the Smithsonian.[17]

The "representations" divide black from white, and the narrator from his "black classmates": "My fellow black classmates pulled such faces I was asked to interpret the anger. Nothing about me could make whites feel bad, as if I had been inculcated against carrying terror."[18] As a "slave in heaven"[19]—a black teenager in a white high school—the narrator refers to himself as the "uninhabited me."[20]

Years later—after university, dropping out, traveling, working—the "uninhabited me" is uncomfortably tenanted:

> The ledger of how to be simultaneously yourself and everyone else who might observe you, the captain's log of travel in the dual consciousness, the white world as the deceptive sea and black world as the armed galley, gave me the comic feeling that I was living alongside myself, that there

was a me and a ventriloquist's replica of me on my lap, and that both of us
awaited the intervention of third me, the disembodied me, before we
could begin the charade of dialogue.[21]

And as his world widens, the narrator's crisis develops around his growing
certainty that others see him as an individual example of a generic type: "I
bumped against television images and wet newsprint, against people in the
street."[22]

I cannot do justice to this narrative, which laces and unlaces again and
again, around the narrator's relationship to his grandfather—which ultimately
(and explicitly) becomes the relationship of the past to the future: "Perhaps the
old-timers were right to insist that we, the Also Chosen, live wholly in the
future. . . . I used to wonder how they managed to be all-inclusive. It never
occurred to me that they might be making it up as they went along and
sometimes backing down."[23] And in this reclaiming of his personal presence
in the space created by the dissolution of the past and future, the narrator at
last finds the grief that has become the object of his quest. Finally, playing on
the trope of the imagined future, he imagines his own old age, from which he
looks back on his generation's emblem:

> One day—if it comes— . . . I may elect myself a witness and undertake
> to remember when something more important than black, white, and
> other as lost. Even now I grieve for what has been betrayed. I see the
> splendor of the mornings and hear how glad the songs were, back in the
> days when the Supreme Court was my Lourdes, and am beyond consola-
> tion. The spirit didn't lie down and die, but it's been here and gone, been
> here and gone.[24]

I have drawn on Pinckney's novel for its evocation of a young African
American coming of age in the *Brown* generation—indeed, *as* the *Brown*
generation. The links to *Brown*, and to specific rhetorical strategies in *Brown*
are explicit in the novel; I have emphasized these in the passages quoted.
Brown claimed to mark the narrator's generation for a special future, but the
crisis of the novel is the narrator's discovery that there is no autobiographical
interval to connect him to that future; that future is not, in the end, a time for
him, but, instead, certain imperatives of meaning. Significantly, the narrator
recovers a personal life only when he abandons the genre of autobiography
altogether—at least, as defined by the single-stranded "progress" that the civil
rights generation was supposed to embody.

Living Fictions

Let us turn now from a fictional life story to a "real" life story—the autobiography and biography of Justice Clarence Thomas, as constructed in the course of
his confirmation hearings in 1991. I will focus on the parallels—a triple
parallel—between *Brown*, Pinckney's rendering of the *Brown* generation, and
the public construction of Thomas's life story. These three "takes" draw atten-

tion to the ways "race" precludes conventional notions of authorship and agency.

The relationship between authorship and agency is explored by Bakhtin:

> The author-creator moves freely in his own time: he can begin his story . . . at any moment of the events represented without violating the objective course of time in the event he describes. Here we get a sharp distinction between representing and represented time. . . . [The] author-creator, finding himself outside . . . the world he represents in his work, is nevertheless not simply outside but as it were tangential to [it].[25]

One way of summarizing this essay so far is to observe that the *Brown* Court's construction of "race" as a field of federal power *and* contingent agency catapults the iconic African American life "outside . . . the world he represents [and] . . . tangential to it." My example in this section derives from a context in which this exteriority was politically potent: the U.S. Senate's confirmation hearings on the nomination of then-Judge Clarence Thomas to the Supreme Court in 1991. In that year, Thomas was forty-three years old; both his age and his story suited him to be what he became, an emblem of the civil rights era, as viewed from the right.

By the time the hearings began, Thomas's nomination was the object of intense partisan controversy, and his life story already had rhetorical uses beyond—well beyond—personal narrative. Senator Sam Nunn, on that first afternoon, narrated Thomas's biography as a preemptive rhetorical strike against interest groups arrayed against him:

> Our duty is not to create or deny another vote on abortion or sex discrimi-nation or affirmative action or any other particular issue. Our duty, as I see it, is to confirm a Supreme Court Justice who, subject to good behav-ior under the Constitution, may serve for many years on the Court, indeed, may serve for life. I doubt seriously, Mr. Chairman, that many of today's—maybe most of today's—burning issues will still be raising the blood pressure of our nation seven years from now when Judge Thomas is 50, much less when he reaches the still relatively young judicial age of 60. (Hearings, 3)[26]

Before Thomas took the stand for the first time on September 10, 1991, his life story had been told—in condensed or extended form—eight times that same day by different senators, most of whom spoke for his confirmation.

The relevance of Thomas's life story—the "climb" (as Nunn and others labeled it) from poverty and discrimination in Pinpoint, Georgia, to success and power in Washington, D.C.—was thus well established in the hearings even before Thomas told it himself. Narrators stressed the comprehensive aspect of Thomas's life story, in repeatedly juxtaposing his unpromising ori-gins and his present success. This aspect of his story was then leveraged rhetorically against the narrow interests of any particular interest group. His success story was also invoked as an inspiration to others. But primarily, Thomas's life story was offered as the promise of his future memories as a

Justice, memories that would inspire him to fight for "fairness and equal justice" (Nunn, Hearings, 3). As in the novel, "difference" emerges not as a presence, nor in the present, but in the empty space between the past and the future—a linear temporality that is fundamental to the cultural apparatus of the nation state.

Significantly, the life story as the principal idiom of qualification was the work of Thomas's supporters, but Thomas was a full participant in the collaborative narrative of his autobiography. As he said at the beginning of his opening statement, "I hope these hearings will help to show more clearly who this person Clarence Thomas is and what really makes me tick" (Hearings, 11). It was Thomas's supporters who referred to him familiarly in the third person as "Clarence" (Senator John Danforth) or, more often, "Clarence Thomas"; his critics tended to refer to him more formally as "Judge Thomas."

Thomas's life story was inflected with a selective doubling of certain of its features; it is this doubling (and, more generally, repetition of specific themes and questions) that leads me to "read" them as key features of his presentation. In a unique comment in the course of his welcome to Thomas, Senator Joseph Biden referred to a strong physical resemblance—a fictional twinning—of Thomas's son, Jamal, and Thomas: "Jamal, welcome. You look so much like your father that probably at a break you'd be able to come back in, sit in there, and answer questions—so if he's not doing it the way you want it done, you just slide in that chair" (Hearings, 10).[27] Just as the life story brought the young Clarence Thomas to the fore, that young man could literally be seen—literally, that is, in Biden's introduction—in the hearing room. At numerous junctures, Thomas was also provided with (and provided himself) with another surrogate, that is, his grandfather, whose aphorisms and experience Thomas cited with frequency and fervor. Occasionally, his grandfather also was given a surrogate, in another senior black male figure to whom Thomas was said (most directly by Senator Orrin Hatch, Hearings, 8) to be heir—Associate Justice Thurgood Marshall. The fictive kinship linking Marshall (= grandfather) and Jamal (= Thomas) lengthened the linear dimension of Thomas's life story, heightening its symbolic association with the national civil rights "story." This association also provided the basis for equating Thomas with both the senior and junior men—with Marshall, whose seat Thomas now occupies on the court, and with his "double," Jamal—as if Thomas's own life story in a sense could encompass both the past and the future.

In context, these evocations and recitations of Thomas's life story by himself and others repeatedly made reference to Thomas's physical presence as an African American, though in highly selective and patterned ways. His racial identification as such was repeatedly dissociated from his candidacy and the confirmation process, though both supporters and critics referred to their belief that his race had symbolic value—in very different ways. The prevalent direct racial references were to the *past* and *future* relevance of Thomas's identification as an African American—in the past, as a target of racist discrimination during his childhood in the South; in the future, anticipating his service as Associate Justice as the fruit of Justice Marshall's harvest from his years on the Supreme Court (there were numerous references to Marshall, e.g., Hatch's reference to Thomas as Marshall's "heir"; Hearings, 8). Otherwise, Thomas's "race" tended to frame the story of his upward mobility, the fact of his success contrasting with what were repeatedly said to be the stronger probabilities against it; for example, Thomas recalled watching a group of criminal defendants board a bus from the window of his EEOC office and thinking, "But for the grace of God, there go I" (Thomas, Hearings, 4). Thus, Thomas's exceptional life called forth assertions of what were said to be more typical, and more typically negative, African American lives.

Other references to Thomas's "race" had less (or little) to do with his experience as an individual than with the canons of his thought and the public relevance of his nomination. For example, after reciting Thomas's life story in his own opening remarks, Senator Arlen Specter shifted to an otherwise uncontextualized quotation from Martin Luther King:

> Mr. Chairman, it was 28 years ago that Martin Luther King stood on the steps of the Lincoln Memorial and gave a speech that I believe helped shaped [sic] the conscience of this nation. He said, "I have a dream that my four little children will one day live in a nation where they will not be judged by the color of their skin, but by the content of their character." We're here to learn more about the judicial philosophy of Judge Thomas, but I must say I am flatly and frankly impressed with the personal background and the character of Judge Thomas. (Hearings, 54; see also Senator Strom Thurmond, Hearings, 24)

In a related vein, Hatch made one of several references by senators and by Thomas to King and Lincoln as advocates of natural law theory:

> Well, . . . it seems to me it's apparent that you follow in the footsteps of Abraham Lincoln and Martin Luther King, Jr., who argued that natural law informs the Constitution. Do you agree with that? [Thomas:] I think it informs and inspires it the way we conduct ourselves in this country, Senator, in our political processes. [Hatch:] Well, I agree with that too. (Hearings, 70; see also Thomas, Hearings, 36)

These isolated (though patterned) allusions to "race" intensified toward the end of the first hearings, as senators sought some rhetorical means of summing up "the process" and the nominee. Senator Howard Metzenbaum made direct reference to Thomas's race, in dismissing race as the explanation for the intensity of the committee's scrutiny. Most others were less direct. Hatch evoked and inverted a powerful television image from the civil rights era, alluding to the possibility of a liberal filibuster over Thomas on the Senate floor, and equating it with the conservative efforts to block the expansion of civil rights by filibuster a generation before (Hearings, 9). In the same speech, he borrowed the rhetoric of choice from the abortion debate context, and reintroduced it as the senators' "right of choice" in relation to accepting Thomas's testimony. Even more vividly, Hatch made metaphorical reference to Thomas's "working on the plantation" of the liberals or the conservatives (Hearings, 9–11).

Though race was not generally the explicit subject of the Thomas hearings, the dominance of his life story—as it was told and retold in context—structured the hearings around conventional racial stereotypes, particularly the stereotypical identity of an African American man. In context, this stereotype blended with the rhetorical figure of the future citizen evoked in *Brown*. In other words, the relevance of Thomas's life story was established as the life story of *an* African American man who had overcome the negative aspects of his identity and kept the positive ones. Those positive features were rhetorically reduced to his "memory," his "sensitivity," and his availability as a "role model" to others, presumably younger African American men.

That this "climb"—this "life"—had been possible was simultaneously situated in the civil rights era and in Marshall's specific legacy. Thomas's own use of such references to his life story deepened his (and his advocates') implicit and explicit claims that his life served as the frame within which all interests could find a touchstone (see also Senator Dennis DeConcini, Hearings, 21, for such a reference). More particularly, his own autobiographical references tended to broaden the context in which apparent changes in his positions on legal questions or questions of philosophy could be reassessed as superficial or moot. He stressed that his views were based on his *life* experience, an experience that permitted neither the time (in response to Senator Patrick Leahy on his views on *Roe v. Wade* while a student at Yale Law School, Hearings, 5–6) nor the context for theorizing: "I did not just simply sit around and spend time just trying to spin theories. I had certain experiences that prompted me to think about some of these issues, and with respect to the issue of having a right to—to run my grandfather's business, for example, I simply looked at what in theory was his right" (in response to Senator Heflin, Hearings, 19).

On several occasions, Thomas responded to questions about the development of his views on specific matters of policy during his tenure at the Equal Employment Opportunity Commission or constitutional issues with references to his grandfather or his own childhood perceptions, as when he recounted reflecting on the implications of gender discrimination at the age of eight (in response to Senator Kennedy, Hearings, 28; for related references to childhood or youthful experiences in response to a range of policy questions, see also responses to Senators Edward Kennedy, 24; Howell Heflin, 19; Hank Brown, 26–27; Paul Simon, 32). Though such references were contested by some (e.g., by Biden, 15), they were compelling to others:

> I [Specter] do believe it is very important that Judge Thomas will serve as a role model for young African Americans and he brings a very different perspective to establishment positions and to the political process which is a by-product. Not a reason for supporting him, but in essence, I have more confidence and I pay more attention to his roots than to his writings, and I intend to vote for him. (Hearings, 26)

In many respects, Thomas' treatment by the committee—and to some extent, his own references to himself—were strikingly disembodied. While critics made reference to "two Clarence Thomases" (Simon, 38) or questioned the existence of an "authentic" Clarence Thomas (Senator Herbert Kohl, Hearings, 43), his supporters also rhetorically separated the person from the nominee. For example, introducing Thomas to the committee on the opening day, Danforth claimed that "[o]ther than the nominee himself, I know Clarence Thomas better than anyone who will appear before this committee" (Hearings, 7). In his own opening statement, Thomas also seemed to stand outside himself assessing his life ("I have grown and matured," Hearings, 12). Under evident stress, Thomas (as well as most of the senators) often began statement of belief with such constructions as "I thought that I thought . . ." (or similar) (e.g., Thomas, Hearings, 38). In general, optical metaphors from architecture, cinema, and stage pervaded senators' efforts to define Thomas's position as nominee in the confirmation process. For example, Leahy, speaking against Thomas, referred to wanting "to kind of look into the window of your soul, if I could, although I find the shade down quite a ways" (Hearings, 40). Senator Alan Simpson, speaking for Thomas, rhetorically offered him "the Oscar on judicial temperament" (Hearings, 83). Later, Simpson characterized the entire confirmation process as a "very disturbing ritual" and "a charade" involving "caricature" and "cartoon" (Hearings, 17). On the Senate floor, Danforth defended the relevance of Thomas's life story with the argument that the Court did not need a "bottled brain" (Hearings, 18–19). Hatch, in perhaps the most vivid example of Thomas's simultaneous absence and presence from the first hearings, concluded by congratulating him, adding, "You've added a lot to these proceedings" (Hearings, 21).

In the context of the first hearings' close on September 27, 1991—when, it is now known, at least some of the committee were aware of the sexual harassment report concerning Anita Hill—the contest to characterize Thomas accelerated and changed shape several times. Critics tended to narrow the issues. For example, Leahy deflected the life story canon by referring to Thomas's professional accountabilities (Leahy, 14); more generally, critics reiterated themes of the balance of powers, the current state of the Supreme Court, and the criteria of judicial qualification. Supporters, on the other hand, tended to broaden the issues, referring to the quality of Judge and Mrs. Thomas as people ("I know what kind of quality people they are," Simpson, Hearings, 16) and the unanimity of Thomas's support from people who knew him at the EEOC ("Not one person in this city that I have yet found knows this man and said a single negative thing," Simpson, Hearings, 16).

In the first hearings, Thomas and his supporters invoked his life story as a way of defining African American identity as an identity of discrimination reversed by the civil rights gains during the period of his childhood and young adulthood. In this way, Thomas's personal success was cast as the nation's success. To the extent that the discussion of his professional qualifications claimed center stage, the hearings centered prominently on his EEOC experience as the yardstick of his philosophy and capabilities as a lawyer and future judge, participating in the very agency—indeed, as the very agent—of civil rights.[28]

Overall, the collaborative construction of Thomas's life story appears to have prestructured the meanings, risks and responses inherent in the hearings. While several senators lamented that the sexual harassment "charge" derailed the confirmation process, my own reading of the hearings is that it was Thomas and his supporters who had already defined the grounds of qualification in terms of Thomas's body. The first hearings made his African American body the canvas of a personal and professional life publicly constructed as exceptional—and explicitly in reference to other African American men of his own generation. This was the body he was required to occupy, as it were, by his supporters who cast him as the particular representative of African Americans in the federal context. Whether or not there is "a real Clarence Thomas," even Thomas referred to that person in the third person, as a silent witness to the public figure's life.

Reading the National Life

Pinckney's narrator and Thomas the nominee are constructed out of many of the same signs; I have stressed the elements that I believe to be drawn most directly from *Brown*'s rhetoric and substance. Fictional hero and judicial nominee: both are men of the same age, and both were raised in the *Brown* generation. Both are made to embody—made by their families, teachers, friends, employers—the national life envisioned in *Brown*'s rhetoric. Beneficiaries of opportunities made available by federal power, their very lifetimes confirm the end of an era. The contest over this proposition is to be found in the narrator's inner struggle, and, in very different terms, in the public debate over the Thomas nomination in the Senate and beyond.

Further, the post-*Brown* life story is at the very least a double rhetoric. The "but for" aspect of the life story is explicit in Thomas's personal narrative (gazing out the window at criminal defendants boarding a bus); however, in the fictional narrator's difficulties and self-doubts one finds instead the senses of vulnerability explored in *Brown*. Both "lives" are representative lives, and, from their different perspectives, so are their risks; the issue of representation is explicit in the hearings and in the novel. Both "lives" confirm that the capacity of one life to represent *any* other betrays the fact that a life story is not made of personal stuff; it already belongs to the public. Both Thomas and the narrator must work within or against the knowledge that their individuality is (for the public) only a second-order derivative of their generic function as icons in the national life. Or, to put this another way, their life stories represent national interests, not their own personhood. Indeed, in discussing the public constructions of these images and icons, we are not talking about persons—although we probably ought to be.

Homi Bhabha considers this aspect of the relationship between the nation and difference in his proposition that the "cultural construction of nationness" is "a form of social and textual affiliation" involving "complex strategies of cultural identification and discursive address that function in the name of 'the people' . . . and make them the immanent subjects of a range of social and literary narratives."[29] *Brown* itself emerged from an intersection of literary tropes and patterned social experiences. My reading of *Brown* in retrospect, across Pinckney's novel and Thomas's confirmation, suggests some directions of *Brown*'s enduring affiliations in texts and social practice.

Bhabha views "cultural difference" as an index of the disruptions of the nation's time and space; as we have seen, signs of difference are borrowed from the signs of the nation. This construction of difference cannot create "plurality" since it entails no real referent; rather, "difference" in the nation creates a "double."[30] Such differences always "add up," but they do not "add *to*."[31] Although he does not consider civil rights legislation in his discussion, Bhabha's essay is suggestive for our purposes, underscoring the importance of the ways *Brown* rhetorically resolves the disjunctive status of "Negroes" with the invocation of a future in which African Americans will be productive citizens.

This returns us once again to the issue of "difference" and its unsteady salience in the deictics of time and space in the life of the nation. In Bhabha's formulation, "the nation" is not composed of the stories of its people, but the reverse: citizens are constructed from the nation's identity claims, as figurations of particular contradictions encompassed in the nation itself. As we have seen with respect to *Brown*, while time and space are crucial to the semiotics of the nation, these are not time and space in any ordinary sense. The nation's time is not history; the nation's space is not place.

Cultural pluralism or "multiculturalism," then, cannot be more than a hypothesis predicated on the relations of power that emanate from and instantiate federal power; indeed, it is fair to say (but beyond the scope of this paper to confirm) that "the nation" recognizes only those expressions of difference that federal power *can* mediate. Pinckney's fictional narrator and Thomas's "life" as litanized by his Senate supporters are striking for their play on this inseparability of the curriculum vitae and federal power. Pinckney parodies the federal claims to the meanings of race in the narrative organization of his book (with chapter titles like "The New Negro," "The Color Line," "Equal Opportunities," and "Minority Business"). In Thomas's case, as we have already discussed, the nominee's unwillingness to discuss any aspect of his life or thought other than those elements that conformed to the national life is (in my view) indicative of the power of the federal trope over his narrative to the exclusion of elements that the federal trope does not contain or consider. This raises an important difference between the two "lives."

Although Pinckney's novel is particularly keyed to *Brown*'s rhetoric and the cross-currents of its legacy, the book shares with other contemporary fictional analyses of inequality in the United States a vision of legal or extralegal segregation and its reversals. In more complicated ways, contemporary fiction reverses the deictics of a European semiotics of race and sexuality that makes the "other" into the "non-verbal marker [of] *here* and *there*, *this* and *that*."[32] It is *this* use of people's bodies to separate them from their own times and places that the novels refuse most forcefully. In the novels, the "other" is the sign of the law's absence, civil rights notwithstanding.[33] As in Pinckney's novel, fiction refuses the iconic life, except, perhaps, as a parodic or ironic narrative form, or as a source of specific images and cultural critiques.

Meanwhile, in the life story presented by Clarence Thomas and his supporters, the legalities of race and racial discrimination are cast entirely in the past—certainly no more recently than Thomas's own beginnings, which coincided with the *Brown* decision and Thurgood Marshall's own triumph. Strategically, these had to be explicitly acknowledged, but their purpose was entirely different than in the fictional examples whose contours I have just sketched. Thomas's "life" is made to cancel any possibility of irony in relation to federal civil rights powers; it is offered almost explicitly as proof that *Brown*'s vision of equality has been fulfilled in Thomas. In stressing Thomas's value as a role model, rather than legal interpreter, his supporters cast contemporary inequalities into the domain of individual choice. This brings us to the present, when one hallmark of postmodernity is public anxiety over national practices of recognition, and certain political efforts to sustain these by denying the legitimacy of claims beyond their scope. Under conditions of postmodernity, the "but for" scenario—the dangerous and unproductive citizen—plays a particularly important and insidious role.

Conclusion

Recent cultural politics of the United States has involved currents whose force is accelerated by deepening tensions between race and class as principles of mobilization and reform; the widespread legibility of presidential candidate George Bush's "Willy Horton" ad is a convenient icon of these changes, but the ad was neither their cause nor their onset. Moreover, such tensions are by no means limited to American ground. The globalization of markets for labor and capital has had well-documented impact on urban life in metropolitan centers, particularly in relation to parallel transformations in the globalization of cultural politics.[34] These translocal developments yield compelling comparative problems, as Gilroy and others have shown in their studies of Afro-Caribbean experience in Thatcher-era Britain.[35]

Elsewhere, I have argued for a definition of *modern* society (in any historical period) as any political order whose cultural legitimacy rests on its management of cultural diversity. Correspondingly, a *postmodern* society (again, in any period) cannot abandon the central claims of modernity as to the integral relation between cultural management and political legitimacy, but maintains them primarily by means of a retemporalized present that removes difference from the future.[36] To put this another way, a modern state is one whose legitimacy rests on the promise of future inclusiveness; a postmodern state is one whose promise of inclusiveness is affirmed as its past achievement.

Our present world is postmodern in precisely this sense. Specifically, the epistemological basis of order in the United States (and perhaps elsewhere) shifted significantly in the late 1970s and early 1980s, away from the Enlightenment "social contract" paradigm that prevailed through the civil rights era as liberal pluralism. The intellectual development of sociolegal studies from its roots in and across various academic disciplines originates in this paradigm also. When I refer to the possibility of there having been a paradigm shift, I mean that the "need to know" about difference has shifted from a paradigm whose ideological basis involves hypothetical exchanges among moral equals to one that contemplates highly asymmetrical relationships—judgments and accountings—among actors who are posited as morally unequal. The contrast between the universal affirmations of equality among citizens in *Brown* and the highly pejorative Willy Horton advertisements (which figured dangerous criminals with an African American man) in the first Bush campaign illustrates the differences between the two paradigms. More broadly, the media coverage of the violence in Los Angeles in 1992 has now been generalized to the point that the semiotics of difference have become explicitly coded for violence in a wide variety of everyday contexts.[37] These are not isolated examples, but signs of changing times.

In one variant of the national discourse we have been discussing, difference itself has become criminalized. Criminalization heightens (in reversed form) the constitutive power claimed by the state in relation to subaltern groups. It also heightens the "but for" aspect of the life story trope.[38] The force of such judgments is so pitched that one must consider whether the Enlightenment's social contract paradigm has not given way to a criminal trial paradigm as the new template for public discourses of social order and civility. The sources of evidence for a paradigm shift are not only in academia's internal critiques and tonalities. Just as civil rights made race the paradigm of *identity*, so the new criminal trial paradigm makes race the template for social *judgments*. The modernist affirmations of pluralism have not vanished, but (I would argue) it is the *limits* of pluralism that now occupy the center of public debates about culture, law, economy, politics, and the "world order" in general.

The efficacy of the criminal trial as the vantage point from which to know and (refuse to) reconcile difference is not new (Wright's *Native Son* was published in 1940); this is part of the literary legacy to which *Brown* itself is heir, as I noted at the outset. Still, hallmarks of the new era are a public moral insistence on a stable point of view as an appropriate moral optics (e.g., a refusal of nonconvergent pluralisms), heightened discourses of social responsibility and guilt (e.g., "the deserving poor"), and the active disqualification of individuals and groups from participation in their own futures (e.g., criminalization of AIDS; social control of pregnant women; forcible detainment of refugees). In practice, the criminal trial paradigm reveals an element of the national life that *Brown* captured profoundly, and that is the extent to which one can celebrate a life story without acknowledging the life that *makes* the story.

These concluding reflections might appear to have roamed some distance from the opening discussion of *Brown's* vision. Their link is in the rhetorical construction of the generational interval and its iconic individuality, the state's intervention in the public management of difference, the justification for that intervention in terms of specific social dangers, and the centrality of that role in the state's cultural self-legitimation. For rights advocates, *Brown's* children were the evocations of real human beings and their future well-being. In the current climate, these have become figures of another kind of economy altogether. Since the *Brown* generation has now reached middle age, the benefits of equality having been made available (so this reasoning seems to go) ,inequality is no longer the public's responsibility, but the lifestyle choice of intrinsically inferior citizens. This is an inversion of the "but for" scenario in *Brown,* all the more cruel for its inversion of *Brown's* particular hopefulness.

To put all of this another way, *Brown* defined a version of the classic ethnic success story that has been central to twentieth-century discourses of the nation.[39] For immigrants, the "American dream" and the "melting pot" might have proved elusive, but it was available to them—available to them one at a time, linking generations. Immigrants—as is obvious in the recent California vote for Proposition 187—are also vulnerable to "but for" stereotypes, but their chances were never limited to a single generation. As I say, the current paradigm of criminalized identities is too widespread to be *Brown's* legacy alone, but *Brown's* cultural impact in the United States does make it difficult to imagine a concept of difference that is not also—for better or for worse—a map of federal power.

Notes

I am grateful to Cynthia Werner, Ann Reed, and Teresa Adams Lester for their research assistance. Indiana University and the Rockefeller Foundation's Bellagio Study Center provided support for the larger project on which this chapter draws. Conference participants at Amherst provided helpful readings. Particular thanks go to Peggy Davis, Paul Gewirtz, Robert Gooding Williams, and David Wilkins—and to our host, Austin Sarat, for a challenging question. Some material in this chapter was adapted from Carol J. Greenhouse, *A Moment's Notice: Time Politics across Cultures,* chapter 6. Copyright © 1996 by Cornell University Press. Used by permission of the publisher, Cornell University Press.

1. For discussion of "law and order" in British electoral politics, see Centre for Contemporary Cultural Studies, *The Empire Strikes Back: Race and Racism in Thatcher-Era Britain* (New York: Routledge, 1982).

2. I base this characterization of the plaintiff's position and the Supreme Court's opinion on 98 F. Supp. 797, 387 U.S. 483; also, Daniel Berman, *It Is So Ordered: The Supreme Court Rules on Segregation* (New York: W. W. Norton, 1966); Leon Friedman ed. *Argument: The Oral Argument Before the Supreme Court in* Brown v. Board of Education of Topeka, 1952–55 (New York: Chelsea House, 1983), esp. pp. xxxvi–xxxviii; Richard Kluger, *Simple Justice* (New York: Alfred A. Knopf, 1975); Gabriel Moens, *Equality for Freedom: A Critical Study of Unresolved Problems of School Desegregation Cases in the United States* (Wien-Stuttgart: Universitäts-Verlagsbuchhandlung, 1976); J. Harvie Wilkinson, III *From* Brown *to* Bakke: *The Supreme Court and School Integration* 1954–1978 (New York: Oxford University Press, 1979); Mark Whitman, *Removing a Badge of Slavery: The*

Record of Brown v. Board of Education (Princeton and New York: Markus Wiener Publishing, 1993), chs. 1 and 2.

3. Experimental findings included the famous "doll test" by Kenneth Clark, which established a connection between racism, commodity culture, and children's self-images. This test, too, supplied an important image to subsequent literature; see, for example, Toni Morrison, *The Bluest Eye* (New York: Washington Square Press, 1970).

4. 347 U.S. 483.

5. See Anthony G. Amsterdam, "Telling Stories and Stories About Them," 19 *Clinical Law Review*. I am indebted to Peggy Davis for drawing my attention to Amsterdam's essay.

6. Subsequent civil rights legislation accelerated this layering; see Carol Greenhouse, "Figuring the Future: Local and Global After Los Angeles," in *Power and Justice in Sociological Studies*, Bryant Garth and Austin Sarat, eds. (Evanston, IL: Northwestern University Press, forthcoming, 1997).

7. Richard Wright, *Native Son* (New York: Harper Collins, 1993 [1940]).

8. Allison Davis & John Dollard, *Children of Bondage: The Personality Development of Negro Youth in the Urban South* (Washington, D.C.: American Council on Education, 1940).

9. St. Clair Drake & Horace Cayton, *Black Metropolis: A Study of Negro Life in a Northern City* (Chicago: University of Chicago Press, 1993 [1945]).

10. Kluger, supra note 2, at 421.

11. Darryl Pinckney, *High Cotton* (New York: Penguin, 1992).

12. Id. at 3.

13. Id. at 4; emphasis added.

14. Id.

15. Id. at 6.

16. Id. at 26–27.

17. Id. at 49.

18. Id. at 107.

19. Id.

20. Id. at 123–24.

21. Id. at 220.

22. Id. at 291.

23. Id. at 304

24. Id. at 309.

25. M. M. Bakhtin, *The Dialogic Imagination*, Michael Holquist ed. (Austin: University of Texas Press, 1981), at 254–56; passage quoted is from pp. 255–56.

26. References in the text are to the published hearings of the United States Senate Judiciary Committee, Nomination of Judge Clarence Thomas to be an Associate Justice of the Supreme Court of the United States: Hearings before the Committee on the Judiciary, 102d Cong. 1st sess. September 10, 11, 12, 13, 16, 1991. (Hereafter Hearings.)

27. I am grateful to Fred Aman for pointing out that Biden's spontaneous remark involves an implicit contrast between Thomas's "climb" during the civil rights era, and Jamal's instantaneous success—the hallmark of full equality in the post–civil rights era.

28. It is worth noting that while the second hearings, involving Anita Hill, aimed at tightening the seams in Thomas's adult life story (Thomas's own metaphor was to a lynching, Hearings, 9), Thomas appears to have felt constrained by the

biographical narrative of his life during the earlier hearings, too. Thomas repeatedly sought to disaggregate his professional autobiography to account for his various silences. While Thomas readily accepted (and offered) a narrative version of his life that stressed the sequence of his commitments, he just as quickly expressed reluctance to permit his written and spoken record to speak for him (in general, see statement of Clarence Thomas, Hearings, 44, distinguishing between policy-making and judicial roles). Anticipating confirmation, he declined to express his views on numerous legal issues on the grounds that they might compromise his impartiality later (see statement of Clarence Thomas in response to Senator Metzenbaum, Hearings, 39). In the context of questions on constitutional guarantees of abortion, for example, Thomas consistently equated the expression of opinion with a compromised vote.

These rhetorical efforts to create some space *within* his autobiography culminated in Thomas's references to the need to "strip down" (that is, refrain from expressing personal views) in accepting a judicial position (statement of Clarence Thomas in response to Senator Kohl, Hearings, 10). The autobiographical frame within which Thomas and his supporters presented his career paradoxically highlighted Thomas's commitment to silence on these and other matters, and provided the rhetorical basis for his critics' challenges on substantive policy (and other) questions.

29. Homi Bhabha, *The Location of Culture* (New York: Routledge, 1994), 140.

30. Id. at 154.

31. Id. at 163.

32. Hortense J. Spillers, "Introduction: Who Cuts the Border? Some Readings on 'America,'" in *Comparative American Identities: Race, Sex, and Nationality in the Modern Text*, Hortense Spillers ed. (New York: Routledge, 1991), 8.

33. For a discussion of the relationship of self, absence, other, law, and accountability in Morrison's *Beloved*, see Mae G. Henderson, "Toni Morrison's *Beloved*: Re-membering the Body as Historical Text," in Spillers ed., supra note 32, at 62–86, esp. 82–83. Henderson argues that "[f]or Morrison, the absent is only the 'other' of the present—just as the repressed is only the other of the conscious" (p. 83).

34. In general, see Saskia Sassen, *The Mobility of Labor and Capital* (Cambridge: Cambridge University Press, 1988); Sassen, *The Global City* (Princeton: Princeton University Press, 1991).

35. Center for the Study of Contemporary Culture, supra note 1.

36. Carol J. Greenhouse, *A Moment's Notice: Time Politics Across Cultures* (Ithaca: Cornell University Press, 1996). I prefer to use the terms "modern" and "postmodern" in spite of their misleading evocations of a periodization of states and styles, on two grounds. First, the terms will be familiar to readers, as will my claims that they stand for very large-scale cultural developments with implications for the conditions—at every level—in which people live. At the same time, I want to use the terms to contest what I view as their overuse—particularly that of the "postmodern," which seems to have become a term to describe any two ideas, styles, or things that do not obviously "go" together. In the text, below, I suggest that the issue of what goes with what arises from the criminal trial paradigm, i.e., that "hybrid expressivity" (as Houston Baker terms it) is hybrid precisely in relation to (and against) the criminal trial paradigm's tacit assertion of the moral necessity of maintaining a single, stable point of view.

37. See Robert Gooding-Williams ed. *Reading Rodney King/Reading Urban Uprising* (New York: Routledge, 1993).

38. These connections are made plain in Houston Baker's essay on the public condemnation of "black youth" following the arrest of several young African American men accused of rape (the so-called wilding) in New York's Central Park. Implicitly and explicitly, Baker uncovers the discursive links between the criminal trial and the ordinary language of social description. Once difference is criminalized, sociological description, too, becomes a language of social judgment.

39. Phyllis Pease Chock, "'Illegal Aliens' and 'Opportunity': Myth-Making in Congressional Testimony," 18 *American Ethnologist* (1991), 279.

8

GARY PELLER

Cultural Imperialism, White Anxiety, and the Ideological Realignment of *Brown*

Brown I itself did not need to rely upon any psychological or social-science research in order to announce the simple, yet fundamental truth that the Governement cannot discriminate among its citizens on the basis of race. . . . As the Court's unanimous opinion indictated: "In the field of public education the doctrine of 'separate but equal' has no place. Separate educational facilities are inherently unequal." . . . At the heart of this interpretation of the Equal Protection Clause lies the principle that the Government must treat citizens as individuals, and not as members of racial, ethnic or religious groups. It is for this reason that we must subject all racial classifications to the strictest of scrutiny.

Clarence Thomas, 1995[1]

This essay considers the transformation from the color blindness ideology embodied in *Brown v. Board*[2] to the more recent emergence of "cultural pluralism" and "multiculturalism" as the dominant categories through which progressive American whites think about racial justice. For many of us throughout the sixties and seventies, the Supreme Court's *Brown* text and the eventual federal court enforcement of school desegregation policies were emblematic of progressive law reform, if not idealized as the epitome of liberatory social change through litigation. But, as I discuss in this essay, the kind of racial integration envisaged in the *Brown* consciousness embodied conservative assumptions about culture, identity, and difference. The contemporary (though belated) embrace of "color blindness" by the right is partly linked to a "principled" reading of what *Brown* stood for and what the opinion meant as a broader symbol of civil rights reform in American society—including some of the very ideals that moderate and left-leaning whites used to champion but have come, in the ensuing decades, to experience as backward and regressive.

The rejection of "color blindness" in favor of "multiculturalism" as the frame through which progressive whites understand racial justice is, to my mind, a positive development in American racial dynamics. One strand of this essay traces the discursive terrain traversed by progressive whites in the decades since *Brown*, and, conversely, maps the route by which *Brown* has been symbolically appropriated in the 1990s by a new racial conservatism, articulated by Justice Clarence Thomas and others. The aim is to reread *Brown* through the lens of contempory assumptions about culture, race, and ethnicity in order to explain its recent ideological realignment.

A second strand of this essay highlights a particular link between the multicultural sensibility and the recent lack of progressive white activism around issues of race. A paradoxical tendency towards cultural isolationism has often been associated with the embrace of multicultural ideology by whites. As I see it, intense anxiety about the risks of exercising "cultural imperialism" over "other" groups has led many whites to view cultural nonintervention as the guiding norm for their social practices. This response is understandable in light of the belated realization that the racial consciousness symbolized by *Brown* represented a false form of universalism blind to the mores of white American culture as they were imbedded in the everyday life of workplaces and schools. Self-doubt is probably preferable to the worst forms of cultural presumptuousness characterizing the racial dynamics of the recent past. But anxiety about the limits of our own cultural position also tends to leave progressive whites silent and passive in the face of politically conservative and often authoritarian representations of the interests of minority communities.

Section I describes, in very general and basic terms, the ways that progressive whites today tend to view racial and ethnic difference, and the central place that the injunction to avoid "cultural imperialism" occupies within that contemporary racial ideology. Section II relates the multicultural sensibility to the Clarence Thomas/Anita Hill controversy, focusing on how the image of African American cultural particularity was deployed to immunize Thomas's harassment of Hill and to immobilize white criticism. In Section III the noninterventionist posture is contrasted with the broad-scale regulation of southern life that *Brown* represented and that progressives of the period proudly supported. Section IV traces the genealogy of contemporary progressive white race ideology from *Brown*, to the Black nationalist critique of *Brown*'s integrationist assumptions, and, through their contrasting interpretations of *Brown* and the general course of the school desegregation effort, to the various features of the 1960s black nationalist ideology that have been appropriated by both conservatives and progressives today. In Section V, I set forth an analytic critique of the general idea of deferring to the self-determination of "other" cultural groups; I argue that this imagery of deference and nonintervention echoes, at the level of groups, the assumptions that free market ideology makes about individuals and that progressives have already properly rejected as incoherent. I also suggest that there is a link between this "laissez-faire" way of thinking about relations between cultural groups and the conservative presentations of group identity that mark recent right-wing appropriation of 1960s Black Nationalist rhetoric. The essay concludes by suggesting an alternative way to think about race, a "postmodern" attitude about cultural difference and nationalist integrity that seeks to retain a liberatory aspect of *Brown*—the social will to intervene, even forcefully and coercively, to transform oppressive social structures.

A few words about method:[3] In this essay, I treat *Brown v. Board* as a cultural symbol for a set of recognizable, though constantly reinterpreted and contested, ideologies about race in America. There are many other ways to approach *Brown*—as standing for particular philosophical principles[4] or social policies that might be debated, or as posing a specific doctrinal approach to the legal issue of the appropriate interpretation of the Constitution, or as the actual causal agent for public school desegregation. Part of the significance of *Brown*, of course, is that its literal text was produced in the American legal arena, so that its meaning is bound up with more general notions about legal authority and specific, localized controversies about legitimacy and the role of neutral principles in judicial decision making. But in this essay, I take *Brown* to signify a broader "text" as well, one that includes not only the specific moment of the Supreme Court's opinion but also the ways that *Brown* consequently has been interpreted, constructed, rejected, and appropriated in American racial ideologies. While the debate about the legal or institutional legitimacy of the Supreme Court's rulings in *Brown* and its progeny is important, my focus here is on reading *Brown* both as a still contested and highly charged cultural icon, and more specifically as a historical demarcation point from which to analyze the dynamics of transformation over the last several decades. From this perspective, *Brown* is both a reflection of and a constituent factor in ongoing struggles over how to comprehend and describe race and its place in the social world. The particular legal institutionalization of the racial consciousness reflected in *Brown* is only one part of that story.[5]

Finally, given my specific interest in viewing *Brown* through the lenses of contemporary multiculturalism, I take as starting-point assumptions that there is such a thing as cultural difference between groups in American society and that African Americans and whites in general inhabit significantly—though of course not totally—different cultural spaces.

I. The Racial Predicament of Progressive Whites

Later in this essay, I trace the steps that progressive whites followed in the decades after *Brown* leading to the adoption of multiculturalism as the organizing norm of racial justice. Rather than start chronologically with *Brown*, however, I want first to depict, in very general terms, the problem of "cultural imperialism" as it is situated in contemporary progressive white conciousness, in order to provide a point of contrast for the *Brown* history.

As I use the term, "multiculturalism" refers to a recognizable ideology, associated with left-of-center politics and social style and manifest in a loosely connected set of attitudes and practices sharing, in one way or another, the notion that American society should be understood as a collection of diverse cultural groups rather than as a single, unified national body on the one hand or as simply an aggregate of atomized individuals on the other. It is distinguished from the traditional liberal civil rights vision evoked by Clarence Thomas in the passage that opens this essay in that it takes the status of group membership as a positive, meaning-generating value rather than an irrational or arbitrary attribute. Unlike the governmental color blindness that Thomas advocates, a multiculturalist sensibility implies that the government must recognize and respect if not nurture the diversity and integrity of racial and ethnic communities.

Stated in this amorphous way, I am suggesting that a wide range of social phenomena—the appearance of Afrocentric schools, political support for bilingual education, university campaigns for "diverse" faculty hiring, legal consideration of the "culture defense," campus hate speech codes, the official institutionalization of "Black History Month," sidewalk tolerance of "Free Mike Tyson" sweatshirts, and so on—are linked by a recognizable, shared ideology about the nature of race, ethnicity, and difference. The point is not that this is all new—clearly, bits and pieces have been contained in past efforts at "cultural appreciation" and the like—but rather that, in the mid-1990s, a notion of cultural integrity has replaced antidiscrimination as the main frame through which progressives understand racial justice. Multiculturalism in this sense is not meant as a philosophical position or social theory, but rather a vaguer, less worked-out background sensibility.

It is within this new sensibility—that racial justice means respecting the integrity of diverse cultural groups in the social fabric—that the idea of "cultural imperialism" assumes a central place. Again, it is not as if this notion is totally new by any means—it is, after all, a metaphor referring to the classic colonial relationships between "nations"—but instead that it has been centered in a recognizable and particularly contemporary racial ideology.

The idea of "cultural imperialism" is that one cultural group will impose its norms on another. The "cultural" side reflects the notion that colonialism is not always imposed by visible material force nor according to the boundaries of formally constituted nation-states. The "imperialism" side embodies the understanding that disparate power is at issue.

The well-known controversy over whether Westerners should condemn female genital mutilation[6]—despite claims that it is an integral ethnic ritual when seen from within particular African tribal worldviews—puts the cultural imperialism issue in clear focus, given the international context and the clear history of European colonial domination in Africa. But the international rights debate is only one, relatively distanced (for virtually all Americans) site where the colonialism framework operates; anxiety about cultural imperialism is more local and common. There is a sense in which it looms in the background of everyday relations between whites and blacks, Anglos and Latinos, and so on, as less a worked-out ethical dilemma and more an undercurrent of social interaction in America.

Anxiety about exercising cultural imperialism is the manifestation of two different kinds of impulses that progressive whites want to respect. First, as progressives we strive to make the world a better place, to relieve suffering, and to effect a more egalitarian distribution of wealth, power, and recognition. These commitments suggest active intervention in the social world. Second, we simultaneously believe in rights of community self-determination and the correlate principle that white cultural norms should not dominate the cultures of other people, particularly historically disempowered groups. The prevailing norm is to defer to the mores and wishes of other cultural groups.

Given these two impulses, progressive whites have faced a repetitive dilemma. The substantive impulse to reform the world in a progressive fashion is met by a procedural impulse—with its own progressive pedigree in the language of anti-imperialism—to respect and celebrate, or at the very least tolerate, difference. The result of this tension has often been paralysis: the inability to resolve, in a series of particular contexts, whether it is acceptable to criticize and intervene in an attempt to influence another group, or whether this intervention constitutes cultural imperialism; whether progressive whites should actively intervene in race politics, or simply defer to the decisions of people of color; and so on.

A general consequence of progressive preoccupation with this set of issues has been that, while conservatives in America have articulated a substantive and existentially evocative vision of how the world should be, liberals and progressives have instead struggled over whether it is acceptable to take a position at all. Conservatives have staked out a stance in the "culture wars" and clearly marked their territory, as boring, square, and false as their picture might be to a left-leaning constituency. Liberals and progressives, however, have spoken less in terms of substantive visions and more in terms of procedural-type values such as inclusion and respect for other cultures. This phenomenon is particularly evident among Anglo, straight males who do not identify as members of structurally victimized communities (indeed not as members of any socially constructed group at all), but it is also apparent with respect to how whites relate more generally to people of color.

I believe that the injunction to respect the autonomy and self-determination rights of other cultural groups reflects real progress on the part of progressive whites. It was not that long ago, after all, that whites unselfconsciously dominated and directed major civil rights organizations, or, as I discuss shortly, integrated public schools primarily by closing black schools and replacing black teachers. After years of painful critique on this score, we have come to understand that our "help" can itself constitute a form of domination.

On the other hand, I also think that the centering of cultural imperialism has provided a discursive framework seeming to confirm that it is progressive not to act in many instances when intervention would make the world better. As I discuss below, the idea of avoiding "cultural imperialism" cannot resolve the difficult but inevitable issue of what whites should do with the racial power that we actually possess; not exercising this power does not make it disappear. I am not claiming either that the kind of white anxiety I am describing is the most important problem of contemporary race dynamics, or that whites should stop paying any attention to these concerns. I address "cultural imperialism" simply as one trope among the many complex and cross-cutting strands of our racial landscape; my particular interest is in exploring how this belief structure has helped disempower progressive forces in cultural and political conflict with conservatives.

This general description of "multiculturalism" and "cultural imperialism" is meant to evoke a recognizable piece of our cultural landscape. More than a set of "ideas" or "premises" in a theoretic model, the point is that, as a social ideology, this sensibility is a lived part of, and helps constitute, everyday psychocultural experience. Accordingly, its range of influence sets the boundaries not only for what is considered acceptable in the realm of public policy and official institutional culture, but also for the terms of microencounters in everyday social life—think of the way that many whites adopt black vernacular in integrated social settings. In the next part of this essay, I explore how the "ideas" I've just described helped frame social perception and regulate political energy in the context of the Clarence Thomas/Anita Hill confrontation.

II. Clarence Thomas, Anita Hill and a "Down Home Style of Courting"

> With his mainstream cultural guard down, Judge Thomas on several misjudged occasions may have done something completely out of the cultural frame of his white, upper-middle-class work world, but immediately recognizable to Professor Hill and most women of Southern working-class backgrounds, white or black, especially the latter. . . . I am convinced that Professor Hill perfectly understood the psycho-cultural context in which Judge Thomas allegedly regaled her with his Rabelaisian humor (possibly as a way of affirming their common origins), which is precisely why she never filed a complaint against him. . . . [S]he has lifted a verbal style that carries only minor sanction in one subcultural context and thrown it into the overheated cultural arena of mainstream, neo-Puritan America, where it incurs professional extinction. . . . [M]ost of Professors Hill's supporters seem to be middle-class white women. My own daughter, Barbara, a post-feminist young woman brought up by two feminists who came of age in the 60's, believes along with her friends that Judge Thomas did say those raunchy things, should have been told at once what a 'dog' he was and reported to the authorties by Professor Hill if his advances continued to annoy her. But they cannot see the relevance of Judge Thomas's down-home style of courting to his qualifications for the Supreme Court.
>
> Orlando Patterson, 1991[7]

To get a more concrete sense of the contemporary ideological situation, think back to the Anita Hill/Clarence Thomas hearings. One of the explicit charges made against Anita Hill was that she represented white feminism, directly, in the sense that white feminists were putting her up to testifying and advising her while the controversy went on, and indirectly because a white feminist ideology had problematized "sexual harrassment" as a trope in the first place. Orlando Patterson, an esteemed black male Harvard sociology professor, articulated this analysis of Hill quite explicitly in the *New York Times* op-ed piece from which I have quoted. His argument is an exemplar of what is commonly called "the culture defense," the idea that taboos are culturally specific and thus what would be a transgression in one culture may not be in another. Underlying its deployment is the premise that the stronger group should not impose its norms on the weaker. [8]

Patterson's editorial is actually a vivid example of the twists and turns required by an argument based on an accusation of cultural imperialism and invoking the authority of the "subcultural group." Patterson's overt argument is that Hill in a sense perpetuated a culture fraud on mainstream American culture by pretending that she did not recognize Clarence Thomas's behavior simply as "down-home courting" rather than sexual harassment. Patterson's authority to expose her fraud is, apparently, his own status as an African American, signifying a culture he claims they share.

But as soon as that authority is expressed, it is immediately evident that it is insufficient. If this is an issue of possible gender domination, it makes no more sense for a male like Patterson to adjudicate it than it would for "[white] mainstream, neo-puritan America" to adjudicate the mores of Hill and Thomas, two African Americans. Given this reflexive tendency of Patterson's brand of the culture defense to turn on itself, it is not suprising that he awkwardly deploys the authority of "my own daughter . . . along with her friends." Yet even that deployment is suspect, from the viewpoint of sensitivity to the risk of imperialism: he gives as his daughter's main credential that she was brought up by "two feminists," reverting obliquely around to his own authority as a "good male" while manifestly claiming to be invoking the authority of females.

It is not that we should ignore Patterson because his "argument" has these internal contradictions. These limitations do not matter because the effectiveness of his intervention depended on the particular anxiety cultural imperialism that whites *already* experienced. Patterson's editorial was one example of the many ways that this dynamic played out during the Thomas/Hill confrontation. The gist was that Hill represented white feminism, and thus supporting her meant violating the norm of cultural and racial self-determination. It is a sign of its strength that it is not only progressive whites who honor the principle, but moderates as well: Senator Sam Nunn, a centrist from Georgia, openly justified his vote by pointing to the overnight poll results showing overwhelming support for Thomas among Georgia blacks. [9] There was, in all of this debate, no need to justify or argue about the underlying premise of cultural deference because cultural deference was a key implied component of the reigning multicultural sensibility.

The Thomas/Hill confrontation also implicated a second dimension of the "cultural defense": its deployment in service of a conservative, traditionalist, and allegedly authoritative representation of a "culture." The force of Patterson's argument against intervention depends on two assumptions: first, the idea that whites must respect the cultural integrity of the African American community, and second, that Patterson himself was authentically representing the black community's dating mores. Given the cultural geography that multiculturalism celebrates, most whites are in no position to challenge the accuracy of "indigenous" descriptions of native cultural space. However, if Hill's depictions were accurate, as Patterson assumes, to me it does not reveal a distant courtship ritual practiced across cultural boundaries. Instead, her account describes a common, recognizable—albeit particularly awkward and bizzarre (the "pubic hair on the Coke can")—genre of male sexual acting out with which most people in both black and white culture are familiar. (This is not to say that it is a universal or inevitable phenomenon.)

The progressive white community, however, is politically and culturally vulnerable to the accusations of improper intervention as exemplified by Patterson's editorial. It would be silly to claim that Patterson as an individual contributed in a significant way to Thomas's confirmation. On the other hand, the attitude expressed by Patterson was, I believe, part of a wider point of racial confrontation that undercut the will and the confidence of white opponents of Thomas and contributed to his ultimate confirmation.[10] Patterson's accusation that Hill was a tool of white feminism directly addressed white liberal anxieties about engaging in cultural ethnocentrism; it equated feminist reformism with white imperialism, thus linking feminist criticism to the "lynching" metaphor of Thomas's testimony.[11]

The high-profile nature of the Thomas/Hill confrontation made the deployment of cultural difference against white progressives particularly obvious. But progressive whites face this same hurdle of cultural legitimacy at various points of cultural contact, ranging from broad doctrinal questions about various forms of the "culture defense" or debates about American foreign policy, to specific questions of how whites ought to react to Minister Louis Farrakhan or the O. J. Simpson verdict. As crystallized in the Thomas/Hill confrontation, the question was what white progressives thought Sam Nunn should have done when presented with the apparent self-determination of the black community manifesting approval of Thomas? Within what understanding of racial and cultural justice was Nunn to oppose Thomas, without reverting to the discredited tradition of vicious Old South paternalism represented by Nunn's Georgia predecessor, Herman Talmadge?

In the remainder of this essay, I want ultimately to defend an "interventionist" orientation against the reigning notion that whites must defer to the dominant voice of "other" communities or be guilty of cultural imperialism. The motivation for this argument is a general belief that, under the rubric of

"respecting the self-determination rights of cultural communities," whites
have often neglected some of the best aspects of our progressive tradition, the
willingness to intervene to create a more just social world. [12]

III. *Brown* and the Colonization of the South: Replacing Down-Home Schooling with New South Technocracy

> Local control results in the same kind of intellectual parochialism that
> characterizes schools in totalitarian countries. . . . National survival
> now requires educational policies which are not subject to local
> veto. . . . It is becoming increasingly clear that local control cannot in
> practice be reconciled with the ideals of a democratic society. . . .
> Local control is a major cause of the dull parochialism and attenuated
> totalarianism that characterizes public education in operation.
>
> Myron Lieberman, 1960[13]

In this section, I utilize the multicultural sensibility I have sketched above as
the framework to describe the enforcement of *Brown*'s desegregation ruling as a
colonialist intervention of northern—more specifically, northeastern—power
and cultural ideology in the South. My aim is to provide a point of contrast
from which to reconsider today's reflexive deference to "other" cultures.

Contemporary caution about the dangers of cultural intervention is mark-
edly different from the confidence and sense of righteousness that characterized the specific federal enforcement of *Brown*'s desegregation ruling in the
South, and that marked the more general assurance, openly expressed by
Lieberman and others, that the parochialism of southern culture could be
transcended by centrally administering southern schools. Seen through the
filters of contemporary concerns about "cultural imperialism," the relationship between the Northeast and the South during the 1960s looks, in retrospect, classically and unabashedly colonialist. *Brown* appears as one face of a
broad northeastern intervention into what might be seen as the indigenous
culture of "the South" as it existed prior to the mid-fifties, an intervention that
included elements of physical and material coercion; the delegitimation of the
justificatory ideology of natural order and divine authority; the substitution of
the discourses of technocracy, professionalism, bureaucratic expertise, and
competent management; and the associated replacement of the former ruling
aristocrats with a New South leadership more pleasing to northeastern sensi-
bilities. [14]

The material dimension of northern intervention was dramatic. Armed
troops enforced the *Brown* ruling, albeit after official legal delay and massive
resistance including "Impeach Earl Warren" billboards sprinkling southern
highways. The famous Little Rock television coverage—the nationally broad-
cast images of coolly professional, armed federal officers protecting a fright-
ened black girl arriving for the first day of school with a bookbag and a
lunchbox and facing a venomous mob of screaming white adults—remains
powerful and compelling even today. The visual images combine the dra-

matic quality of the intervention through coercive, militaristic power with a moving portrayal of the existential basis for the exercise of that power.

Less dramatic versions of the Little Rock scene were reenacted in school after school across the South in the mid-to late 1960s. Even after the first wave of white parental resistance subsided, students typically started the first school year in desegregated schools under the shadow of bayonets held by federal or national guard soldiers perched on the roof "in case of trouble." The presence of troops to enforce federal court desegregation orders was a visible and clear reminder that power was being exercised from the outside, by an authority structure external to and superior to the locals who had administered the southern version of American apartheid.

But the "takeover" of the South did not consist simply in the enforcement of legal rulings under *Brown*, although that was its most dramatic point of visible coercive intervention. *Brown* was part of a broader critique of and intervention into the status quo culture of southern life; in general terms, the trajectory of northern regulation was to replace the all-white, Old South patriarchal ruling class with a somewhat integrated, rationalist and technocratic New South leadership, both literally in terms of political office, and more generally in terms of everyday cultural and ideological legitimacy in diverse institutions.

It accordingly made sense that federal courts banned school prayer, a common and significant ritual in southern schools, at about the same time that they implemented *Brown*. In the ideology of federal intervention, both reforms consisted of replacing the parochialism and narrowmindedness of southern schools with the rationality of northern professionalism and expertise. At the level of cultural symbolism, racism and religiosity were linked as irrational and ignorant belief structures, to be contrasted with the face of northeastern legitimacy, the enlightenment of science and the rationality of the rule of law.

By the time that the various facets of northern intervention had played themselves out, the transformation of everyday southern culture was striking, particularly with respect to schools. By the mid-1970s, public education in the South proceeded for the most part on a legally desegregated basis,[15] virtually all school prayer had ceased, and, more generally, the kind of centralized professionalism advocated by Lieberman replaced virtually any semblance of local southern influence over schools. Significantly, the rest of the traditional school practices—paddling, singing, an informal maternal network of educators, curricular education in moral virtues and social values—were, without any legal compulsion from the North, replaced with the latest in standardized instruction, evaluation, curriculum, and administration. Ultimately, the schools became in most respects—with the notable exception of the students' and faculty's accents—indistinguishable from those in the Northeast. The colonization of southern schools was accomplished over little more than a decade between the appearance of armed troops and the ultimate administration of the modernization project by a heralded "New South" suburbanite class recruited to manage the new order. In terms of the excercise of cultural power, it was as if alien educational institutions designed in the Northeast had simply been placed in the midst of southern communities by an occupying force with superior might and ultimately the ability to impose a new ideology of legitimacy and authority.

Support for the federal government's coercion of local southern school boards on matters of race and religion, and the correlate critique of southern white culture as parochial and backward, constituted an important part of what identified one as a progressive during the sixties and seventies. As the image of the thickly accented "redneck" was explicitly utilized by the popular media as the comical signifier of uncivilized stupidity, the possibility that one should respect the "cultural differences" of white southerners simply did not appear on the progressive ideological screen.

The point here is not to bemoan the destruction of the dominant southern white culture of the pre-*Brown* period, nor to condemn the implementation of *Brown* and the associated reform of the South on the ground that it all constituted a form of colonialism with respect to the region's "traditions." As I discuss, what might be called the *Brown* intervention was properly understood as in many ways heroic and virtuous; it was a good thing to topple the old regime. Aspects of the intervention also were colonialist and imperialist as well. My aim in framing the description in these terms is to highlight how much white progressives' assurance about the legitimacy of coercive intervention has changed from support for the explicit regulation of the southern social structure to today's reigning anxiety about the risks of engaging in cultural imperialism. It is possible, of course, that *Brown* was not experienced as a colonialist intervention because the group being coerced consisted of other whites (or other "Americans"), and thus white northerners did not experience themselves as excercising power over an "other" cultural group. Alternatively, perhaps southern culture was seen as so bound up with racism that it was deemed worthy of destruction, or, to say this differently, "the issues were so much clearer then." But I do not believe that either of these possibilities accounts for the contrast between progressive whites' enthusiasm for the regulation of the South in the 1960s and 1970s and our contemporary anxiety about intervention.

The next section of this essay examines the substantive racial ideologies that progressive whites held at the time of *Brown* and their subsequent repudiation in order to suggest that the universalist and rationalist racial norms of integrationism and color blindness that *Brown* for a time represented were ideologically linked with the social willingness to intervene across cultural boundaries. While this section treated the *Brown*-oriented transformation of the South as a possible form of cultural imperialism when viewed from the viewpoint of status quo white southern traditionalism, I next consider *Brown* as emblematic of the imposition of culturally imperialist power vis-à-vis blacks themselves, a charge that has, I believe, propelled progressive whites to reconsider and repudiate the ways that racial justice was understood at the time of *Brown*.

IV. The Construction of Multiculturalism and the Reinterpretation of *Brown*

A school system in an all-white neighborhood is not a segregated school system. The only time it's segregated is when it is in a community other than white, but that at the same time is controlled by the whites. So my understanding of a segregated school system, or a segregated community, or a segregated school, is a school that's controlled by people other than those that go there. . . . On the other hand, if we can get an all-Black school that we can control, staff it ourselves with the type of teachers that have our good at heart, with the type of books that have in them many of the missing ingredients that have produced this inferiority complex in our people, then we don't feel that an all-Black school is necessarily a segregated school. It's only segregated when it's controlled by someone from the outside. . . . So, what the integrationists, in my opinion, are saying when they say that whites and Blacks must go to school together, is that the whites are so much superior that just their presence in a Black classroom balances it out. I just can't go along with that.

Malcolm X, 1963[16]

It never ceases to amaze me that the courts are so willing to assume that anything that is predominantly black must be inferior. . . . First, the court has read our cases to support the theory that black students suffer an unspecified psychological harm from segregation that retards their mental and educational development. This approach not only relies upon questionable social science research rather than constitutional principle, but it also rests on an assumption of black inferiority . . . the idea that any school that is black is inferior, and that blacks cannot succeed without the benefit of the company of whites. . . . Given that desegregation has not produced the predicted leaps forward in black educational achievement, there is no reason to think that black students cannot learn as well when surrounded by members of their own race as when they are in an integrated environment. Indeed, it may very well be that what has been true for historically black colleges is true for black middle and high schools. . . . [B]lack schools can function as the center and symbol of black communities, and provide examples of independent black leadership, success, and achievement.

Justice Clarence Thomas, 1995[17]

To understand the stakes of the cultural imperialism charge for progressives today, it helps to consider the genesis from "color blindness" to "difference" as the dominant way of understanding race. When Malcolm X opposed school integration, the civil rights movement, led by Reverend Martin Luther King, Jr. was near its apex. Malcolm X spoke against school integration in the same year as the March on Washington, where King's "I Have a Dream" speech movingly summarized the moral basis for color blindness.[18] And the country had just symbolically committed itself to the coercive enforcement of school desegregation in the South in Little Rock and other sites. Although Malcolm X's rhetoric actually represented a revitalization (and radicalization) of a tradition of Black Nationalist ideology with long roots in the mid-nineteenth century, he was experienced, at least by virtually all liberal and progressive whites, as a militant and somewhat crazy reverse racist, as the black equivalent to the never-say-die segregationists in the South. Both white racists and Malcolm X violated the reigning moral norm that color makes no difference between people and that only irrational and prejudiced people thought that it did. In the dominant perception of liberals and progressives, the key racial conflict was between enlightened integrationists and ignorant segregationists. Malcolm X was simply off the map.[19]

The transformation of reigning racial assumption over the last three decades is dramatically manifest in the way that Clarence Thomas's rhetoric in 1995 echoes Malcolm X's critique of integrationism. Thomas represents a neoconservative ideology fundamentally at odds with the left-leaning and revolutionary worldview of Malcolm X, Stokely Carmichael, the Black Panthers and other Black Nationalists of the sixties and early seventies. No one interprets his rhetoric as suggesting the same thoroughgoing critique of American society that sixties radicals lodged. But both Clarence Thomas and Malcolm X, from opposite ideological commitments, target the (predominantly) white liberal administration of race reform as it was practiced in the desegregation era.

The ingeniousness (if ultimate incoherence) of Clarence Thomas's reconstruction of conservative race ideology is that he has melded an individualist-oriented legal rhetoric of governmental neutrality and color blindness onto the group-based racial self-determination assumptions of contemporary multiculturalism. In doing so, he is able to appropriate strands of Black Nationalist discourse, particularly the self-help thematic, in service of right-wing legal ideology. His view is traditionally conservative in its depiction of the government as a "night watchman" over society, basically staying out of the "private" marketplace except to enforce the ground rules of social competition and struggle. The difference between this view and its traditional nineteenth-century antecedent is that the private marketplace is now conceived as made up of discrete cultural groups, such as African Americans, rather than discrete individuals. In this vision, color blindness serves to permit blacks to establish their own schools and determine their own community needs, rather than providing the justification, as it did in the sixties and seventies, for coercive federal intervention to integrate schools.

It is difficult for progressive whites to oppose rhetoric like Thomas's because, in many ways, it actually matches the implicit assumptions of our own embrace of multiculturalism. To understand how we have arrived at this rhetorical juncture, it is instructive to consider the twists and turns that white progressive race ideology has taken in the last three decades. What follows is a summary and somewhat impressionistic account of the recent history of progressive white race consciousness. *Brown* and the widely shared moral imperative to end school segregation is an obvious and useful demarcation point against which to contrast the multicultural sensibility and from which to trace its development through the succession of racial ideologies held by moderate and left-leaning American whites in the recent past.

As Clarence Thomas states, *Brown* is conventionally understood to have embraced two basic justifications for its ruling that state-enforced school desegregation was unconstitutional. The first, celebrated by Thomas and other conservatives in contemporary discourse (if not at the time of the *Brown* decision itself) was based on the formal principle that government may not take race into account in making decisions about social policy because race is an irrelevant and arbitrary attribute of individuals. The other justification, more controversial within traditional understandings of the appropriate grounds for constitutional interpretation, was that segregation produced psychological ill effects in black children. This conclusion was supported in the *Brown* opinion by cites to social science research and the famous "doll studies" purporting to show that black children in segregated educational settings viewed white characteristics as superior.

Within the arena of conventional legal commentary, the Court's opinion was controversial on both grounds. With respect to color blindness, for example, Herbert Wechsler argued that the idea did not state a *neutral* principle because it improperly privileged those desiring interracial contact over those abhorring it.[20] With respect to the social science basis, mainstream legal scholars contended that constitutional interpretation could not properly be based on historically contingent empirical data.[21]

As a reflection of what would become the dominant moderate and progressive white view of race, however, these criticisms were at first technical and legalistic. For progressive whites, and one supposes for most members of the Court, the two strands of *Brown* were complementary and consistent. Segregation in principle was wrong, and social science confirmed its pernicious effects. It was not until the principle of color blindness seemed to be insufficient to produce desegregation that the two bases diverged into two different and recognizable ways to understand racial justice, with conservatives embracing color blindness, governmental neutrality, and formal equality, and progressives advocating affirmative governmental action to achieve substantive racial equality—understood as integrated social institutions.

The "principled" reading of *Brown* as enshrining color blindness as the reigning constitutional norm matched the dominant way that liberal and left-learning whites of the period understood racial justice. They saw themselves in a struggle against white racists who claimed that race marked essential and inherent differences between whites and blacks, and that blacks were genetically inferior to whites. Enlightened whites characterized racism as an irrational process of attributing difference where there was none; the model was, rather, that blacks and whites were essentially the same and that skin pigmentation was an arbitrary and irrelevant attribute. As a matter of social policy, it made sense from within this worldview that public schools would be the point of reformist intervention. Since racism was based on the ignorance begotten by segregation, children in integrated schools would learn through simple interracial exposure that race made no difference. Over time, this policy would eventually produce a society of enlightened adults in which "ethnic identity will become a thing of the past."[22] Integration accordingly became an affirmative social policy to be achieved, distinct from understanding *Brown* as merely symbolizing a negative prohibition on governmental segregation.

The significance of the centering of integration as a desired norm was that, eventually, the color blindness principle and the real-world achievement of integration would conflict. The progressive position on color blindness, associated with the affirmative integrationist policy, also conflicted with the conservative position, as articulated by Clarence Thomas, which asserted that color blindness was all that was required on the part of the government even if it failed to produce integration.

This divergence emerged as a clear ideological opposition in the legal arena with respect to the enforcement of *Brown* itself. It soon became clear that simply forbidding the state from enforcing racial school segregation would not achieve integrated schools; color blindness in official policy—say, by adopting "freedom of choice" plans permitting students to go to whatever school they chose, or by adopting neighborhood attendance policies—by itself did not produce an end to segregation in fact.[23] At that point, liberal and progressive legal discourse began the first stages of rejecting color blindness, and, ultimately, its associated assimilationist assumptions. Linking the issue of school desegregation and race discrimination generally to the formalism/realism opposition already extent within legal ideology, progressives within the legal arena began associating the color blindness approach with a formalist way of representing the social world. Color blindness became linked to the formal equality espoused by the Supreme Court in the discredited "liberty of contract" era, within which laborers and capitalists were said to have equal rights to contract with respect to wages and other working conditions.[24] According to this kind of racial realism, color consciousness was required in order to identify whether racial discrimination was being practiced, or whether remedies were being implemented in good faith. In the school context, progressives argued for a de facto test that would make constititional requirements turn on the actual achievement of integration rather than merely a cessation of intentional segregative practices on the part of the government; in the employment context, they advocated a disparate effects test that made the identification of discrimination turn on the racial results of alleged job qualification criteria; and in the emerging affirmative action context generally, they contended that a period of benign color consciousness was required in order practically to offset the effects of years of malign racism and to compensate for the "deprivation" that blacks suffered under the segregation regime.[25]

Within the terms of this embrace of "substantive" rather than "formal" equality, the social science research relied on by the *Brown* Court came to symbolize a real-world jurisprudential alternative, opposed to the abstract and formal quality of the conservative commitment to "principled" decision making. The social science strand of *Brown* became the new, positive symbol of realism in law, of making law correspond to the actual social conditions to which it applied rather than to the abstract idealization of formal equality in the face of empirical inequality.[26] In this alternative reading, *Brown* could be interpreted to stand for the proposition that constitutional law must consider racial history, the power relations between groups, the social meaning of particular governmental acts, and so forth. Looking to social science signified opposing formalist and universalist abstraction.

This splitting of *Brown* between a formalist and realist or functional interpretation constituted only the first stage of a progressive reinterpretation of *Brown*. The second part consisted of the less explicit, more subtle rejection of the social science side as well, as it became apparent that the "realism" depicted by social science research itself rested on what we would today call "Eurocentric" assumptions.

The irony of the opposition that progressive legal commentators drew between the formalism of the color blindness principle and the "real world" depicted by social science research was that the social science paradigms of the *Brown* period were themselves in historical retrospect quite universalist and ethnocentric. "Cultural deprivation" was the reigning paradigm in sociology in the late fifties and early sixties for comprehending the underachievement of black students in integrated educational settings. As the phrase suggests, black underachievement was explicitly understood on cultural grounds, as the inferior quality of a black culture rooted in poverty:

> The problem, stated as simply as possible, is that the environment [in] which lower-class Negro children . . . grow up does not provide the intellectual and sensory stimulation they need in order to benefit from the conventional kindergarten and first-grade curricula. . . . [M]iddle class children do, in fact, come already equipped with these skills; they acquire them quite unconsciously from their environment, more or less by osmosis. But the lower class child, as a rule, has not acquired these skills because of the intellectual and sensory poverty of his environment. . . . For example, the Negro youngsters . . . have much less auditory discrimination [because] the noise level in a household tends to be so high that the child is forced to learn how not to listen and [fails] to develop an ability to distinguish relevant and irrelevant sounds. . . . [The] lower class child has not had the experience of having adults correct his pronunciation . . . or ask about school. . . . The nonverbal household [in which] adults speak in short sentences . . . and give orders in monosyllables . . . means that youngsters' memory, as well as their attention span, receive less training. . . . Given this poverty of experience, it is almost inevitable that the Negro child will fail when he enters school.[27]

Although he would later renounce the thesis as racist,[28] Silberman, writing as a concerned liberal sociologist, was a leading exponent of the cultural deprivation thesis. In his account, black schoolchildren failed in integrated educational environments because they tended to come from more crowded living conditions, providing the material frame for a whole slew of learning problems.

The "cultural deprivation" ideology was more than simply the thesis of academic sociologists. It became, for a short time, the dominant framework for a liberal American understanding of race.[29] The idea that black children were culturally deprived and therefore needed enrichment in order to fare well in the educational process underlay the institution of programs during the War on Poverty such as the Head Start program,[30] and the basic, early justifications for affirmative action in many contexts.[31]

The furor that erupted over the publication of *The Bell Curve*[32] is but one notable example of how far mainstream culture has come from the kind of discourse that Silberman employed. The kinds of claims made by Silberman in the 1960s seem downright racist and totally "ethnocentric" today in that he explicitly used the mores of the white middle-class, two-parent family as the baseline norm from which deprivation was determined, and he made patronizing assumptions made about different verbal and familial styles across racial boundaries. Like the lack of consciousness about the possible imperialism implicit in the denigration of southern culture generally, Silberman and other white liberals of the period similarly had little apparent consciousness about the possible imperialism impicit in their depictions of condition of the "plight" of blacks, without any sense of the positive, sustaining elements of the black community. Progressive whites thus experienced militant nationalists like Malcolm X as ideologically indistinguishable from deferential "Uncle Toms" in the black community who opposed segregation because they had bought into the ideology of white supremacy or were too scared to oppose it. In other words, whites saw in black life only the harmful consequences of racial heirarchy and simply never considered the possibility that African Americans had built and constructed a cultural community worth preserving. When nationalists argued for the preservation of black institutions, whites heard only resistance to liberatory change.

The embrace of the idea of "cultural deprivation" also illuminates the particular manner in which the school integration policy was actually implemented. Nothing in *Brown v. Board*, the formal legal decision, and nothing within the analytics of integration as a social policy, dictated that it would proceed primarily by closing formerly black schools, terminating black teachers and administrators—and virtually wiping out for a generation almost the entire class of educators in the black community, a class with a long and important influence in constituting black middle-class culture.[33] Well-intentioned white liberals could think that such a social policy was not problematic from an ideological framework within which the ethnocentric cast of the "cultural deprivation" thesis was invisible and from which, conversely, white schools appeared simply as superior on neutral, acultural terms. In other words, the assumption was that schools themselves did not embody cultural norms, and thus pursuing an integrationist policy that largely integrated black children into formerly white schools did not raise issues of cultural assimilation or, as Robert Browne, a black nationalist intellectual of the late sixties put it, "painless genocide."[34]

By the mid-1960s Silberman and other liberals publicly renounced the "cultural deprivation" thesis as racist in its implications. Instead, mainstream sociologists such as Silberman and Kenneth Clark began embracing what became known in the sociological jargon as "labelling theory," the general idea that black children's underachievement was due to the discriminatory way that schools responded by expecting them to fail.[35] In this reading, the very labeling of black children as "deprived" made their educators expect less of them, imperceptibly communicating to the children themselves that they did not have an equal chance at educational success.

This transformation from "cultural deprivation" to "labelling theory" and "lowered expectations" focused attention away from alleged inadequacies in lower-class African American culture and toward the inadequacies of mainstream public schools. It was, in my reading, symbolically the first step in the ultimate rejection of the assimilationist assumptions of integrationism as it was understood by white proponents of *Brown*. Also, this implicit rejection of the social science basis of *Brown* was concurrently the last step in the implicit progressive rejection of *Brown* as resting on ultimately conservative assumptions about the range of cultural norms of institutional life.

While it would be impossible definitively to account for this change in perspective, it was correlated with, and I believe largely responsive to, the simultaneous explosion of antiintegrationist, nationalist militancy in the black community. While white progressives were, in the legal arena, struggling to extend integrationist norms by requiring actual integration as the test of remedying past segregation and disparate impact to identify present discrimination, and had in general embraced the cultural deprivation account for understanding blacks' relative inability to assimilate successfully into white schools, the nationalist posture of Malcolm X and newly emerging black radicals such as Stokely Carmichael and the Black Panthers put the rejection of color blindness on a more fundamental, substantive plane.

Black nationalists in the sixties and early seventies explicitly asserted that the integrationist policy that mainstream America had by then adopted was colonialist and racist. In their analysis, the instructions into which blacks would be integrated were specifically white in character and culture. Racial integration accordingly meant a further loss of black control over the institutions of their community, insofar as integrationism implied that blacks would be integrated into white schools, economic institutions, and neighborhoods.

With respect to the rejection of the idea of culture deprivation, black nationalist and the liberal academic sociological discourse had similar structural elements. Most importantly, they both located the cause of the problem in the institution into which black integration would be conducted, rather than in the culture of black people, although they pointed in very different directions.

For the liberal sociologists of the mid-sixties, heirs to the color blindness ideology of racial justice and integrationist social policy, the problem that black children were having in integrated classes could be accounted for by bias in how integrated public schools approached them. The problem, from the liberal integrationist point of view, was one of deviation from a supposed neutral norm of how teachers should relate to students in a classroom, "regardless of race." In this discourse, when teachers do not expect as much from black children, black children get the message that they are not expected to do as well. According to labelling theory's contribution, people tend to adapt to the category in which they are classified, and thus black children did not do as well as whites in integrated schools.

The alternative view articulated by Malcolm X and other radical black nationalists of the sixties and early seventies differed at the basic starting point of analysis. While traditional liberal pro-*Brown* integrationists saw the goal to achieve neutral public institutions, purged of specificity and neutral to a diverse population, "regardless of race, religion, creed, etc.," nationalists asserted that institutions like schools were inevitably culturally specific and identifiable as white institutions. Borrowing from the independence discourses of emerging African nation-states, Black Nationalists saw school race issues not as concerned with the identification of bias from a position of neutrality or objectivity, but rather as an instance of colonialism through which a national community was being robbed of important cultural, economic, and educational institutions. The model of racial power in the black nationalist analysis located racial hegemony outside of individuals who may have "biases," to institutions and social structures, conceived in terms of separate white and black cultures. The colonialism framework was vastly different than the model of integrationism because it assumed that there *are* differences based on race and that the proper goal was not to integrate what was wrongly segregated, but rather a kind of respectful coexistence, like friendly nations on the world stage. Malcolm X dramatized this ideological message when, with some degree of seriousness, he sought relief for African Americans as a colonized nation from the United Nations.

It is amazing, in light of how vilified nationalists were in the late sixties and early seventies in mainstream discourse, that they ultimately won the cultural/philosophical dimension of this particular ideological struggle. Over the last two decades, American culture in general and white progressives in particular have moved closer and closer to the basic assumption of the nationalist depiction of the inevitably cultural character of institutions like public schools. While there is no clearly obvious demarcation point akin to the "cultural deprivation" idea or the adoption of "labelling theory" within academic discourse to chart this transition, the trajectory for white progressives has been a subtle and incremental rejection of the color blindness model of racial justice in favor of at least a version of the nationalist analysis.

As described above, the first analytic step in this process was clearly contained within the frame of the substantive vision of color blindness itself: color consciousness was necessary properly to identify discrimination on the basis of race and to ensure compensation for past exclusion. It was the way to ensure in a real-world way that integration was actually taking place. The gradual extension of this idea, that institutions discriminated whenever their processes impacted people differentially based on race, would over time lead to the premise from which Black Nationalist analysis began—that institutions themselves embodied inevitable cultural assumptions. Accordingly, rather than conceive of the continual application of antidiscrimination norms to "purify" schools and other places of their "biases," progressives came to believe instead that schools must be "multicultural" and "inclusive" of various cultural traditions and assumptions.

Of course, this dynamic did not consist simply of a progression of ideas leading logically to "multiculturalism." These transformations all occurred in the social/cultural context of the heated appearance of nationalist ideology on the national scene in the late sixties, the explicit and implicit expulsion of whites from dominant positions in what remained of the "civil rights movement," the disintegration of racial liberation politics in the late seventies and early eighties, the rebirth of nationalist ideology in the African American community continuing through the nineties, the appearance of a radicalized feminist movement simultaneously criticizing antidiscrimination ideology in the gender context as "formal equality" because gender marked real cultural "difference," and the emergence of other ethnic nationalisms, particularly with respect to Latino culture. In addition, this ideological transformation has not been complete and total, by any means. As I see it, white progressive race ideology today still contains bits and pieces of the antidiscrimination vision, even as "multiculturalism" has become the public slogan for understanding racial justice. We bemoan the failure of the current Supreme Court to vigorously enforce school desegregation decrees and its adoption of the de jure model of unconstitutional discrimination—all analytically based on the *Brown* model of integrationism—while we simultaneously celebrate Afrocentric schools and honor ethnic assertions of difference and cultural integrity. The dominance of norms of inclusion, diversity, the celebration of difference, Black History month, and the like in our contemporary discourse about race are at the least versions of the Black Nationalist project in refusing integration on the model of the sameness of all students before a neutral institutional face. But the multicultural sensibility sits alongside the image of racism consisting of bias and prejudice—as if we still believed there was some neutral, acultural, aracial way to constitute institutional life, to set admissions criteria for universities and qualifications for jobs.

The contemporary emergence of multiculturalism is ultimately traceable to various historical factors, and it is only partial; nevertheless, it also seems clear that one of its main, established tenets has been the idea of acknowledging and respecting difference, rather than assuming, like the *Brown* consciousness seemed to, that there was a neutral, acultural institutional reality, in public schools or any other places, that would transcend race. From this vantage point, the social science paradigms of "cultural deprivation" embraced in *Brown*, as well as the confident assertions of color blindness and integration into "quality" schools, seem embarrassingly naive to most progressives. Both of these justifications for the *Brown* ruling have, at least implicitly, been recast as ultimately resting on conservative cultural premises; from a multicultural sensibility, both strands of *Brown* posed as universal assumptions about social reality that over time have come to be seen as culturally specific.

This history of ideological development, I think, accounts most profoundly for progressive white sensitivity to charges of "cultural imperialism." It was, in a sense, culturally traumatic to have confidently embraced as liberatory a way of understanding racial justice that would soon be turned on its head and alleged to be yet another form of white domination. In addition, it also seems clear that another dimension of contemporary white anxiety is rooted in the lack of any perceived substantive basis upon which intercultural activism could be based. That is, taking seriously the ideas of multiculturalism means acknowledging that there may be no transcultural normative basis by which to judge the social practices of another culture. The sense of righteousness and confidence with which progressives supported the coercive enforcement of *Brown* was, in this interpretation, linked to the very universalist premises of the color blindness principle and the "realism" of cultural deprivation that seem so problematic from a contemporary multicultural perspective. The topic of the next section of this essay is whether "deference" to cultural self-determination is a coherent response to this history.

V. Laissez-Faire Multiculturalism

I want to challenge as a false mode of avoidance on the part of progressive whites the image of cultural self-determination that is implicit in the reigning anxiety over "cultural imperialism." As I see it, the issue is whether the dichotomy that I have just described—between a belief in an objectivist, neutral moral imperative like color blind integrationism linked with the will to intervene on the one hand, and a belief in relativistic, multicultural assumptions about differences in mores and an accompanying deference to other identified cultural groups on the other hand—exhausts the realistic possibilities for a coherent understanding of race on the part of whites.[36] Is it plausible to believe simultaneously in the "relativist" norms of multiculturalism and nevertheless be willing to intervene across cultural boundaries to influence and even coerce other cultural groups? Is the *Brown* intervention into southern culture defensible only from now-discredited universalist premises about the possibilities for cultural neutrality on the part of schools and other institutions?

I approach this issue in a negative fashion; rather than provide as affirmative defense of cultural intervention in specific contexts, I want to consider the possibility that the opposition between deference and intervention is a false way of framing issues of interracial and intercultural dynamics. Mutual respect and cultural self-determination are too indeterminate to themselves provide a justificatory compass. This respectful, deferential aspect of multicultural sensibility depends on there being some transcultural basis upon which to identify the cultural boundaries of the other group, and to distinguish between authentic and fraudulent representations of that group's authentic mores. In order to carry out the deference injunction, in short, some way of identifying what is being deferred to is necessary. The more formalist, essentialist, ahistoric, and traditionalist the definition of the other culture's mores, the more compelling the case for deference will seem to be, in that intervention would be posed against a clearly delineated, fixed practice. At the same time, the more formalist, essentialist, ahistoric, and traditional the definition of the other culture's mores, the more it will appear that the practice in question is a contested one within the other group, and that this practice's survival depends on the continued domination of a segment of the community rather than the reflection of their culture as a whole.

The background analytic that informs this approach to cultural issues is an analogy to similar images of deference and self-determination in market ideology. That is, it seems to me that the progressive commitment to the importance of cultural self-determination embodied in the contemporary multicultural sensibility closely tracks, in both substantive motivation and analytic structure, the political and economic theory of the invisible hand in laissez-faire market ideology.

In free market ideology, the norm of government neutrality vis-à-vis the private market was based on the notion that, if the government stayed out of the private sphere, individual actors would freely choose the terms and conditions of their relationships. Through the workings of the market's "invisible hand," society would end up enjoying the fullest possible level of social satisfaction. The resulting distribution of wealth could not regulate and thereby distort free market forces.

The problem, compellingly demonstrated through the American legal realist scholarship of the twenties and thirties, was that it was analytically impossible to conceive of the state playing merely a background role in protecting private property, enforcing contractual agreements based on free will, and refusing to enforce agreements that were the result of fraud, duress, or incompetency. As the realists showed, the "framework" rules of the private market were not merely background, but necessarily regulative as well. The legal rules for identifying what would or would not be protected as "property" served to establish the bargaining position of individuals in the market—and yet there was no way analytically to leave such questions to the market itself, since any market must proceed on the basis of such rules already being in place. Similarly, the identification of the free will of a market actor depended on legal rules that distinguished the permissible from the impermissible deployment of coercive pressure—and yet rules for determining duress, fraud, and incompetency could be drawn in a variety of ways without violating the underlying notion that the voluntary decisions of market actors would be decisive. Again, however, the specific ways that legal rules distinguished free from coerced transactions "regulated" the market to the extent that they favored some transactions at the expense of others. In short, the legal realists concluded that the central idea of a private market free from the regulatory effects of state power was incoherent. The social power of the state, manifest in the choice of a certain delineation of interests that would be protected as private property, or a certain definition of permissible and impermissible market pressure, constituted what laissez-faire economics falsely understood as the private market. The idea of deferring to private market actors was analytically indefensible because the private market itself was constituted by social power. The conclusion that the state constituted the very market it purported merely to facilitate and defer to was hidden from view, the realists argued, only by *formalism*, the assumption that the particular legal rules for identifying property and free will somehow matched up with their actual existence in the world.

The same kind of analytic applies to the identification of and deference to the self-determination of cultural groups. This aspect of the multicultural sensibility depends on the ability to identify an independent culture, just as free market ideology had to identify a private market actor, and to distinguish what is really an integral part of that culture from what is an illegitmate imposition of external and distorting power, just as a laissez-faire approach must distinguish free from coerced market transactions. Short of a formalist or essentialist definition of particular cultures, however, there is similarly no way neutrally and aculturally to identify what practices are worthy of deference because they represent the intrinsic integrity of independent cultural groups. Just as the state inevitably regulated when it appeared simply to facilitate an independent private market, so a similar form of regulation is implicit in the idea of cultural deference.

Take, for example, the issue of African female genital mutilation as it has been constructed in mainstream Western human rights discourse. The common way that the imperialism concern is articulated is with respect to the mores of, say, tribal Sudanese culture. But identifying the relevant self-determination interests as implicating Sudanese culture is a contingent and culturally loaded judgment.

In the international context, we conventionally identify culturally relevant entities in terms of geography, identifying culture with the boundaries of land and territory in which an identifiable group lives. But there is no analytic reason to identify the culturally relevant group in terms of land. In fact, in many ways it seems quite formalist and old-fashioned to think that the most relevant cultural association must be based on physical proximity. Just as there were, within market ideology, alternative ways to identify private property, there are alternative ways to slice up the cultural pie. While we tend to think of culture in terms of a people who have a particular geographic solidarity within which they share cultural mores, there actually are a virtually infinite number of ways to divide up what to call a culture. For example, it is possible to conceive of a "female" culture that exists in the world and flows, perhaps, from the shared experience of childbirth. That's a fairly abstract and general definition. But it is sufficient to see that, from this alternative way of identifying culture, the issue of deference and intervention looks qualitatively different. From this perspective, to the extent that black Sudanese males are encouraging or requiring genital mutilation practices, *they* are regulating, dominating, and intervening in the culture of females. Honoring the principle that no group should impose its power on another cultural group, any female is part of that international culture of females, and therefore from this cultural angle has a basis, under self-determination principles, to "intervene" in Sudanse life.

Or we could identify culture, not by geography, but by age. This approach would build from the realization that, across land-based cultures there are youth cultures, there are cultures of the elderly, and that age also is an important determinant of the way we look at the world. To the extent that Sudanese rituals are practiced on adolescents, one must decide whether to respect the land-based culture of Sudanese tribes, or the age-based culture of rebellious youth. Nothing in the idea of "respecting cultural difference" can determine which cultural frame to utilize.

The point here is not that these alternative ways to divide up cultural boundaries are equally meaningful, or that the choice between them is arbitrary. It is rather that *analytically* nothing in the general idea of respecting difference can determine how difference will be identified. As the realists demonstrated with respect to the *Lochner* era, there is a broad range of ways to identify the voluntary free will of the contracting party, ranging from the formalism of a seal on a document to a substantive inquiry into the fairness of an exchange itself. And the choice of one point rather than another on the continuum implicated the social power of the state into the "private" market. Similarily, there is a broad range of ways to identify the boundaries of a culture and its authentic mores; the difference between ways that seem silly and ways that make sense flows from within *our* own assumptions about what culture consists of.

To carry this analogy to another stage, just as it was necessary to distinguish between coerced and free exchanges within market-oriented legal theory, the idea of cultural deference requires a distinction between cultural practices that are authentic expressions of the cultural community from those that are merely reflections of a culturally contingent victory of a particular group of dominators. For example, consider again the northern intervention into southern culture associated with the enforcement of *Brown*. In order to highlight the arguably colonialist character of the intervention, I described it earlier as if it were clear that there was a "southern" culture that had authentic cultural mores of racial segregation and subjugation, along with religiosity and other characteristics not directly connected to race. But it was possible to describe the whole process in different terms. Utilizing the frame of an "American" culture, the Old South rulers could be seen to have thwarted the self-determination rights of a general American culture. Alternatively, their rule could be characterized as a takeover and domination of an authentic southern culture by a particular, small class of white aristocrats who had themselves perverted its true expression—say, because of their economic drive for free and cheap labor. Just as the possibility of nonenforcement on the ground of duress helps constitute the bargaining power of "private" market actors, the possibility of nondeference when an alleged "cultural practice" is actually a sham cover for domination over the cultural group itself helps constitute power *within* the group. Again, the point is not that these descriptions are equivalent in any sense, other than that they pose the analytic indeterminacy of the idea of deference on the grounds of cultural self-determination.

Finally, the realist idea that the private sphere is constituted by state power also seems applicable in the cultural context. The point is easiest to see with respect to African American culture. The image of deference to African American norms, as it was deployed, say, in the Hill/Thomas confrontation, implies that the African American culture was developed outside of and independent of white American culture, as if their cultural norms had a freestanding, instrinsic life of their own. But, despite some nationalist attempts to invoke a distant African past as the basis for cultural self-identification, the fact is that African American culture has been constructed in large measure in a dialectical engagement with whites in America. Some of the terms of this engagement have been horrific. Others have been ambiguous and complicated. But it is impossible simply to define an African American culture that does not acknowledge engagement, albeit often unwilling, with whites. In fact, one of the ironies of the current racial scene is that, while progressive whites seem anxious to honor the principle of community self-determination and thus publicly to defer to the otherwise objectionable anti-Semitic, homophobic, and sexist ideology of the Nation of Islam and Minister Louis Farrakhan, it is not clear that the current domination of this authoritarian form of Black Nationalist ideology is simply reflective of African American self-determination. From another perspective on the recent history of race relations, the strength of Farrakhan is in some measure due to whites themselves, in the sense that whites helped empower Farrakhan by rejecting and repressing more progressive and sophisticated expressions of black nationalism in the sixties and seventies, leaving the Nation of Islam as the only major nationalist group with the means for institutional survival.

Implicit in the comparison of the idea of deference to the self-determination rights of cultural groups and the idea of deference to the wishes of market actors is an analogy between the state in laissez-faire economic theory and whites in American racial dynamics. The basis of this comparison is the idea of *power.* Whites in contemporary racial dynamics are in an analogous role to the state in market theory to the extent that, as a group, whites currently possess significantly and qualitatively greater social, political, and economic power than any other identifiable cultural group. That is why, of course, the cultural imperialism anxiety runs in a specific direction; I am assuming that progressive people of color similarly committed to multiculturalism are not similarly anxious about the risks that they will culturally dominate whites.

This final link in the analogy—the correlation between the state and whites—is the most troublesome for progressive whites; it brings together the issue of the connection between a substantive basis for intervention with the terms of white identification within a multicultural sensibility. To the extent that the comparison between the position of whites in a race-stratified society and the position of the state in market ideology makes sense, it exposes the problematic character, from within the ideological development of progressives since *Brown*, of whites exercising their racial power. Ever since *Brown*, the demonstration that a particular institutional practice was rooted in white, or Eurocentric, cultural assumptions has been understood to delegitimate that social practice on the ground that it embodied hidden biases against racial minorities. When *Brown* was understood to rest on acultural norms of color blindness and a rationalistic case for integration, the basis for its coercive enforcement was not seen to emanate from culturally specific white norms. When, within the assumptions of multiculturalism, the only basis for action seems to be culturally specific frameworks for perceiving the world, whites are hesitant to act on the basis of white cultural traditions whose identification as white has always been in service of their delegitimation.

Another way of saying this is that, in the multicultural sensibility, there is a missing ingredient—the cultural bearing of the dominant group of whites in American society. Identification with whiteness has traditionally meant an interest in racial domination. No alternative traditions have developed from which whites could understand themselves as acting as whites in a liberatory, nonimperialist, and nonracist fashion. And yet, if this picture of the racial landscape is persuasive, whites must be seen—regardless of various subcultural identifications—to be constituted in the dynamics of American race relations as a specific, identifiable group which has an enormous amount of power on various axes of measurement. It is the anxiety over facing this fact of our own status as a socially constructed cultural group, more than anything else, that has characterized the recent isolation of progressive whites with respect to race politics. We do not want to act *as whites*, and yet no other basis for action seems available from within our own ideological assumptions and historical position.

One way to understand the current ideological situation of progressive whites is to see that we are, in a sense, between ideological paradigms. We have embraced multiculturalism as the norm of racial justice, but perhaps because of the historically imperialist use of race by whites in America, we have not located ourselves within the multicultural social fabric. Instead, our cultural "affiliations" have in a sense been privatized to subcultural groups—as Jews, Irish, gays and lesbians, workers—within the larger white community, groups that themselves seem to be in no direct engagement with the overall racial economy. We have sympathy with postmodern admonishments that cultural groups not be essentialized, that cultural meaning be recognized as contested, in flux and subject to diverse interpretation. But we simultaneously wish to defer to a formalized presentation of the self-determination of other cultural groups in response to our own anxiety that intervention will be a form of imperialism; thus deference is in order.

The problem as I see it is that inaction is simply not an option. Having racial power, however unwilling we may be to admit it, means necessarily acting one way or the other, to delegitimate social practices as forms of domination or to privilege them as forms of cultural integrity, to accept the existing community's dominant voice representing its cultural mores or to support insurgents fighting for change. Either way, we must decide from within whatever framework we have available. The option of simple deference to some independently constituted cultural community is, by and large, an empty set.

VI. Conclusion

Comprehending whites and blacks in terms of culturally distinct communities is a major ideological victory for what I would describe as the most progressive faction of the struggle for black liberation. I personally see the black nationalist analysis as superior to the conventional integrationist interpretation of race issues. I also believe that the exposure of the Eurocentric assumptions of mainstream institutional life is an important stage of racial development in which the culture of the dominant white community, long invisible as simply the background assumptions for social and institutional life, is problematized.

The problem, however, is that the commitment to cultural integrity and to the self-determination rights of other communities is general and abstract; it does not answer the inevitably normative issues involved in identifying culture and distinguishing integrity from domination. But if I am right that simple deference is not an option, and that there is no transcultural ground upon which to decide these issues, then we are in the position that, in my view, we've always been in—of having to make choices, explicitly or implicitly, about how the power we actually have in American racial dynamics will be exercised. While there is no universal basis for deciding when to intervene and when to defer, there remains all the basis that there ever has been—the bits and pieces we can weave together from the imperfect history and tradition of the struggle for racial liberation, including the caution that sometimes white "help" can be a form of domination. In other words, we have in this postmodern understanding both the general commitment to integrity and self-determination, and the realization that there is no formal or determinate way to give these ideas meaning separate from the way that we participate inevitably in their construction. Understanding that culture is historical and constructed rather than given and essential should lead us, as white progressives, to comprehend that "white" culture depends, in part, on how we construct ourselves as whites in the racial economy of American life, and to comprehend that the construction of African American culture is likewise in flux and contested. Our cultural distance from the African American community should give us pause in applying "white" norms to that community. On the other hand, having rejected "formalism" on various grounds and in various contexts, we also know that there is no essential, canonical way to represent the "authentic" mores of that community. Given that a "culture" develops in history, over time, with the terms of community life constantly contested in various ways, we should also pause before reflexively accepting authoritarian or sexist reprensentations of the culture of minority communities as simply an authentic, unchallengeable given. Deferring to sexist authoritarian representations of African American culture, like those promulgated by the Nation of Islam, means actively disempowering black feminist insurgents.

I think it is important that we understand that intervention is always a possibility. Power carries a great deal of existential responsibility. We as liberals and progressives, having played a role in winning an important victory in establishing multiculturalism and cultural pluralism as the norms of our societies, also have to bear responsibility for not allowing this new consciousness to become the excuse for refusing to do good in the world, to become the ground for a progressive version of "benign neglect."[37] It is understandable that, after embracing forms of integrationism that were blind to cultural difference and the cultural specificity of institutional life, progressives would create a way of understanding cultural difference that relieves whites of responsibility for much of African American life, under the idea that the black community is entitled to self-determination. But like the market ideology it echoes, it relies on false images of deference and nonintervention.

From the perspective of contemporary multicultural sensibility, it is apparent that *Brown* represented a coercive culture intervention into southern life. Parts of that intervention were, to my mind, colonialist and oppressive. There was little gained and much lost when white southern culture was repudiated in toto as irrational and parochial, because the antiseptic New South culture of technocracy is, in its own way, alienating and hierarchical. In contrast to the self-understanding of liberal integrationists, the coercive regulation of the South was not justified on the ground that a neutral rationality would replace cultural backwardness; in retrospect, it is clear that the ideologies and institutional practices of transformed southern schools are not acultural and universal, but specifically northeastern. But saying that there was no transcultural ground for the regulation of the South is not to say that it was groundless. Rather, I believe that the coercive overthrow of southern apartheid was right and often heroic, even if its terms were imperfect. It helped (partially) topple a racial regime that was oppressive and unjust; it helped (partially) empower southern insurgents, black and white, whose struggle might have failed but for "external" assistance and legitimation. The ground for concluding that intervention was warranted cannot be a universal, transcultural set of principles, because that does not exist—just as the idea of respecting "difference" could not, at the time, have provided a neutral basis for intervening. It would have meant privileging the rule of Old South rulers. Instead, the justification was historical, existential, and necessarily partial. That's all we ever ultimately have.

Notes

This essay has benefited from the excellent assistance of Elizabeth Watson and Ambrosio Rodriguez, and from comments on an earlier draft from Anthony Cook and Dennis Patterson.

1. Missouri v. Jenkins, 115 S. Ct. 2038, at 2064, 2065 (1995) (Thomas, J., concurring).

2. 347 U.S. 483 (1954).

3. This method is part of a broader "critical legal studies approach" to legal ideology. See Robert Gordon, "New Approaches to Legal Theory," in *The Politics of Law*, David Kairys ed. (New York: Pantheon, 1990); for a broader "critical race theory" approach to the intersection of law and race, see K. Crenshaw, N. Gotada, G. Peller, & K. Thomas ed. *Critical Race Theory: Key Writings That Shaped the Movement* (New York: New Press, 1995).

4. For an excellent "philosophical" treatment of many of the issues considered in this essay, see John Horton ed., *Liberalism, Multiculturalism and Toleration* (New York: St. Martin's, 1993).

5. Just as a legal decision like *Brown* is part of a process of ideological struggle over how the social world will be constructed, so "scholarly" commentary is immersed in similar ideological contestation. This is to say that I do not offer the following as an objective or detached interpretation; my "analysis" proceeds from an impressionistic take on the political and ideological significance of *Brown* and on subsequent developments in American racial dynamics—from my own situation as a full-time, white, critical legal studies–oriented progressive law professor and occasional activist, immersed within the ideological framework that I endeavor to depict.

6. Of course this is a loaded term, as are any terms used to describe the issue. For a discussion of the issues presented, see H. Kim, "Gender-Related Persecution: A Legal Analysis of Gender Bias in Asylum Law," 2 *American University Journal of Gender & Law* (1990), 107, 125–28; Alison T. Slack, "Female Circumcision: A Critical Appraisal," 10 *Human Rights Quarterly* (1988), 439.

7. Orlando Patterson, "Race, Gender, and Liberal Fallacies," *New York Times*, Oct. 20, 1991, at sec. 4, 2.

8. For a discussion of the ways that the Patterson intervention in particular, and the deployment of race particularism in general, worked to split antiracist and feminist forces during the Hill/Thomas confrontation, see Kimberle Crenshaw, "Whose Story Is It, Anyway? Feminist and Antiracist Appropriations of Anita Hill," in *Race-ing Justice, En-gendering Power: Essays on Anita Hill, Clarence Thomas, and the Construction of Social Reality*, Toni Morrison ed. (New York: Pantheon Books, 1992).

9. See Thomas Edsall & E. J. Dionne, Jr., "Core Democratic Constituencies Split: Support for Nominee Reflects Power of Black Vote in the South," *Washington Post*, Oct. 16, 1991, at Al.

10. I do not mean to assert that progressive white groups gave up after Clarence Thomas's invocation of the "high tech lynching" image in his testimony, because they did not. On the other hand, the race turn in the discourse did tend to be met with silence on the part of whites.

11. Of course, this issue has a particular trajectory within the feminist movement. See bell hooks, *Ain't I a Woman: Black Women and Feminism* (Boston: South End Press, 1981), Crenshaw, supra note 8.

12. The anxiety of this argument is that I have completely misjudged the current climate in that white power is still so pervasive and unself-conscious that calling for progressives to exercise more power is irresponsible.

13. Myron Leiberman, *The Future of Public Education* (Lexington, Mass: Lexington Books, 1960), 34, 38, 60.

14. For a more detailed description of the connection between the ban on school prayer and the prohibition of school segregation in general transformation of southern culture in the sixties and seventies, see Gary Peller, "Creation, Evolution and the New South," *Tikkun*, Nov.–Dec. 1987, at 72.

15. This is, of course, not to say that schools were necessarily integrated, given the dynamics of white flight and resegregation within schools pursuant to ability or achievement tracking and other devices.

16. Malcolm X, *By Any Means Necessary: Speeches, Interviews and a Letter*, G. Breitman ed. (New York; Pathfinder Press, 1970), 16–17.

17. Missouri v. Jenkins, 115 S. Ct. at 2061, 2062, (1990).

18. "I have a dream that one day on the red hills of Georgia, sons of former slaves and former slave owners will be able to sit down together at the table of brotherhood. . . . I have a dream my four little children will one day live in a nation where they will not be judged by the color of their skin but by the content of their character." M. L. King, *The Martin Luther King, Jr. Companion: Quotations from the Speeches, Essays, and Books of Martin Luther King, Jr.* (New York: St. Martin's Press, 1968).

19. The reigning discourse on race simply had no way to come to grips with Malcolm X's conception of race as a potentially liberatory aspect of identity, as an affirming but socially constructed charcteristic as opposed to the segregationist/imperialist conception of race as an essentialist, divinely ordained signifier of superiority. In precious work, I have canvassed in detail the clash between integrationist and Black Nationalist race ideologies as they were articulated in the sixties and seventies. See Gary Peller, "Race Consciousness," 1990 *Duke Law Journal*, 758.

20. See Herbert Wechsler, "Toward Neutral Principles of Constitutional Law," 73 *Harvard Law Review* (1959), 1.

21. See, e.g., Edmund Cahn, "Jurisprudence," 30 *New York University Law Review* (1955), 150.

22. These social assumptions were explicitly articulated in sociological literature of the period: "Human beings throughout the world are fundamentally alike. . . . Hence, whenever social distance is reduced, individuals recognize their similatities. The basic differences between ethnic groups are cultural, and conventional norms serve as masks to cover the similarities. Whenever men interact informally, the common human nature comes through. It would appear, then, that it is only a matter of time before a more enlightened citizenry will realize this. Then, there will be a realignment of group loyalties, and ethnic identity will become a thing of the past." Tamotsu Shibutani & Kian Kwan, *Ethnic Stratification: A Comparative Approach* (New York: Macmillan, 1965).

23. See Green v. County School Board, 391 U. S. 430 (2968) (holding that school districts that were once segregated by law came under a duty to produce actually integrated schools, not simply to stop requiring segregation).

24. See Lochner v. New York, 198 U. S. 45 (1905).

25. One way to see this approach as emboding the "victim" perspective is Alan Freeman, "Legitimizing Racial Discrimination Through Antidiscrimination Law: A Critical Review of Supreme Court Doctrine," 62 *Minnesota Law Review* (1978), 1049.

26. See, e.g., Charles Black, Jr., "The Lawfulness of the Segregation Decisions," 69 *Yale Law Journal* (1960), 421.

27. Charles Silberman, *Crisis in Black and White* (New York: Random House, 1964), 269–73.

28. Charles Silberman, *Crisis in the Classroom* (New York: Random House, 1970), 81n.38.

29. See, e.g., Frank Reissman, *The Culturally Deprived Child* (New York: Harper, 1962); John Beck & Richard Saxe eds., *Teaching the Culturally Disadvantaged Pupil* (Springfield, Ill.: C. C. Thomas, 1965).

30. See Edgar Zigler & Jeanette Valentine eds., *Project Head Start: A Legacy of the War on Poverty* (New York: Free Press, 1979), 477–94; Laura Miller, "Head Start: A Moving Target," 5 *Yale Law & Policy Review* (1987), 322.

31. Excerpt from President Johnson's commencement address at Howard University on June 4, 1965. Cited in Alan Freeman's "Racism, Rights and the Quest for Equality Opportunity: A Critical Legal Essay," 23 *Harvard Civil Rights–Civil Liberties Law Review* (1988), 295.

32. Richard Herrnstein & Charles Murray, *The Bell Curve: Intelligence and Class Structure in American Life* (New York: Free Press, 1994).

33. See Derrick Bell, *And We Are Not Saved: The Elusive Quest for Racial Justice* (New York: Basic Books, 1987), 102–09; Harold Cruse, *Plural but Equal: A Critical Study of Blacks and Minorities in America's Plural Society* (New York: William Morrow, 1987), 20–24.

34. R. Browne, "A Case for Separation," in *Separatism or Integration: Which Way for America: A Dialogue*, R. Browne & B. Rustin eds., 1968, 7–15.

35. See Silberman, supra note 27; Kenneth Clark, *Dark Ghetto: The Dilemmas of Power* (New York: Harper & Row, 1965), 129–53.

36. This analysis generally tracks Duncan Kennedy's argument that paternalism is inevitable in the law's construction of contract and tort rules because it is analytically impossible simply to defer to the wishes of individuals. See Duncan Kennedy, "Distributive and Paternalist Motives in Contract and Tort Law, with Special Reference to Compulsory Terms and Unequal Bargaining Power," 41 *Maryland Law Review* (1982), 563.

37. Daniel P. Moynihan, *The Politics of a Guaranteed Income: The Nixon Administration and the Family Assistance Plan* (New York: Vintage Books, 1973).

9

HAZEL CARBY

Can the Tactics of Cultural Integration Counter the Persistence of Political Apartheid?

Or, The Multicultural Wars, Part Two

I would like to begin my reflections on *Brown v. Board of Education* by returning briefly to a set of concerns and specific questions with which I concluded an essay entitled "The Multicultural Wars," published in the fall of 1992 in the journal *Radical History.*[1] There I argued that contemporary debates about cultural intergration most commonly rage under the banner of "multiculturalism" in our schools and colleges but that the content of these debates seemed to me to be a totally inadequate political response to the conditions of social, political, and economic devastation present in the daily lives of those who are poor and designated members of so-called minority populations in the United States.

An enormous amount of our individual and collective political energy in the academy, I am convinced, has been directed toward increasing the diversity of cultural representation through curricular reform. Agitation for increased cultural representation has, of course, a long history in black cultural politics but the specific link to curricular reform in educational institutions is a legacy of the *Brown* paradigm—having fought to integrate our educational institutions should we not now also struggle to integrate the curriculum? However, in many educational institutions across the country it appears that most advocates of multiculturalism are ignoring the fact that forty years after *Brown v. Board of Education* we still live with widespread educational and residential apartheid. Multiculturalists, it seems to me, limit their political imagination and vision to dreams of culturally integrated syllabi instead of agitating for the institutionalizing of a political vision of a just and equitable social formation: indeed, the former seems to be a comforting substitute for the latter. So, some forty years after what is considered to be the victory of the *Brown* decision, it is important that we question the apparent reluctance of these proponents of multiculturalism to confront not only the continuing maintenance but the increasing strength of an apartheid system in residence and education in this society. In addition, it is imperative that we develop a political critique of the discourse of multiculturalism and condemn its lack of a political vision for aggressive political action, action that would not only desegregate this society but would seek to create a just and equitable alternative social order. "I feel it is essential," I stated in "Multicultural Wars," "to question the disparity between the vigor of debates about the inclusion of black subjects on a syllabus, and the almost total silence about, and utter disregard for, the material conditions in which many black people live." The last paragraph of the essay concluded:

> [I]t is evident that in white suburban libraries, bookstores, [movie houses] and supermarkets, an ever increasing number of narratives of black lives is easily available. The retention of apartheid-like structures of black inner city versus white suburban life mean that those who read [or view] these texts lack the opportunity to grow up in any equitable way with each other. Indeed, those same readers are part of the white suburban constituency who refuse to support the building of affordable housing in their affluent suburbs, aggressively oppose the bussing of children from the inner city to their neighborhood schools, and who would fight to the death to prevent their children from being bussed into the urban blight that is the norm for [many] black [and 'minority'] children. For white surburbia, as well as for middle-class students in universities . . . [cultural] texts are becoming a way of gaining knowledge of the "other": a knowledge that appears to satisfy and replace the desire to challenge existing frameworks of segregation. Have we, as a society, sucessfully limited the desire for achieving integration through political agitation for civil rights and opted instead for [a very limited version of] knowing each other through cultural texts?[2]

I reassert this question because I feel that our contemporary discursive legacy from *Brown*, multiculturalism, has at its heart a complete disregard for cultural, political, and economic justice.[3]

Many of the daily practices of multiculturalism have spawned an obsessive engagement on the part of its practitioners with issues of identity politics, a form of politics that has focused upon questions of the personal, the subjective, and the emotive. The emphasis on increasing personal, or subjective, awareness of difference is thought to take place in conjunction with a selection of cultural texts but this process, frequently imagined to be an engagement in cultural politics, takes place at the expense of an engagement with the politics of culture and cultural production. In other words, what is deeply disturbing is that as multiculturalism is currently practiced the attention paid to cultural forms does not necessarily extend to a systematic interrogation of the nature of cultural formations. I would argue that it is not only necessary but urgent that we shift from this intense concentration on cultural forms, on textual representation and the subjectivity of identity politics, to an analysis of the relation between the production of cultural forms and the state of cultural formations, the material conditions that shape our collective as well as our individual existence.[4]

What we need to ask ourselves is if the vision of cultural integration implicit in the paradigm of the discussion of *Brown* at this period of time is, in fact, an adequate conceptual and political framework in which to understand the complexity of our contemporary systems of apartheid. I would argue that it is a very inadequate frame of reference and would evoke Antonio Gramsci's warning about becoming complacent about the nature of the battle in which *Brown* was only an opening sortie: "It was right," Gramsci asserts, "to struggle against the old school, but reforming it," he continues, "was not so simple as it seemed. The problem was not one of model curricula but of men, [and women] and not just of men [and women] who are actually teachers themselves but of the entire social complex which they express."[5] Any analysis of identity politics, of the subjective and emotive expressions of the social order, must be part of an active and rigorous critique of and engagement with the "social complex" in order to embody a vision of social, political, and economic transformation.

Throughout the nineteenth and twentieth century, issues of representation have consistently been present within the spectrum of black politics and political organizations. However, in the academic field of African American studies, which has been in existence for more than twenty-five years,[6] there seems to be an assumption that the cultural politics of textual representation, as first articulated by black modernists, has an integral if not a seamless relationship to issues of political representation and the achievement of equal rights of citzenship. Thus, much of our energy as black intellectuals, cultural producers, or critics has been aggressively directed toward increasing the force of our cultural presence, with pen and paper, in front of or behind cameras, or with paint or clay, as part of a wider political struggle. However, now these cultural forms, particularly mass cultural forms, easily penetrate the boundaries that the black working class or the black poor are forbidden to cross: rap music, or Spike Lee's, Stephen Carter's, and Cornel West's cultural texts become metaphorical substitutes for the presence of young black male bodies in the white middle-class suburb; white suburban schools and towns boast richly endowed multicultural libraries containing multiple copies of the works of Alice Walker, Toni Morrison, and Maxine Hong Kingston but have few or no black or women of color who have access to them. Now, I want to stress that it is not a problem of authorship or of artistic practices that I am trying to name. The fact that our cultural forms have a social mobility and accessibility that is denied to the majority of black people is a structural issue with which the field of African American studies should be centrally concerned. What I want to contest, here, is an assumption of cultural integration that has dominated African American humanist thinking: an assumption that if cultural forms embody our undeniable humanity they will help advance our demands for justice and equality in the society at large.

In African American studies we can loudly applaud our own "difference" and assert our distinct cultural presence in ways that resemble the valorization of difference within the discourse of multiculturalism, but we do so at great risk, if not at our peril.[7] As Paul Gilroy has argued, theories of cultural difference are becoming as absolute in their demarcation of the racial boundaries of humanity as the biological theories that supported scientific racism.[8] Indeed, the most notable feature of contemporary racist formations is that they no longer have to depend upon theories of biological heredity for their existence but, on the contrary emphasize "the insurmountability of cultural differences" instead. Rather than "postulate the superiority of certain groups or peoples in relation to others," what is articulated is "only the harmfulness of abolishing frontiers, the incompatibility of life-styles and traditions." As Etienne Balibar has characterized this shift, this new racism is "a racism without races . . . a differentialist racism," in which culture functions like nature. What has changed, he continues, is that contemporary racist discourse "naturalizes not racial belonging but racist conduct."[9]

Our contemporary facination and obsession with cultural difference and cultural belonging is, thus, entirely compatible with a hegemonic ideology of apartheid that structures our contemporary social formation. An emphasis on cultural difference and cultural belongingness supports, for example, one of the most pernicious practices of university administrations and departmental politics, a practice which is frequently justified by appealing to the discourse of cultural integration. On a daily basis university administrators and departmental chairs conflate the need to increase the presence of minority faculty with particular fields of knowledge. For example, African American faculty are drafted to teach African American studies, Latino and Latina, Chicano and Chicana, and Asian American professors are considered *only* in the context of a variety of ethnic studies programs. We, therefore, exist in the academy as professionalized ethnic or racialized presences. It was not the vision of *Brown* but maybe it is its legacy that our professionalized ethnicity, or professionalized blackness, has become a required academic commodity—a commodity that is in demand and can be utilized as a type of academic currency.

If *Brown* was about the practice of inserting bodies into integrated educational environments, are the current academic practices of reducing bodies to spheres of knowledge a crucial element of the insidious and pervasive practices of physical and mental ghettoization? And is the physical and mental ghettoization experienced by so many so-called minority faculty the more comfortable, though still unacceptable, academic equivalent of the brutal residential and educational apartheid of the wider society? If you exist as a racialized or ethnicized intellectual, it is difficult to speak or to be heard outside the boundaries of the body/field of knowledge equation: of casting a critical eye upon the narrow reach of mainstream disciplines, for example, or of daring to confront the structures of masculinity and patriarchal practices that shape and penetrate the academic world. But, unfortunately, the reduction of bodies to spheres of knowledge also has the effect of constructing those fields of knowledge as political turfs, as fields of influence over which ethnicized and racialized intellectuals feel that they have an exclusive claim or within which they consider, usually quite correctly, that they have their only chance to gain an academic job.

The metaphor of war that I intentionally evoked through my title of the 1992 essay, "Multicultural Wars," was not used lightly. On the contrary, I would describe the state of "minority" intellectual presences in the academy, as students and as faculty, as embattled. *Brown* was only one of many charges that we are going to have to make against the forces of racist reaction and retrenchment and maybe we should revise our strategies of war to take account of what we did not achieve through the *Brown* decision. Antonio Gramsci's analysis of the difference between wars of position and wars of maneuver I have found to be very useful in thinking about the complexities of our struggle for justice and equality.

> [I]n wars among the more industrially and socially advanced States, the war of manoeuvre must be considered as reduced to more of a tactical than a strategic function. . . .
>
> The same reduction must take place in the art and science of politics, at least in the case of the most advanced States, Where "civil society" has become a very complex structure and one which is resistant to the catastrophic "incursions" of the immediate economic element (crises, depressions, etc.). The superstructures of civil society are like the trench systems of modern warfare.[10]
>
> The same thing happens in the art of politics as happens in military art: war of movement increasingly becomes war of position and it can be said that a state will win a war in so far as it prepares for it minutely and technically in peace time. The massive structures of the modern democracies, both as state organizations, and as complexes of associations in civil society, constitute for the art of politics as it were the "trenches" and the permanent fortifications of the front in the war of position: they render merely "partial" the element of manoevre.[11]

The cultural politics of multiculturalism, far from being a war of movement, a wing in a larger war for radical transformation of which *Brown* was a part, has, in fact, become merely a discursive strategy in a war of position. Whereas proponents of multiculturalism like to see themselves as part of an attack on the racist formation, they have actually become stuck in the first line of the trenches of textual representation and seem incapable of climbing the next hurdle and challenging the injustice and inequity of our contemporary racialized social order. Indeed, I would go even further and suggest that our legacy of cultural integrationism works in harmony with not in opposition to the anti–civil rights hegemony first secured during the Reagan and Bush years and now being elaborated through an anti–affirmative action backlash and the Republican "Contract with America." The liberal consensus on the attainment of justice and equality as it was embodied in the demands of the expanded civil rights agenda of the sixties and seventies and which we believed was the legacy of *Brown* has clearly been revoked, and instead we are offered a vision of cultural integration, multiculturalism, as a pacifier, an antidote to the anger and outrage that we bitterly repress.

Forty years or so after *Brown v. Board of Education*, the interests of the white and a significant portion of the black bourgeoisie are aligned in a battle over one of our most important public resources—the public school system. In a maneuver that increasingly resembles the historical mobilization of states rights to retain the disenfranchisement of masses of black southern residents, the white suburban middle class, rallying to the cry of "the right to local control," are virtually privatizing sectors of the public educational system in their own class interests. Now that corporations, rather than the middle class, control capital accumulation, the bourgeoisie seek to retain control over the production of what Immanuel Wallerstein has called "human capital."

> Human capital is what these new style bourgeois have in abundance, whereas our proletarian does not. And where do they acquire the human capital? . . . [I]n the education systems, whose primary and self-proclaimed function is to train people to become members of the new middle-classes, that is to be the professionals, the technicians, the administrators of the private and public enterprises which are the functional economic building-pieces of our system.

In a situation in which the children of the bourgeoisie can no longer be assured of inheriting capital, the middle class is in a battle to retain its control over quality education as a legacy for its children.[12] Many members of the black middle class are aligned with the white bourgeoisie in this struggle and have adopted similar political strategies, either by supporting the establishment of black private schools or through attempting to gain privileged access into magnet schools as a legacy for their children. The result is an apparent social consensus on the significant drain of economic, physical, and material resources away from the poor.

The paradigm of *Brown* from a legal perspective is completely inadequate to counter this drain of resources. Indeed, the current role of the courts is to support the bourgeoisie as our educational system has entered the front line of this political struggle. We need, therefore, to drastically revise our perspective on the role of the law in the achievement of change. We need to interrogate the history of the role of the courts in the achievement of legal definitions of cultural integration while we develop a critique of the contemporary role of the law in the defeat of social justice and equality. As Jonathan Kozol has argued, the legal redress offered by *Brown* has been invalidated by the Supreme Court rulings in *San Antonio Independent School District v. Rodriguez* and *Milliken v. Bradley*, decisions which have effectively denied the legitimacy of claims for educational equality and justice.[13]

Surely, in the face of the despair and suffering of poor black, Native American, Latino(a) and Chicano(a) children we must try to develop an alternative to the *Brown* paradigm, a paradigm that asks us to place our hopes for radical social transformation in the courts of this land. The question is,

Who will take up the cause for social justice and equality that the courts refuse to defend? Our public school system must be defended as a public resource that no group has the right to use or abuse in its own narrow class interests. Through which channels do we articulate what we want to demand of a public education system in a democracy?

"Democracy, by definition," Gramsci stressed, "cannot mean merely that an unskilled worker can become skilled. It must mean that every 'citizen' can 'govern' and that society places him, [or her] even if only abstractly, in a general condition to achieve this."[14] Or, to make the point through the phase that C. L. R. James used as the title of one of his essays, "Every Cook Can Govern."[15] Our present language of cultural integrationism, multicultural-ism, must be replaced by an active politics of social, political, and economic transformation, a politics that is not satisfied with understanding and bewail-ing inequities but seeks to redistribute wealth through a socialist vision of the future in the present. To conclude in the words of Etienne Balibar, the "destruction of the racist complex presupposes not only the revolt of its vic-tims, but the transformation of the racists themselves and consequently, the internal decomposition of the community created by racism."[16] This is our actual legacy from *Brown*, a legacy that should force us to undertake the work that *Brown* left undone, to confront and dismantle the forces that not only protect but nurture the racist community.

Notes

1. See Hazel V. Carby, "The Multicultural Wars," 54 *Radical History Re-view* (Fall 1992); 7. I am taking this opportunity to address some of the issues raised in response to that article. In particular, I intend in this essay to implicate those working in African American studies. As Thelma Foote stated in response to "Mul-ticultural Wars": "[A]lthough Carby provides an incisive critique of multicultural-ism's failings, she limits her analysis to the consequences those failures hold for the political awakening of white middle-class students, while ignoring the fact that curricular reforms have important consequences for politicization of black students also." Foote, "The Black Intellectual, Recent Curricular Reforms, and the Dis-course of Collective Identity," 56 *Radical History Review* (Spring 1993), 51, 52.

I am not assuming that this volume's reader is familiar with the earlier essay, so I reproduce here some of its main arguments, in a slightly revised form.

2. Carby, supra note 1, at 10–11.

3. The term "cultural justice" has been coined by Andrew Ross in the follow-ing context: "I see cultural studies as the quest for cultural justice, which is my preferred term for political correctness." Ross, "Cultural Studies Times Inter-views," 1 *Cultural Studies Times*, no. 2 (Fall 1994), All.

4. See Eric Lott, *Love and Theft: Blackface Minstrelsy and the American Working Class* (New York: Oxford University Press, 1993), 10–11, for a similar argument, which is elaborated in his critique of strands of cultural studies in North America.

5. Antonio Gramsci, *Selections from the Prison Notebooks* (New York: Inter-national Publishers, 1971), 36.

6. The African and Afro-American Studies Program at Yale University was established in 1969. It was preceded by a conference in the spring of 1968, one of the first in the nation to examine the nature of Afro-American studies. The program formally changed its name to African and African American Studies in 1994. Thank you to Lorrie Trotter in the Office of Public Information, Yale University.

7. See Etienne Balibar, "[I]t is not a question of setting a collective identity against individual identities. *All identity is individual*, but there is no individual identity that is not historical or, in other words, constructed within a field of social values, norms or behavior and collective symbols. . . . The real question is how the dominant reference points of individual identity change over time and with the changing institutional environment" (emphasis in original). Etienne Balibar & Immanuel Wallerstein, *Race, Nation, Class: Ambiguous Identities* (London: Verso, 1991), 94.

8. I absolutely agree with Paul Gilroy when he states, "[W]here black art and aesthetics are debated in conference after conference it is becoming harder to dislodge the belief that ethnic differences constitute an absolute break in history and humanity." See Paul Gilroy, "Cruciality and the Frog's Perspective: An Agenda of Difficulties for the Black Arts Movement in Britain," 5 *Third Text* (Winter 1988/89), 37.

9. See Balibar & Wallerstein, supra note 7, at 21–22.

10. Antonio Gramsci, supra note 5, at 234–35.

11. David Forgacs ed., *An Antonio Gramsci Reader: Selected Writings 1916–1935* (New York: Shocken Books, 1988), 226–27.

12. Balibar & Wallerstein, supra note 7, at 150.

13. Jonathan Kozol, "Romance of the Ghetto School," *The Nation*, May 23, 1994, at 703.

14. Forgacs, supra note 11, at 318.

15. C. L. R. James, *The Future in the Present: Selected Writings* (London: Allison and Busby, 1977), 160–75.

16. Balibar & Wallerstein, supra note 7, at 18.

Index

and the language and structure of
oral arguments in *Brown*, 8–9,
23–48
legal, harm of, Kateb on, 10–11,
91–109
and multiculturalism, 201–10
psychological damage of, 5–6, 11,
16n22, 25, 31–32, 91–109, 171
and the revolution in the interpretation of the Constitution, 9–10,
49–73
Seidman, Louis Michael, 67n18
self-definition
and the language and structure of
oral arguments in *Brown*, 24–27,
42
national, 9, 24
"separate but equal" doctrine, 137,
154, 171. *See also Plessy v. Ferguson*
Friedman on, 54
Kateb on, 94
and peonage cases, 58
and scientific racism, 59
Warren on, 5–6
sex discrimination, 12, 110, 111–13,
118, 121–22, 180
sexism, 214, 217
sexual harassment, 112, 180–81, 196–
98
sexuality
European semiotics of, 183
sexual orientation, 110, 115–16,
118, 214–15
sharecroppers, 56
Shelley v. Kramer, 59
Silberman, Charles, 205–7
Simmons, William, 62
Simon, Paul, 180
Simpson, Alan, 181
Simpson, O. J., 197
slavery, 5, 117
abolition of, 56, 92
and the annulment of family rights,
30
and the harm of legal segregation,
92, 95, 97, 99, 103–4
and peonage cases, 58
voluntary, 103–4
Smith, Frances, 39–40
Smith, Gerrit, 23
Smith, James M., 23–24
Smith, J. Clay, 157n4
SNCC (Student Nonviolent Coordinating Committee), 151, 153

"social contract" paradigm, 184–85
social engineering, 137–69
social justice, cause of, 10, 14, 137–
69
Social Security System, 114
sociology, 53–54, 58, 61–62, 203–5
Socrates, 101
Souter, David, 78, 80, 81
South Carolina, 5, 24, 31–33, 92
South Carolina Convention of 1865,
33
Sowell, Thomas, 161n34
Spann, Girardeau, 143
Specter, Arlen, 179
standing, principles of, 28
Stefancic, Jean, 50
stereotypes, racial, 62, 127, 141, 146,
180
Stewart, Potter, 80
Stone, Harlan Fisk, 75
Strauder v. West Virginia, 54, 106
Sudan, 212–13
Sweatt v. Painter, 58, 94

Talmadge, Herman, 197
taxpayers, 28–30
Taylor, William L., 50
technocracy, 198, 199
Texas, 58
Texas Southern University, 140
Thatcher, Margaret, 184
Thirteenth Amendment, 56, 57, 94,
95
Thomas, Clarence, 4, 8. *See also*
Thomas hearings
on the assumption of black inferiority, by the courts, 3, 201
on the psychological effects of segregation, 16n22
Thomas hearings, 193, 201. *See also*
Thomas, Clarence
and Hill, 181, 187n27, 191, 195–
98, 214
and the nationalization of the life
story, 13, 171, 176–82
Thoreau, Henry David, 99–100
Time Magazine, 51
Title VII (Civil Rights Act), 113, 120,
122–23
Tocqueville, Alexis de, 4, 98
tolerance, ideal of, 124
trading places, idea of, 102–3
Trans World Airlines Inc. v. Hardison,
123
Trubek, David, 18n51